For every season, there is a purpose.
And in every season, Tracey McBride helps you fulfill it by . . .

- Gracing your home with flowers, laughter, and peace

- Adorning your walls, tables, and windows with vintage china, romantic laces, and rescued linens

- Combining magnificent decorations for your holidays with the joy of family gatherings

Don't miss:

- Mysterious May Day Chocolate Chip Cookies . . . from a recipe found tucked into a tattered book, the best chocolate chip recipe yet. (p. 30)

- The optimism of list-making . . . for spring cleanup or winter transformations, a master list provides a rebirth of optimism and enthusiasm. (p. 39)

- Favorite secrets for cultivating quiet graces . . . ice cold milk served in a chilled silver pitcher, a cluster of fresh ferns on the table, and many more unique touches. (p. 42)

- The language of herbs—mint is for cheerfulness, lavender brings good fortune. Make a bouquet magical by noting the symbolic meanings of botanicals. (p. 114)

- Fall soups . . . a cornucopia of recipes for the heartiest, most satisfying stocks and soups . . . and serving them in style. (p. 189–192)

- Theme trees . . . low-cost decorations that make your Christmas even more fun and special. (p. 233)

**And everything you do, from pretty parcels to inspirational verses,
will be delivered with love.**

Frugal Luxuries by the Seasons

Also by Tracey McBride

Frugal Luxuries:
Simple Pleasures to Enhance Your Life
and Comfort Your Soul

Frugal Luxuries by the Seasons

Celebrate the Holidays with Elegance and Simplicity on Any Income

Tracey McBride

BANTAM BOOKS

New York • Toronto • London • Sydney • Auckland

FRUGAL LUXURIES BY THE SEASONS

PUBLISHING HISTORY
Bantam trade paperback / November 2000

Library of Congress Cataloging-in-Publication Data
McBride, Tracey.
Frugal luxuries by the seasons : celebrate the holidays with elegance and simplicity on any
income / Tracey McBride.
p. cm.
Includes bibliographical references and index.
ISBN 978-0-553-37995-2
1. Holiday cookery. 2. Low budget cookery. 3. Holiday decorations. 4. Handicraft. I. Title.
TX739 .M22 2000
641.5'68—dc21
00-039755

Published simultaneously in the United States and Canada

Bantam Books are published by Bantam Books, a division of Random House, Inc. Its trademark,
consisting of the words "Bantam Books" and the portrayal of the rooster, is Registered in U.S.
Patent and Trademark Office and in other countries. Marca Registrada. Bantam Books, 1540
Broadway, New York, New York 10036.

146659772

&

This book
is dedicated to
God,
and was written
for my beloved family.
It is an archive
for all who seek
to reconcile body and soul.
And it is for those who wish to
cultivate an appreciation
for the host of practical *and* intangible
wonders, wisdom, and graces
that surround us
always.

Contents

～

Part III The Still Small Voice of Autumn

Part IV The Magic and Majesty of Winter

Appendices

Foreword

How to Balance the Blended Being

"We are but fragments of what man might be."
—PLATO

Two worlds exist: one the permanent yet invisible spiritual world of perfect order and design; the other, the transient material world, with motion and change its only constants. From day to day, we watch the rising and setting of the sun and moon, the changes in weather, the movement of the stars in the night sky. After a time, we are able to discern that there is something more behind what Shakespeare describes as the "fixed and stately march of the planets and the seasons of the year." And if we observe long enough and think deeply enough, we may discover, as others who have gone before, that there are deep and essential connections between the two worlds.

The human soul is, as Plato tells us in the *Phaedrus,* driving a chariot with two horses, one a "gallant and gentle steed," straining continually to go upward, keeping his eyes ever on the divine world, which he aspires to return to. The other horse, "unruly and . . . obstinate," plunges downward and drags the chariot behind him.

When I first heard this metaphor, I was struck by its accuracy. I immediately thought of the many times I had been involved in a soul-inspired meeting of the minds with a kindred spirit when, with a sudden jerk, I was pulled down to earth by a growling stomach, a baby's helpless wail, or a messy room.

Because we are blended beings, composed of many diverse fragments, the golden mean is forever being sought. The human need to balance the material and the intangible is as perennial as the seasons. Yet, once we consciously recognize that God created us this way on purpose, it becomes simpler to find ways to reconcile body and soul. This knowledge of things divine and human can become your best ally in living a happy and productive life.

The goal of *Frugal Luxuries by the Seasons* is to offer you the necessary tools with which to keep the "two horses" somewhat level, so you will not always feel as if you are being pulled in two directions at the same time. I also hope it will help you cultivate the ability to untangle the maze of earthly phenomena from what Plato describes as the "invisible, pure and immutable essence of things."

With my very best thoughts,

Tracey McBride

Tracey McBride

Prologue

~

Works of Wonder and Quiet Graces

"A miracle is a wonder, a beam of supernatural power injected into history . . .
An opening in the wall that separates this world and another."
—*TIME*, DECEMBER 30, 1990

Our lives are filled with wonders, beginning with the miracle of birth. Children seem to begin life accepting this comfort. And as they grow from infancy into childhood, you can see their natural awareness and acceptance of the miracles around them. Each moment seems to be a discovery, a wonder, a joy.

Sadly, as people grow older, they become involved with the tasks of living—so much so that they lose sight of the miracles that are sent to them, as well as the author of those miracles. Oftentimes they are discouraged during life's more challenging moments. Still, it is in these darkest of times that they should seek out and draw forth the wonders working within their own lives. Consequently, they may discover that they are able to reach beyond themselves and positively touch the lives of others as well.

In looking back at the many quiet wonders in my own life, I see that a great many of them were linked to a larger one—one that went virtually unrecognized by me at the time. The value of small actions and decisions is immense, for these are often but segments of a larger whole. How many times have you ignored an instinct? How many times have you thought, "Wonders never happen in *my* life, so why waste the effort and time to even try to see them?" How many times have you been blind to the smaller graces that can lead to larger ones?

Take a moment, now, before delving into this book, to think about the quiet graces and works of wonder that have happened in your life. Think of recent ones; consider childhood memories. Perhaps it was something you shrugged off as coincidence or, because you couldn't explain it, you tucked it into the recesses of your memory. It could have been the time you lost a large amount of money in a public place and it was returned to you. Maybe a friend loaned you a book that only an hour earlier you had strongly wanted to read—and reading that book dramatically influenced your life for the better. Sometimes the miracles are as mundane as stumbling across a coveted set of serving bowls and platters that match your now obsolete china pattern at a yard sale— on the weekend before your big party. Think back on small events that developed into a chain of events, which led to the discovery of a new best friend, a positive role model, a marriage partner, or to the positive realization of your life's work.

𝒐𝒃

Please take a moment to fill in the following lines with
a list of quiet wonders that have positively touched your life.

_____

_____

_____

_____

_____

_____

_____

You may reclaim your gift of wonder, and *Frugal Luxuries by the Seasons* will show you how. To begin, you need only develop an awareness of the quiet graces that surround you. They are waiting for you to notice them, dormant, as seeds are dormant, expecting to be planted and watered so that they may sprout and bear fruit. To neglect them may cause you to miss so many of the blessings God has in store for your life. Wonders and graces are not ancient faraway occurrences, they are here, now, today—just as they have always been.

Living a Luminous Life

"A light, a glory, a fair luminous cloud enveloping the Earth."
—SAMUEL TAYLOR COLERIDGE

While exploring the philosophy of *Frugal Luxuries* you will find that our primary goal is happy living. This is accomplished, in part, by making the best of your own circumstances—because what you focus on grows—and creating a lifestyle rich in beauty, grace, and wisdom.

Frugal Luxuries dispels the long-held fallacy that luxury and economy do not mix.

On the contrary, our philosophy happily marries these opposites by taking the finest frugal strategies and mingling them with achievable ideas for luxurious living. The result blends the best of both worlds, while reconciling body and soul.

Life Festivals

"Little, ebullient, patches of delight."
—C. S. Lewis

There is a human *need* for celebration. Why? Celebrations allow for a rededication of hope, rest from labor, and reassurance that good and happy things will continue to occur, despite the transient nature of the world in which we live. A majority of the great and humble festivals of life are joyfully guided by tradition. Should we examine them closely we might find them wondrous in the expectations they excite and fulfill—and very diverse in their meanings.

Born from the Latin word *festivus,* festivals are a part of every known culture and have been observed for *thousands* of years. They are expressions of opinion and emotion, patterned experiences that serve a multitude of purposes, one of which is to unite and inspire groups of individuals with a common bond. And while there are many classifications of festivals (solemn and joyous, religious and secular) they are nearly always held in commemoration of some great event or blessing and are the pegs on which we hang the ornaments of the year.

The survival of many ancient festivals, albeit with strange transformations and enrichments, is a testament to their value, offering us a valuable link to those souls who peopled the past, while unifying today's sometimes fragmented culture. To honor the traditions of each season is to "assist" (as the French say) in their survival—to participate in serious pleasure. By so doing, year after year, we are ensuring their continuity, thereby (often unconsciously) forging a link to future generations.

This humble volume offers ways in which you may continue beloved holiday traditions or develop new ones. You will discover descriptions of seasonal festivals and associated recipes as well as varied ways to elegantly embellish your holidays without exhausting your energy, time, or budget.

Creating Home Graces

"The grand idea of home is a quiet, secluded spot, where loving hearts dwell."
—L. W. Yaggy

Regardless of where you live, we will share with you, in each seasonal chapter of *Home Graces,* how to use simple inexpensive elements to create or enhance the delightful, relaxing retreat of your dreams. You do not need a country farmhouse, a mountain cabin, a penthouse apartment or a cottage at the beach to turn your dreams into reality. You can experience your ideals beginning wherever you live today.

A balanced environment for a human being includes more than simply the four walls of a house. Since the time of cave dwellers, home walls have been decorated with paintings and drawings to satisfy our eternal hunger for beauty. And one of the hallmarks of a civilized society is that its people are not content to live in an unadorned space. Thus, in each season *Home Graces* offers a multitude of tangible ideas unique to each specific time of year. These can enable you to easily decorate your abode in an artful yet inexpensive manner. It extends as well many basic, yet often overlooked ways to create the most prized home-ornament of all: *home peace.*

Understanding the Gift Pantry

"The only thing we ever have is what we give away."
—Louis Ginsberg

The *Gift Pantry* feature (along with the year-round Christmas planning guide) may become your most valuable tool for celebrating each phase of the year in a joyous, creative, and *simple* fashion. For those of you not familiar with the concept, a Gift Pantry is a collection of gifts and packaging materials—homemade, home-grown, and/or purchased—kept readily available for future use. By stocking a Gift Pantry year round you may discover, as I have, that you will save time as well as money. Most important, a Gift Pantry greatly contributes to your peace of mind, allowing *you* to relax and enjoy the festivals of the seasons.

Enriching Extras

Besides the seasonal offerings of *Festivals, Home Graces,* and *The Gift Pantry,* you will find that this little book harbors a plethora of extra riches for you to enjoy. This material is diverse in subject (as is life), so that much of it didn't fit properly into the framework mentioned above. Thus, I have scattered it throughout the book, in what I hope is a somewhat orderly and reasonable fashion.

Alexander Pope tells us that "order is Heaven's first law," and I thoroughly agree. Thus I highlight this philosophy with suggestions for spring cleaning. I believe the first step to getting yourself on track for upcoming holidays (as well as the daily round) is the creation and maintainance of home order. I can think of no better season than spring, that ancient first month of the natural year, in which to accomplish just such a feat.

Throughout civilization an individual's wardrobe has been a language unto itself. In today's modern world, many of us are looking to cull attractive, quality clothing that will express our inner self to the outer world, while allowing us to remain faithful to a budget. In Summer, I address the concept of acquiring and organizing a frugally luxurious wardrobe.

Whenever I think of abundant and delicious foods I automatically find myself conjuring up images of autumn! I suppose this is why I chose that season in which to include my favorite recipes for soups, stews, and *very* quick breads and biscuits. In *Autumnal Offerings* you will find a cornucopia of tried-and-true recipes, and suggestions on how to serve them in style.

Each chapter ends with an *Illuminated Fragment,* my chance to share with you simple observations, philosophies, ideas, wonders, and time-honored wisdom that may help you to better temper and appreciate both the tangible and intangible graces that surround you on a daily basis.

The appendices brim with lovely letters from *Kindred Spirits* who share their creative and unique ideas for living a frugally luxurious lifestyle. You will also learn how you can share your own ideas and philosophy of life with others.

Frugal Luxuries by the Seasons was designed to inspire you to view your life, circumstances, and time with renewed wonder and value. However, be prepared. Should you implement even a small number of the tangible and intangible wisdoms offered in this simple book, you may discover your home filled with flowers, laughter, and peace; your walls, tables, and windows adorned with vintage china, romantic laces, and rescued linens; your holidays celebrated with grace, elegance, and ease; and your soul comforted by an awakened appreciation for the blessings and frugal luxuries that already exist within your own life.

Prepare to transform your life.

Part I
Spring's Promise

*"The year's at the spring
And the day's at the morn."*
—Robert Browning

Chapter 1

Festivals of Spring

~

"Is it so small a thing to have enjoyed the sun,
To have lived light in the spring,
To have loved, to have thought, to have done;
To have advanced true friends? . . ."

—Matthew Arnold

The Feast of Saint Patrick

"Cead mile failte!—One hundred thousand welcomes!"
—Ancient Gaelic greeting

In the Irish countryside, March 17—the anniversary of the death of Saint Patrick—is a day of visiting relatives and friends, and a fitting occasion to sing, feast, and partake of concerts and plays honoring the patron saint of Ireland. Most towns and cities hold a large parade in honor of the day, during which everyone wears green, for "the wearin' of the green" is a celebration of the emerald green of Ireland herself, as well as a symbol of springtime.

When I was young, my mother would celebrate Saint Patrick's Day by speaking with an Irish brogue all day, although she is American by birth. After our traditional Saint Patrick's day dinner of corned beef, cabbage, potatoes, and carrots, she and my father would sip Irish coffee from shamrock-encrusted Irish crystal glasses (purchased on a visit to Ireland) while enjoying Gaelic melodies playing on the stereo. I would lie on the floor at her feet and listen as she delighted us with amusing tales about her day posing as an Irishwoman (giggling with fun at the thought that so many people had believed her brogue to be authentic) and reminisced with my father about their sojourn to that ancient isle of green.

Traditional Saint Patrick's Day Corned Beef Dinner

"People will not look forward to posterity who never look backward to their ancestors."
—EDMUND BURKE

Corned beef, a brine-cured savory meat, is the mainstay of many a Saint Patrick's Day boiled dinner. In old-time Irish households, a platter of this delicious meat was the centerpiece of the evening meal, served with boiled potatoes, carrots, and cabbage. After dinner sweet songs of Ireland were heard throughout the house, as well as the sound of feet that danced a jig, proclaiming Gaelic heritage.

(Note: In store-bought corned beef, a spice packet is often included, thus making the first three ingredients unnecessary)
    1 teaspoon ground allspice
    1 teaspoon ground cinnamon
    1 teaspoon ground cloves
    1 corned beef brisket (store-bought or home-cured)
    2 medium onions, sliced
    7 carrots, sliced in chunks
    1 cabbage, quartered and cored
    6 to 8 potatoes, peeled and quartered
    Optional: 1 turnip, peeled and sliced
    Enough warm water to cover

Use spice packet, or combine allspice, cinnamon, and cloves in a small bowl, and rub the mixture over the corned beef. Place the meat inside a large kettle and cover completely with water. Keep the pot covered while gently simmering the meat about 3 to 4 hours. When meat is nearly done cooking, add the vegetables. Cook until tender. Thinly slice the meat, *against* the grain; this is best done after the meat has been removed from the cooking heat for about 15 or 20 minutes. Serve on a large platter with the cooked vegetables wreathed around it; this recipe serves 4 to 6 generously.

You may also cook corned beef in a slow-cooker, with lovely results. However, unless you enjoy the taste of the corned beef spices in your vegetables, cook the vegetables separately (directly before serving the meat) when using the Crock-Pot.

If you enjoy using corned beef in other recipes, you may wish to stock your freezer during the month of March, when corned beef is on sale. If you cure your own, perhaps make a double batch. Leftover corned beef can make delicious sandwiches (as follows).

Remains of an Irish Feast

"Small cheer and great welcome make a merry feast."
—William Shakespeare

When I was a young girl, my father would make sandwiches from leftover corned beef in one of two ways: steamed and served hot on a soft French roll (with lots of yellow mustard and a garlicky dill pickle on the side); or as a type of Reuben sandwich (on toasted rye bread, with lots of cheese, sauerkraut, and mustard). The secret to either of these delicious sandwiches was the proper draining and chilling of the corned beef itself. Papa would put the remaining hunk of cooked meat inside a colander (with a pie plate beneath it to catch any drippings) and refrigerate it for two or three days. This allowed the excess moisture to drain away from the meat, thus drying it out so that when he finally sliced the corned beef we were rewarded with tender, wonderfully thin, deli-style sandwich slices.

While my own children are not always enthusiastic about the traditional corned-beef-and-cabbage meal of St. Patrick's Day (I believe it has something to do with the cabbage) they *are* more enthusiastic when we serve these delectable corned beef sandwiches from the remains of our feast-day meal.

An Ancient Curing Process

"With the ancient is wisdom."

—Job 12:12

Although corned beef is fairly inexpensive and easily available, I am including an ancient recipe for curing your own brisket of beef, for those who crave a new culinary experience. Unless you already have the pickling spices on hand, however, making corned beef at home may be more expensive than purchasing it already cured from the market.

If you wish to serve this home-cured corned beef on Saint Patrick's Day you must begin curing the meat on the first or second of March, as it will take fifteen days.

A 6- or 7-pound piece of fresh, lean, beef brisket, boneless rump, or top-side roast
1 pound pickling salt (available at most grocery stores)
1 cup light brown sugar, packed well
3 bay leaves, crumbled well
1 tablespoon mustard seed
1 teaspoon whole peppercorns
2 rounded teaspoons saltpeter (available at most drug stores)
1 teaspoon whole allspice
1 teaspoon freshly grated nutmeg
1 teaspoon cracked coriander
1 teaspoon dried ginger, powdered or crushed

Blend together all of the dry ingredients until well mixed. Place your beef in a large glass or earthenware pan. With clean hands, rub the spice mixture thoroughly over the surface of the meat. The salt, saltpeter, and spices will destroy any bacteria, thus the rubbed meat will not spoil. Store the cured meat, tightly covered with aluminium foil or a sturdy lid, inside the refrigerator. Flip the meat over once a day for one week. For the remaining eight days, repeat the daily turning of the meat, and rub the spices from the bottom of the dish onto the meat when doing so. After fifteen days the meat should be red all the way through (and *officially* be corned beef) and ready for cooking. At that time, remove beef from the dish and rinse well with cool water. Pat dry. Store cured beef in the refrigerator until ready to cook. (The meat will keep well in the refrigerator for three to four days and, when well wrapped, will keep in the freezer for about three months without losing too much of its flavor.)

&

Papa's Steamed Corned Beef Sandwiches

"May the road rise up to meet you . . ."
—IRISH BLESSING

Fully cooked, well-chilled corned beef (trim all fat), thinly sliced, enough for
    about six slices per sandwich
Yellow mustard
Optional: Swiss or sharp cheddar cheese
Very fresh, soft French-style sandwich rolls, split down the center
Very sour, very garlicky dill pickle spears—to serve on the plate next to the
    sandwich

Over gently boiling water, place your sliced corned beef inside a steamer or colander (keeping it away from the water itself). Heat for about 5 to 8 minutes, or until meat is warmed thoroughly. Turn off heat and, using a fork or kitchen tongs, carefully place the meat on prepared sandwich rolls. (We children were in charge of preparing our own rolls. Once this was done, we stood in line at the stove, holding our plates while, one by one, Papa carefully placed the hot meat on our sandwich rolls for us.) Eat immediately and enjoy.

Papa's Reuben Sandwich

"May the wind be always at your back . . .
And may God hold you in the palm of His hand."
—IRISH BLESSING

This sandwich, inspired by our favorite delicatessen, was sometimes accompanied by a cup of soup and dill pickles, but most of the time it was a meal in itself.

Rye bread slices (we liked to use the rectangular-shaped rye loaves, as those slices
    seemed to hold the sandwich ingredients together well)
Mustard (Papa preferred the spicy brown mustard, while we children put on lots
    of the vinegary yellow mustard)
Swiss cheese, sliced (enough for at least one generous slice per sandwich)
Sauerkraut, well drained (we usually used the store-bought variety, in cans or jars)
Chilled corned beef (be certain that it is as lean as possible—trim all fat before
    slicing) sliced thin—enough for three to four slices per sandwich

Butter the bread slices on one side and place them on a baking sheet. Lightly toast the bread about four inches from the broiler (1 to 2 minutes). Remove from heat. Spread mustard on *all* of the bread slices. On *half* of the bread slices continue to add cheese, drained sauerkraut (about one tablespoon), and sliced corned beef that has been warmed in a microwave or steamer. Top sandwiches with remaining pieces of toast, and halve. Serve immediately with crunchy dill pickles, soup, and/or fried potatoes, french fries, or onion rings.

IRISH LINEN SACHETS

*"I have loved flowers that fade, within whose magic tents
Rich hues have marriage made with sweet unmemoried scents."*
—ROBERT BRIDGES

Did you know that March is National Craft Month? Every month is craft month in our house, but we will happily use this designation as an excuse to create a frugal luxury from recycled handkerchiefs (found at yard sales or flea markets) or hemmed scraps of good-quality fabrics you have on hand in your craft or sewing pantry. I have used green-and-white cotton gingham, as well as small square damask napkins imprinted with a clover design. If you have heirloom handkerchiefs, this is a lovely way to transform them into useful gifts to pass along to your daughter, niece, or granddaughter. Or you may cut squares from the better parts of worn but beloved baby clothes, childhood dresses, and the like.

1 square handkerchief or hemmed piece of square fabric (the fabric may be any size but it must be square in order for this project to work properly)

Sewing needle and thread to match your fabric

Dried potpourri, such as lavender, rose petals, scented geraniums, or shredded orange, lemon, or apple peel

Essential oil to scent (optional)

Small amount of cotton batting or several cotton balls

14 to 18 inches of ½- to ¾-inch satin, grosgrain, or chiffon ribbon (wired ribbon looks attractive as well)

Optional: Attractive vintage buttons to ornament your sachet

Place handkerchief right-side down and form an envelope with it by bringing three of its four corners to meet in the center. Stitch the corners in place (be certain you don't stitch through to the other side). Leave the fourth flap loose. Turn the fabric envelope right-side out.

Use ribbon to form a hanging loop by cutting it in half and stitching or gluing one piece of ribbon to the top corner of each side. Bring ends together at the top and tie into a bow. Fill the fabric envelope with potpourri and cotton batting or cotton balls (put essential oil on batting or cotton balls, if you opt to use it). Close the flap of the fabric envelope. You may leave it loose or stitch it closed.

This charming sachet looks lovely hanging inside your clothes closet, on the handle of the bathroom door (inside and out), or from an attractive pewter hook to scent a room. If you are feeling ambitious, make several of these sachets as additions to your Gift Pantry—they make lovely token gifts to present to teachers, friends, and hostesses on this and other festive days.

ൠ

Irish Scones

"Over buttered scones and crumpets . . . a hundred A B C's"
—T. S. ELIOT

When my daughter Katie's fourth-grade class held a Saint Patrick's day party, each child was asked to bring a specific Irish dish. Wanting something delicious but simple to prepare, I chose to make Irish scones. After baking, I sprinkled the large scones generously with powdered sugar, surrounded them with fragrant green geranium leaves from my herb garden, and served them in wedges from atop a pedestaled cake plate. The resulting scones were such a delicious surprise—yet so simple, frugal, and easy to make—I would feel remiss in not sharing the recipe with you.

As well, for the sake of novelty, I prepared a fresh pot of Irish Creme–flavored coffee (decaffeinated) and added to it generous amounts of rich whipping cream and sweetener. I brought this beverage to Katie's school in a lovely silver coffee carafe and served it in tiny white cups. Needless to say, the coffee was quite a success with this party of nine- and ten-year-olds, as were the still-warm scones.

 2 cups all-purpose flour
 4 teaspoons baking powder
 2 tablespoons granulated or powdered sugar
 ½ teaspoon salt
 4 tablespoons butter
 2 eggs
 ⅓ cup cream or milk

Mix and sift together all of your dry ingredients into a large mixing bowl. With a fork, pastry blender, or your fingertips, work butter into the dry mixture. In a separate dish, beat eggs (reserving a very small amount) and add eggs and cream to the butter and flour mixture. Toss dough on a lightly floured board. Pat and roll the dough into a large circle, about ¾ inch thick (try not to overwork the dough). With a serrated knife, cut the circle of dough into triangular wedges. Lightly brush the top of the dough with the reserved egg that you have diluted with about 1 teaspoon of water. Bake in a 450° oven for about 15 minutes. You may sprinkle granulated sugar on the dough *before* baking, or dust with powdered sugar *after* baking. Serve the scones plain or with pots of jam, jelly, honey, or sweet creamy butter. Makes 8 to 10 scones.

Pesach (Passover)

*"This day [Passover] shall be unto you for a memorial; and
ye shall keep it a feast to the Lord throughout your generations."*
—THE SECOND BOOK OF MOSES, CALLED EXODUS

On the fifteenth day of Nisan (usually in late March or early April, near or coinciding with the Christian Easter), the second of the Three Pilgrimage Festivals—Pesach (Passover)—is observed. This festival of spring and of unleavened bread commemorates the escape of the children of Israel from slavery in Egypt more than three thousand years ago. This widely observed (and perhaps best-loved) Jewish festival is one of the few holidays that is celebrated primarily at home rather than at the synagogue.

In memory of the Israelites, who fled Egypt in such haste that there was no time to allow the dough for their bread to rise, leavened foods are forbidden during Passover. For many Jews, flour products, baking soda, baking powder, yeast, and, in some instances, legumes are prohibited during the eight days of Passover. During such time, matzo (unleavened bread) is the mainstay of the week's diet, and matzo meal, matzo cake meal, and potato starch replace leavened staples. (Needless to say, this poses a creative challenge for those who cook for this holiday.)

A vital part of the celebration of Passover (and of keeping the holiday's meaning alive) is relating the story of the Israelites' exodus at the seder meals, which are held on the first and second evenings of the holiday and are based on the last meal eaten by the Israelites before beginning their flight to freedom. The seder begins with the reading of the Haggadah, an account of the Jews' flight to freedom from Egypt. During this ceremonial portion of the meal, the seder plate holds the symbolic roasted lamb bone, symbolizing the lamb's blood marking Jewish homes, protecting them from the Angel of Death; parsley, betokening the green of life and of springtime; bitter herbs, usually horseradish, symbolizing the suffering of the Jews in Egypt; a hard-boiled egg, symbolizing life; matzo; and haroset, a mixture of nuts, apples, and wine, representing the mortar used by the slaves. These foods hold religious and historic meanings that are explained during the seder service. Once this tradition has been observed and honored, the family feast ensues.

Songs of the Passover are chanted and sung, and rites of the festival are observed: the symbolic washing of the hands; the drinking of the four cups of wine; the opening of the door for the Prophet Elijah (that ancient wonder-worker and symbolic personage of the Jewish people); and the keeping of an extra glass of wine for Elijah.

Solemn Joy

A friend of mine shared the story of how she hosted a seder meal for three genera-tions of her family. Instead of using the formal dining room, however, she set a long table, low to the ground, with all of the traditional foods of the feast. To further enhance the atmosphere, she replaced the chairs with a series of thick pillows and cushions.

Once the solemnities had been observed and respected and the meal cleared away, the guests (still gathered around the table) continued to visit. As the evening pro-gressed, the festive atmosphere intensified to the point that some of the guests began performing traditional dances down the center of this low table—accompanied by the clapping and singing of the rest. I was told that this specific seder has evolved into a personal favorite Passover memory, and continues to be fondly spoken of by many members of her family.

Tradition is the focus of Passover, and great pleasure is taken in preparing and serv-ing the same dishes that have been passed down through the generations. This is an ideal example of the value of passing sacred knowledge, skills, and faith from one gen-eration to the next.

Linda's Chicken Soup with Matzo Balls

Make chicken stock according to the recipe found on page 189 (chill and skim solid-ified chicken fat for use in the matzo ball recipe). Add the matzo balls (see recipe page 13) and simmer, covered, until the matzo balls are thoroughly heated. To serve, first put the matzo balls into a bowl, and then ladle the hot broth over them. You may wish to garnish each bowl of soup with small sprigs of fresh dill before serving.

Homemade Matzo Balls

4 tablespoons rendered chicken fat (use the chicken fat skimmed from the broth
  for this purpose, or you may find it in the meat department of better food
  markets)
4 large eggs, lightly beaten
2 teaspoons kosher salt
¾ cup matzo cake meal (this is available at most major supermarkets during
  Passover)
¾ cups matzo meal (also available at most major supermarkets during Passover)
4 tablespoons water or chicken broth

Whisk together, in a small bowl, chicken fat and eggs until well blended. In a separate
bowl, stir together the salt and matzo meal. Combine the egg mixture with the matzo
meal mixture, and add the water or broth. Cover and chill for at least 20 minutes (if desired, you may make this a day ahead, and refrigerate overnight).

To shape the matzo balls, form rounded teaspoons of the mixture into balls with
your clean, slightly wet hands. Once you have shaped all the mixture into balls, transfer them into a large kettle of salted, simmering water and poach them, covered, for
about two hours (these will take longer to cook than other recipes because they are
quite dense). Do not take the cover off the pan to peek while the matzo balls are poach-
ing. Remove from heat and allow the matzo balls to cool, keeping them in the water in
which they were cooked. You may prepare these matzo balls well ahead of time and
freeze them for up to six months. To freeze them, place the balls on a waxed-paper-
lined cookie sheet (keeping a space between each) and place them in the freezer until
they have frozen solid (one or two hours). Remove the frozen matzo balls from the
freezer and wrap them individually in plastic wrap. This recipe makes about 22 one-
inch matzo balls.

Eastertide

*"The men were amazed and asked, 'What kind of man is this?
Even the winds and the seas obey him!'"*

—MATTHEW 8:27

On the first Sunday following the first full moon on or after March 21, the Christian feast day of Easter is celebrated. In the first centuries of Christianity, Easter and Whitsuntide were probably the only feasts celebrated by the followers of Christ. But once the church was liberated from the restrictions of the Roman persecutions, and legally recognized, Christian feast days were gradually increased and celebrated on a wider scale.

The word *Easter* is of Saxon origin, being derived from *Estera*, a Saxon goddess to whom sacrifices were offered at about the same time as the Passover was commemorated. How a clearly pagan holiday transformed into the holiest feast day of the Christian faith has much to do with the often ingenius conversion strategies of the early Christian church.

During the second century A.D. Christian missionaries spread out north of Rome, to other regions of what is now Europe. Whenever possible they tried to quietly integrate and transform non-Christian practices into ceremonies that were in accord with those of Christian doctrine. Aside from being a subtle way to spread the new religion, there was another, very practical reason for implementing this strategy. At that time new Christians were often severely oppressed. By not participating in the pagan ceremonies of the day they became obvious and easy targets for persecution. However, if a Christian rite was celebrated on the same day as a pagan one (and if the worshiping style was similar) then the new converts might live and thus convert others.

Today, *Easter* is the English name for the festival of the resurrection of Jesus of Nazareth. This feast is considered by those of every Christian denomination to be the most solemn of all holy days and is the keystone of the religion's hope and faith.

Come Easter Morn

"An egg is dear on Easter day."

—OLD RUSSIAN PROVERB

The happiness of children is much thought of and often well provided for at Easter (although not quite to the extent of the Christmas holidays). In our home the Easter

Bunny is a welcome visitor who fills large vintage baskets with small gifts and an abundance of candy. On Easter morning the children enjoy a family egg hunt before breakfast.

After attending religious services, the remainder of the holiday is filled with a delicious feast of baked—fresh or cured—ham; Grandma Ruby's potato salad; freshly baked dinner rolls; a lettuce-and-tomato salad; and the first fresh green beans of spring—tossed in a light butter sauce and sprinkled with slivered almonds. After dinner you will often find us enjoying a yellow or white cake baked into the shape of an Easter bonnet and covered with a layer of pastel-colored icing, its brim surrounded by satin ribbon and fresh, edible spring flowers.

Elegantly Glazed Baked Ham

"It isn't so much what's on the table that matters, as what's on the chairs."
—WILLIAM S. GILBERT

There is nothing quite so elegant as a glazed baked ham at the Easter table. It is simple to prepare and very tasty. Today we are blessed with the convenience of buying fully cooked hams (marvels in that they have been carefully trimmed of excess fat and often deboned), so they are ready for instant serving after being quickly heated. And during a busy holiday such as Easter this type of convenience is truly a blessing. With the addition of an easy glaze, you can present a delicious feast to your family and friends with a minimum of effort and money. (Because food markets usually offer wonderfully low prices for ham during this season, I often purchase an extra ham to put in my freezer for later use.)

    1 fully cooked whole or half ham
    2 or 3 cups thick peach or apricot preserves (you may substitute drained, pureed
        canned peaches that have been packed in syrup if you don't have the preserves
        on hand)
    1 to 3 cups honey or light corn syrup (use a little more if you are using canned
        peaches instead of preserves)
    3 tablespoons vinegar
    1 teaspoon Worcestershire sauce
    ¼ teaspoon ground cloves
    ¼ teaspoon ground ginger

Place the ham on a rack in a shallow, uncovered baking pan. In a 325° oven, heat ham as directed on the label, or until a meat thermometer inserted into the thickest part of the ham reaches 130°—this will take about 3 hours for a 10- to 12-pound ham, 2 hours for a 6- to 8-pound ham, 1¾ hours for a 4- to 5-pound ham.

Prepare the glaze while the ham is cooking. In a saucepan, combine the preserves or peaches with the honey, vinegar, Worcestershire sauce, and spices; stir and heat for about one minute (simmer for 2 or 3 minutes, stirring constantly, if you are using peaches instead of preserves). Thirty minutes before the end of the ham's baking time, turn the oven up to 375°. Brush ham with glaze, then return it to the hot oven for ten minutes. Brush again with glaze and cook 10 minutes more, then brush on a final glaze before serving. This recipe makes about 1 cup of glaze, which is enough for a large (10- to 12-pound) whole ham.

Grandma Ruby's Potato Salad

"What small potatoes we all are, compared with what we might be!"
—Charles Dudley Warner

This unusual and delicious potato salad was adapted by my mother-in-law, Ruby McBride, from a recipe her mother and grandmother used while she was growing up on a farm in southern Illinois.

6 medium russet potatoes—boiled, with peels on, until tender (to save time, boil your potatoes at the same time you put your eggs on to boil—using a separate kettle for each)
Salt and pepper (to taste)
1 medium sweet red onion, finely diced
¼ cup celery, diced fine (Grandma Ruby likes to use the celery hearts for this recipe)
3 or 4 medium sweet pickles, diced
6 slices of bacon (about one slice per potato), fried until it is very well done—crispy but not burnt. Note: If the bacon is very lean, do not drain the fat. However, if your bacon is extremely fatty retain no more than ¼ cup of drippings in your frying pan (spoon out the rest). Reserve the pan, with the bacon drippings.
1 heaping teaspoon yellow mustard
¼ to ⅓ cup sweet pickle vinegar (taken from a jar of sweet pickles)
3 or 4 hard-boiled eggs—don't boil them too long

Note: Because the egg yolks contribute a pretty golden color to this salad, it is important to not overcook the eggs. Grandma Ruby suggests taking the eggs from the cooking water immediately after they have cooked thoroughly and immersing the hot eggs into a bowl of cold water. This keeps the yolks golden yellow.

Peel potatoes when they are cool enough to handle and dice them into bite-size pieces (do not refrigerate until the salad is complete). Place them into a large bowl. Add salt and pepper, then set aside. Dice onion, celery, and pickles, and add these to your peeled and diced potatoes.

In the same frying pan that holds your bacon drippings, crumble the six slices of cooked bacon, add the heaping teaspoon of yellow mustard, and mix well. With the heat on low, deglaze the pan by adding the sweet pickle vinegar, gently scraping the bottom of the pan while mixing all of the ingredients together. Once this is completed, carefully add the vinegar mixture to the bowl holding your potatoes and other ingredients. Mix so that all of the ingredients are thoroughly blended.

Peel and dice into large chunks all but one of your cooled hard-boiled eggs. Lightly fold the diced eggs into the potato mixture. Slice your remaining hard-cooked egg and use it to garnish the top of your potato salad. The salad may be served hot or cold, and serves 8 to 10.

An Easy Easter Bonnet Cake

*"Come, take and eat thy fill!
It's Heaven's sugar cake."*
—EDWARD TAYLOR

Although this cake sounds quite complicated to create, it is surprisingly easy, fun, and quick to prepare. It may be baked in advance and frozen, unfrosted, for up to two weeks.

> 1 package white or yellow cake mix (enough to make a 9-inch two-layer cake)
> White buttercream frosting (homemade or canned), enough to cover a 9-inch two-layer cake (see recipe on the next page)
> Blue and red food coloring (to tint frosting)
> 1 12-inch pizza pan (this pan *must* have at least a one-inch-high rim) in which to bake the brim of the cake's bonnet
> 1 oven-safe bowl (I use a small stainless steel mixing bowl) that will be used to bake the bonnet's crown

Preheat oven to 350°. Generously grease and flour your pizza pan and your oven-safe bowl. Set aside. Prepare the cake mix according to directions on the packaging. Pour about 3 to 4 cups of the prepared batter into the oven-safe bowl; pour the remainder of the batter into the pizza pan, spreading evenly. Bake the batter in the pizza pan for about 15 minutes, or until the top springs back when lightly touched. When done, remove from heat and allow to cool on a rack for about 10 minutes, then invert the cake onto a wire rack to finish cooling. While this is cooling, bake the batter inside the oven-safe bowl for about 45 to 50 minutes at 350°, or until a toothpick inserted in the center of the cake comes out clean. Allow the cake in the bowl to cool for 10 minutes on a wire rack. Using a thin spatula, loosen the cake and invert it onto a wire rack to cool completely.

While the cake is cooling, prepare your icing. Put about ¼ cup icing each into two small bowls and lightly tint one with red food coloring (very lightly, so you will have a pastel pink color). Blend well. In the other bowl tint the icing with blue food coloring. Add only a few drops to start with, to keep the pastel colors light. Blend well. Cover both bowls with plastic wrap to keep icing from hardening, and set aside for later use.

Place the cooled cake brim onto a flat cake plate or tray and spread about 1 cup of the white icing evenly onto it (you may need to occasionally dip the spatula into a bowl of water to smooth out the frosting). Once this has been done, place the rounded cake crown onto the center of the iced cake brim and cover with icing. (If the bottom of the baked cake crown is puffed up or uneven, simply cut off a thin slice to make it flat—I use a serrated bread knife for this task, with very good results.)

If you like, you may spoon the remaining white icing into a small decorating bag with a petal tip, and pipe a ruffle along the edge of the cake brim (but the cake looks lovely even without this ruffle). Spoon pink icing into a small decorating bag with a small writing tip attached to it. Use this to pipe small pink dots on the cake's surface. Repeat this process with the blue frosting, until the entire cake is decorated with tiny pink and blue dots.

Note: If you don't have an icing bag and tip, you may achieve a similar result simply by putting the colored icing into heavyweight plastic bags. Using a toothpick, create a very tiny hole in one corner of the bag. Use this to pipe the frosting dots onto the cake.

I enjoy wrapping an appropriate length of satin ribbon around the iced crown of the cake. Tuck clean, edible flowers (pesticide-free) around the ribbon. Finally, I place a simple bow (made of the same satin ribbon) at the back of the cake bonnet and set it on the Easter sideboard. To serve, simply remove the flowers and ribbon before cutting.

Buttercream Frosting

1 pound confectioners' sugar (or you may substitute powdered sugar)
¼ cup softened butter or margarine
1 teaspoon good quality vanilla extract
3 tablespoons milk (if you are using ordinary powdered sugar, use 3 tablespoons of boiling water instead)

In a large mixing bowl, beat together sugar, butter, vanilla, and milk until smooth. Add more milk if needed, until frosting is of a spreading consistency. If desired, add a few drops of food coloring. Stir to blend. Makes enough to frost a 9-inch 2-layer cake or a 13-inch sheet cake.

EASTER FANCIES

"I submit my fancies to your eyes . . .
What great creation
What dole of honor."

—WILLIAM SHAKESPEARE

In my mind, the emblems of spring will be forever linked to those of Easter. New shoots of green grass and the classic shape and shades of nature's eggs evoke the spirit of hope and renewal that this season brings with its arrival.

In honor of these symbols, the children and I enjoy lightly decorating our home with small tokens, some purchased, others hand-crafted. Quite often we make these in multiples in order to share with friends, neighbors, or family members—or to stock our Gift Pantry.

A Lucky Bird's Nest   Birds' nests have long been symbols of good fortune and prosperity. And while it is a rare but wonderful find to discover a real bird's nest to use in your spring decor, you may create your own simple, attractive nests using excelsior, an inexpensive, coarse, grasslike material that you can buy to line gift baskets. To make nests, mix several handfuls of excelsior with wallpaper paste (you may substitute white glue, but glue is a bit more difficult to work with) in a metal or plastic mixing bowl and mold it into the shape of a bird's nest with your hands (wear rubber gloves for this project). Place your wet nests on a cookie sheet lined with wax paper and allow them to dry thoroughly. You may leave these natural, or spray-paint them white, blue, silver, or gold. For a lovely Easter centerpiece, display your eggs inside a nest placed atop a raised cake plate, and covered with a clear glass dome. You may also enjoy making tiny nests, filling them with marzipan eggs, and setting them at each place setting, to enhance a spring brunch or dinner party.

Note: A fun variation of this simple project is to substitute well-dried pine needles for the excelsior. However, you must use a heavy wallpaper paste for best results.

Mysterious Bunny Tracks One Easter morning we woke up to discover powdery white bunny tracks leading up the walkway and stopping at our front door. At the time, Mike and I each thought that the other had placed them—yet it was not he or I. To this day we do not know who made those whimsical tracks. (I have a hunch, however, that it may have been the retired couple who lived next door to us at the time, although they never confessed to it.) You may create magic for the children in your life by dipping three fingers in flour, then pressing them against the floor and tables. The pleasure of seeing the children marvel at the mystery of the bunny tracks is sheer bliss.

Easter Baskets Ever since I purchased my first vintage Easter basket for my son Clancy—at a yard sale, fifteen years ago—I have reused the same baskets on Easter morning from year to year. How? Each year, two or three weeks before the holiday, we bring out our vintage baskets—one for each child—and display them upon a tabletop (similar to the manner in which stockings are hung as decorations before Christmas). Inside the empty baskets we place our large and interesting collection of eggs—mingling the decorative eggs with the useful, pastel-colored plastic eggs that the Easter bunny fills with small pieces of candy and coins and hides. (We keep the pastel eggs from year to year as well, supplementing our supply as needed.) On Easter morning the children hunt for these eggs.

Easter Grass Advanced planning will allow you to enjoy a flat of wheat grass—planted three to four weeks in advance—to ornament a buffet table, or to use as a centerpiece. Or you could purchase a square of sod from your local nursery; these often sell for less than five dollars for a piece two feet square. The sod is very easily cut with a serrated knife—over a thick matting of newspaper to capture any mess. Nestle the cut sod pieces into your favorite baskets, terra cotta pots, or wooden flats. Add a few of your prettiest eggs, a large raffia bow, and you have an inexpensive, easy, and elegant decoration that will grace your home during this festival of spring.

ॐ

Remains of an Easter Feast

"Nothing helps scenery like ham and eggs."
—MARK TWAIN

Ham was always the traditional entrée at our Easter table when I was growing up, and it inevitably appeared on our plates *after* the holiday as well. While ham and scalloped potatoes remain my favorite made-over meal, other artful and delicious ways in which to make use of the remains of the Easter feast are diced ham scrambled with eggs; traditional ham-and-cheese sandwiches on fresh rye bread; a delicious yet simple ham spread, used on sandwiches or spread across fresh crackers or rye crisp and offered as a snack or appetizer; and, of course, that humble, time-honored meal of bean soup flavored with the hock (bone) of the Easter ham.

Papa's Ham-and-Scalloped-Potato Casserole

"Papa, potatoes, poultry, prunes and prism are all very good words for the lips."
—CHARLES DICKENS

2 cups chopped cooked ham (trimmed of all fat)
4 to 6 large raw russet potatoes, peeled and sliced very thin
2 cups simple white sauce (or 1 can of a cream-based soup such as cream of celery, cream of potato, or cream of mushroom, mixed well with ½ cup of milk)
Salt and pepper
Optional: ¼ cup shredded cheddar or Swiss cheese to use as a topping

Butter a large casserole dish and spread about one third of the sliced potatoes across the bottom of the dish and sprinkle with one third of the diced ham. Evenly pour one third of your white sauce or soup mixture over this layer. Salt and pepper lightly. Repeat this process two more times. Cover your casserole tightly with a lid or aluminum foil and bake for about 1½ to 2 hours in a 350° oven (or until potatoes are tender). This makes a wonderful lunch or dinner when served with a tossed green salad and fresh or canned fruit. Makes 6 servings.

Simple Ham Spread

"All work is as seed sown; it grows and spreads, and sows itself anew."
—Thomas Carlyle

I enjoy using this easy-to-create ham spread in tiny tea sandwiches or—combined with crisp lettuce and slices of ripe tomatoes—in hearty sandwiches that I pack in my children's school lunches. It also serves as a wonderful appetizer, spread across fresh crackers before a light meal of soup and salad. If you are having a party, it is delicious as a filling for hollowed-out cherry tomatoes served as an appetizer (these may be made a day in advance and refrigerated).

> A food processor or blender that is capable of chopping meat
> 1 ½ to 2 cups lean ham, coarsely chopped
> 1 8-ounce package of cream cheese, cut into cubes
> 3 tablespoons dijon-style spicy mustard
> 2 or 3 tablespoons brown sugar
> ¼ teaspoon ground cloves
> ¼ teaspoon ground ginger

Combine the ham and the cream cheese in a food processor or blender and pulse or puree until the mixture is smooth. Add your mustard, sugar, and spices, and blend until these are well combined. I like to transfer this mixture into an attractive crock and chill, covered, for at least 2 hours. Serve with bread, rye crisp, or crackers. Recipe makes 2 cups of spread.

Note: Grandma Ruby used to make a similar dish substituting mayonnaise for the cream cheese. Using a traditional meat grinder, she first ground the ham, then added mayonnaise, and sometimes the other ingredients, to make what she called a ham salad.

Mother's Ham Hock and Beans

". . . A noble dish . . . a sort of soup, or broth, or brew."
—WILLIAM MAKEPEACE THACKERAY

When the ham was almost gone from the bone (hock) my mother and father would make yet one more meal from the remains of the Easter feast . . . ham hock and beans, served with homemade corn bread slathered with soft creamy butter, and garnished with fresh, diced green and yellow onions. This old-fashioned soup was a welcome meal to come home to on a blustery spring evening. I can think of no other meal that better exemplifies honest, comforting sustenance.

Beans are excellent fare because they are warming, nourishing, and extremely economical. Dried beans double in bulk when cooked; for example, one cup of dried beans will make about four servings. However, you may wish to cook more than is needed for a single meal because, contrary to popular belief, cooked beans can be frozen quite easily. And while dried beans take a bit of time to cook, they require little supervision and may be made ahead of time and reheated without problems. Cooked beans or bean soup will often keep well in your refrigerator for up to ten days without spoiling.

Note: While this particular recipe calls for small white northern beans, you may substitute other dried legumes, such as split peas, lima and kidney beans, or a combination of all of these, in this recipe.

2 cups dried, small white northern beans
12 cups cold water
1 yellow onion, sliced
1 ham bone (ham hock) minus fat and gristle
1 stalk of celery, diced (optional)
1 large carrot, peeled and diced (optional)
1 large potato, peeled and diced (optional)
1 large bay leaf
Salt and pepper to taste
1 cup finely diced yellow and/or green onion as garnish

Note: On rare occasions, my mother would add a bit of tomato sauce to this soup and it became a lovely pumpkin color, but most of the time we all preferred its natural pale hues.

In a colander, wash your beans with cold water and pick out and discard any cracked or broken pieces and stems. Drain well, then soak washed beans in water overnight. The next morning, drain the beans. Place beans and cold water in a clean kettle along with your onion, bay leaf, and ham hock. Simmer soup for 3 or 4 hours, or until beans are soft. Using a slotted spoon, remove the ham hock and allow it to cool, then pull off tender pieces of ham remaining on the bone and put these back into the soup. Add celery, carrot, and potato, bring to a light simmer for 15 to 20 minutes. Discard the bone (quite often we would save it as a treat for our black labrador, Rufus).

The Mystic Egg

"Heaven is like an egg, and the earth is like the yolk of the egg."
—Chang Heng

The tradition of decorating the shells of eggs spans many countries and centuries. It is so diverse that the exact origin of this ritual is somewhat obscure. We do know that the egg has long been a symbol of the mysterious miracle of birth and renewal. The fascination for this ancient symbol continues into modern times, where eggs of all sizes and compositions continue to be dyed, etched, painted, bejeweled, decoupaged, and transformed into lovely decorative elements that impart a charming whimsy to tabletops and bookshelves, and are especially nice to display during the season of spring.

Dyed Eggs The children and I have enjoyed the process of traditional one-color egg-dyeing for years. Yet, on occasion we have veered from tradition to experiment with unique designs and textures. One such strategy is to create a marbled effect on the eggshells by drizzling them with melted wax from a candle before dyeing. (You may also do this with dry dyed eggs for a multicolored effect). For those occasions on which we try more ambitious projects, we like to blow out the egg beforehand (this will remove the uncooked egg from the shell) so that we may keep our creations from one year to the next. It takes a bit of patience to blow out an egg from its shell, but the process is quite simple. To do so, take a large sewing needle and press it firmly but gently into one end of a fresh uncooked egg until you have made a small hole. With your finger over the hole, tilt the egg over and repeat the process on the opposite end, but make your second opening wider than the first (about the size of a pea). Blow through the smaller opening (over a bowl) until the egg comes out of the larger hole. Once the egg is empty, wash it well, using water and a few drops of chlorine bleach. Once it has dried completely, you may decorate it however you wish (I cover the larger hole, using my glue gun, before decorating). These eggshells will keep indefinitely (be gentle with them, however, as they are still fragile).

Decoupaged Eggs Several years ago I saw lovely vintage Easter eggs composed of cardboard and covered with the most enchanting floral papers. Unable to find these in my price range, I decided to try my hand at duplicating them by way of decoupaging hollow eggshells, using scraps of pretty tissue and wrapping paper (these have a very small scale, old-fashioned design imprinted onto them) and decoupage glue. The results are charming, the process quite easy, and the eggs remain beautiful from year to year.

Eggs of Clay Make eggs of air-hardened clay and paint them your favorite colors (I think they look best when painted gold, silver, white, green, and blue). The advantage of these hearty eggs is that you may make them as tiny or as large as you wish, and you do not need to concern yourself regarding their fragility.

Almond Eggs Almond paste, also known as marzipan, is a fun and easy way to create edible eggs for Easter baskets, to embellish the top of an Easter cake, or simply to arrange around your home in pretty grass baskets. Almond paste is available at many grocery stores (in the baking aisle) or at stores that carry cake-decorating or candy-making supplies. For under five dollars I have gotten enough marzipan to make a few dozen miniature eggs (we call them hummingbird eggs because they are so tiny). Simply roll a bit of the paste until it takes on the size and shape that you desire. If you would like to color your marzipan eggs, work one or two drops of food coloring into the dough while forming them. This project is so incredibly easy that six-year-old Rosie has made charming marzipan eggs that rival any of my own.

The First Day of May

"You must wake and call me early, call me early, mother dear;
Tomorrow 'ill be the happiest time . . . the maddest, merriest day;
For I'm to be Queen o' the May, mother, I'm to be Queen o' the May."

—ALFRED, LORD TENNYSON

When I was a young child, my mother was constantly in and out of hospitals. In my childish way, I always endeavored to bring her a token of my love when visiting her in these sterile establishments. Quite often my gifts took the form of a small shred of a fern that grew next to the driveway, or a yellow dandelion plucked from the front yard. Even so, my mother always expressed immense appreciation for these artless presents. She would hold my humble gift to her heart and recite, "A rose to the living, if graciously given before the hungering spirit is fled, is more than sumptuous wreaths to the dead." And she always substituted (for my sake, I like to think) the word *flower* or *fern* for the word *rose*. She quoted this Nixon Waterman verse so often that I took it quite for granted until, as an adult, I stumbled across it in book of poetry.

As I write about May Day I cannot help but notice that the habit of presenting flowers on the first of May to friends and neighbors is an ideal opportunity to practice the rare art of appreciation. It is very important that you express your love and appreciation to those people who touch your life in a positive way *while you have the opportunity to do so.*

This merry-hearted holiday that celebrates the advent of spring is a very pretty festival that can be full of fun for children. In sixteenth-century England, May 1 was a day spent gathering bunches of flowering shrubs and budding branches of hawthorn and sycamore, and fastening them upon the doors of those neighbors and friends who, as tradition mandated, lived good lives and cultivated kindly habits.

Another romantic custom of the day was performed by maids and matrons, who would gather the morning dew with the earliest rays of the sun, and bathe their faces in this magic fluid (some even gathered enough to bottle and hold for later use). Doing this was thought to render the face beautiful for the next twelve months. And while they were out collecting dew, maidens would also gather blossoms. The choicest blooms would be fashioned into a crown for the young maiden who was to be crowned Queen of the May.

Many of the ceremonies of May Day as we know it were brought to the United States by English settlers in colonial days. And a few of these still survive in some form or another. Young people often create baskets or cornucopias to fill with flowers, and leave these anonymously at the doorstep of friends. And at many colleges the traditional crowning of the May Queen is a beautiful, time-honored ceremony.

May Baskets

"Look, here is a basket."

—William Shakespeare

The gentle little baskets that are used to hold and deliver May Day flowers are generally of home manufacture, constructed of a variety of materials and shapes. My favorites are all very simple to make and take very little time or money to create.

The Classic Cone Shape   The simple cone-shaped basket is made from a six-inch-square piece of heavy paper or cardboard (we have covered recycled cardboard with scraps of pretty wallpaper for this project, with lovely results). To make the cone, roll the cardboard into a cone shape and glue the edges using a glue stick, white glue, or rubber cement (a hot glue gun does not work well for this project). Hold the edges together with paper clips or clothespins while the glue dries. Once the glue has thoroughly dried, cover or paint the cone. Cut a piece of ribbon to about one foot in length; this will become your handle. You may staple the ribbon to each side of the cone to make a handle, covering the staple by gluing a small bow, button, or dried flower over it. If your cardboard is very sturdy, you may wish to punch a small hole on either side of the cone (about ¾ inch down from the rim) and thread and knot your ribbon through either side.

The Box Basket   To make a box basket, you must have a sturdy, lidless, cardboard box, such as a small shoe box or perhaps a microwave popcorn box (with the lid flaps cut off). Before painting, use an awl to carefully bore two small holes, one inch apart and one inch down, on each end of your box—these are for your handle. To cover any printing on the box you may decoupage it with wrapping paper printed in a spring motif, or (my favorite way) paint it. For a polished look, remember to paint the bottom and the inside of the box. I have used flat wall paint, left over from another project, to paint the boxes—one coat is usually all that is needed. Once the paint has dried, I stencil ivy and/or hydrangea shapes onto the sides of the box. Or, I paint vertical stripes of pale lavender, blue, or yellow over a white or off-white base coat (or combinations of these colors). Cut two equal lengths of coordinating ribbon about six to eight inches wider than the box (French wired ribbon works well for this project). Thread and tightly knot each ribbon through the corresponding holes of the box, creating a double handle.

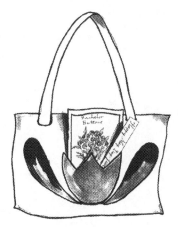

May Day Basket for Late Bloomers For those years in which spring is late in arriving (and thus fresh flowers not so readily or inexpensively available) you may wish to sew tiny (four-inch-square) cushions from pastel-colored gingham. Glue a tulip-shaped felt pocket onto the front, and sew a ribbon handle at the top. Insert a small packet of flower seeds into the pocket and hang on the doorknobs of your favorite neighbors, teachers, and friends.

Fill your baskets with flowers, candy, or our sentimental May Day cookies (be sure to wrap these in cellophane if you are putting them inside a painted box) and show your appreciation by making your secret deliveries.

Mysterious May Day Chocolate Chip Cookies

"God moves in a mysterious way,
His wonders to perform."
—WILLIAM COWPER

As an alternative to flowers, you may wish to bake a batch of these May Day chocolate chip cookies to include in your May baskets.

I discovered this old recipe, handwritten on an index card, inside a vintage cookbook I purchased at a yard sale on May Day, a few years past. I was on the lookout for a good chocolate chip cookie recipe at the time, and this one turned out to be, by far, the easiest, tastiest, and most reliable chocolate chip cookie recipe I have yet to find. To whoever wrote it and tucked it into that old, musty book, I send a delicious "Thank you."

1 cup white sugar
1 cup brown sugar
1 cup solid shortening
1 cup oil
1 egg, lightly beaten
1 tablespoon milk or cream
1 teaspoon cream of tartar
1 teaspoon salt
1 teaspoon vanilla
1 teaspoon baking powder
3 to 4 cups sifted white flour
1 pkg. (1½ to 2 cups) chocolate chips
Optional: ½ cup nut meats

Preheat oven to 350°. Combine the above ingredients in the order given. Drop the dough onto cookie sheets with a teaspoon (keep cookies about 3 inches apart) and bake for 7 to 9 minutes, or until light golden brown. Makes 2 dozen cookies.

Note: If you are feeling especially ambitious, use this recipe to create cookie-flowers. Simply shape the dough into large cookies (about the size of the rim of a teacup) and press a clean Popsicle stick into the dough to create a stem. Place only 2 or 3 cookies on an ungreased baking sheet (keep them three or four inches apart). Bake for 10 to 12 minutes, or until done. After they have cooled, ice the cookies with a buttercream frosting to make them resemble daisies. Makes 5 to 7 cookie flowers.

We often make double batches of this dough and freeze it. Or I roll it in sheets of wax paper (until it forms a tubelike shape), tying the ends like a gift. It will keep in the refrigerator for several days. This is our version of the store-bought "slice and bake" cookie doughs.

Mother's Day

"We are govern'd with our mothers' spirits."
—WILLIAM SHAKESPEARE

There is only one absolutely unselfish and God-like love, and that is of a good mother for her offspring. And the swiftest and most powerful thing in all the universe is a mother's prayer. Kipling knew this when he wrote, "If I were damned of body and soul, I know whose prayers would make me whole, Mother o' mine." If we searched the annals of ancient Greece or Rome we would find no greater name than *Mother*. For most of us, much of that which is sweet, beautiful, and lovely is clustered in that name.

It is little surprise then that the idea of setting aside a special day on which to honor mothers has ancient roots. The British tradition of "Mothering Sunday" has long paid tribute to the maternal parent on the fourth Sunday of the season of Lent. Yet, the American observation of this holiday was not nationally recognized until May 8, 1914, at which time the United States Senate approved a proclamation designating the second Sunday in May to be known as Mother's Day.

Today, Mother's Day is a national celebration when children of all ages pay tribute to, and show appreciation for, "Mother."

Easy Mother's Day Breakfast
⚭

Menu
Baked Eggs In Mock Crepes
Breakfast Fruit Crisp
Katie and Rosie's Berry Good Tea
⚭

Baked Eggs in Mock Crepes

"They are up already, and call for eggs and butter."
—William Shakespeare

This elegant egg dish is surprisingly simple to prepare, and makes an unusual and artful presentation. It is easy for preteens and teens to prepare on Mother's Day, as long as you plan ahead and have these ingredients available (supervise at your own discretion). Or prepare this for yourself, then relax and enjoy the day.

3 tablespoons melted butter or olive oil
8 large spring-roll wrappers (these are available in the refrigerated delicatessen
    section of most major grocery stores, and are quite inexpensive)
8 tablespoons feta cheese, crumbled
8 teaspoons finely minced fresh herbs such as oregano, thyme, and basil, or
    2 teaspoons of dried Italian seasonings
8 fresh eggs
Salt and pepper to taste
8 teaspoons heavy cream
Fresh sorrel or watercress leaves, washed and patted dry
Optional: Sour cream, bacon bits, and chopped parsley to garnish
Nonstick cooking spray
1 eight-sectioned nonstick muffin tin

Preheat the oven to 400°. Spray the muffin cups generously with nonstick cooking spray. With a pastry brush, spread melted butter on one side of each of the spring-roll wrappers. Place these inside the muffin cups, butter side down, and allow each to pleat naturally.

Mix cheese and herbs together. Drop about 1 tablespoon of the cheese mixture into each lined cup. In a small bowl, break one egg, then slide the egg into the muffin cup, on top of the cheese mixture. Repeat this process with the remaining eggs until all the cups are filled. Before baking, season with salt and pepper, then drizzle 1 teaspoon of cream on the top of each egg. Leave wrapper open (as you would a one-crust pie).

Bake on a cooking sheet for 20 minutes or until eggs are cooked to your preference.

Note: I always check the eggs after only 10 minutes of cooking, to ensure that the spring-roll wrappers are not overbrowning. If necessary, remedy this problem by tenting the pan with aluminum foil during the last ten minutes of cooking.

Remove the pan from the oven and loosen each wrapper by running a narrow spatula or butter knife around the outer edges. Carefully lift the hot egg cups out of the pan using the same spatula.

Serve egg cups (while still warm) on pretty serving plates that have been lined with sorrel or watercress. Garnish the top of your egg with a dollop of sour cream and a sprinkling of bacon bits and parsley.

Breakfast Fruit Crisp

"The earth bringeth forth fruit of itself."
—MARK 4:28

"And in's spring became a harvest," Shakespeare noted, and it is quite true—spring is the season in which trees blossom and begin to bring forth fruit to nourish and refresh us. This fruit is especially welcome once winter has edged away. And, happily, the harvest is often so very bounteous that I am challenged to discover unique and tasty ways in which to prepare and serve the delicious fruits of the season.

One morning, as I surreptitiously consumed a plate of apple crumble for breakfast, I became inspired to adapt the fruit crisp into a legitimate breakfast dish. Peaches, pears, plums, blueberries, blackberries, raspberries, even strawberries and apples are all quite delicious in a crisp. However, you needn't confine yourself to only one fruit; combining fruit is a delicious, frugal, time-honored way to make use of small amounts of a variety of fruit. Many berries mingle together beautifully—blackberry, raspberry, and boysenberry—as do peaches, nectarines, apricots, and plums. You are limited only by your resources and/or your imagination. If fresh fruits are not available, you may use drained canned fruit for this recipe.

Blend 1 cup toasted oats (or granola cereal), 1 cup flour, ½ cup brown sugar, and ½ cup butter or margarine

Wash and prepare fresh fruits as you would for a pie filling. Quite often I add approximately ¼ cup of sugar or honey for each 5 or 6 cups of prepared fruit. (For fruits such as peaches, nectarines, apricots, and apples I sometimes add small amounts of raisins, cinnamon, nutmeg, allspice, ginger, and cloves to the prepared fruit before cooking.)

Spread fruit in a shallow casserole or baking dish (about 4 to 6 inches deep), sprinkle topping evenly over fruit, and bake for 30 to 40 minutes in a 350° oven. I enjoy using attractive baking dishes so that I may serve the dish at a breakfast buffet—this will also allow it to look pretty on the breakfast table. Serves 6.

Garnish each dish of baked fruit crisp with a dollop of flavored yogurt (you may want to use vanilla with apple or pear crisps—berry-flavored for berry—and the like).

Note: This dish is very easy for older children to assemble, and may be prepared in ad-

vance. It is a lovely, easy, light breakfast in itself, or as an accompaniment to a fuller menu. It is also fun to make this fruit crisp as a surprise treat for your family or tasty breakfast before a busy day of school and work. And, of course, it is a wonderful holiday breakfast.

Katie and Rosie's Berry Good Tea

". . . Is there honey still for tea?"
—RUPERT BROOKE

In our tea-drinking adventures the girls and I always enjoy variations of our favorite beverage. The girls have made delicious concoctions when steeping fresh blackberries (plucked from my father's garden every year on Mother's Day) with ordinary black tea. Simply add fresh berries (or frozen ones that have been thawed) to your teapot along with your tea leaves and allow them to steep for about ten minutes. The berries will impart their very delicious essential oils into the brew. You may serve the hot tea directly into cups (use a strainer to capture tea leaves and berry remnants), adding honey or sugar if desired. On very hot days, we strain the warm, freshly brewed tea directly into a pretty glass pitcher, add a sweetener, and serve it in tall frosted glasses filled with ice. This is a lovely and simple luxury.

You may also use other fruits, as well as spices such as cinnamon and ginger, to enhance ordinary tea. The peels of apples or oranges and other citrus fruits are also quite delicious tea enhancers when added to tea leaves as they are steeping.

Memorial Day

"While memory holds a seat in this distracted globe. Remember . . . !"
—WILLIAM SHAKESPEARE

"A memory is what is left when something happens and does not completely unhappen," noted British author Edward de Bono. Certainly this is never more true than when remembering those souls who have fallen in defense of any good nation. In the United States, Memorial Day was designated a federal holiday in order to keep green the memory of those who have paid the ultimate price, so that freedom—as Abraham Lincoln phrased it—"shall not perish from the earth."

Since this holiday was mandated in 1868, its true meaning has become somewhat obscure in some areas of the country. Many people look on it as merely a fun-filled, three-day weekend marking the end of spring. I must confess that, until several years ago, I was among this group. My attitude changed, however, when Mike, the children, and I visited the southern Illinois town where his mother had been raised.

As we ambled through this hamlet, we noticed that a small brass band and a large crowd of people had gathered around a weathered monument in the town square. Taking our place in the crowd, we watched as about one dozen veterans formally placed a large bunch of flowers at the base of this memorial and did an unusual thing for these puzzling, modern times: They said a public prayer, a sincere offering of appreciation, honoring the soldiers whose names were engraved on the plaque. This war memorial listed every hometown boy who had lost his life fighting for America, from World War I to the Korea and Vietnam conflicts.

But it wasn't the ceremony that amazed me. It wasn't even the fact that these men, long dead, were being so honored. *It was the reverence of the crowd.* Young couples, teenagers, the elderly, and children of all ages were nodding their heads in respectful silence. They were listening to the member of the VFW (Veterans of Foreign Wars) as he described the great sacrifices made by the men whose names were chiseled onto that monument. He spoke about the providential nature and near perfection of the Constitution of the United States, and the freedoms that it ensured. It was this, he quietly and firmly stated, that these men died for. The freedoms we now enjoy, he reminded us, were paid for by these men, and the hundreds of thousands of others like them.

The memory of that Memorial Day ceremony continues to haunt me. Having lived in southern California for most of our lives, we were unfamiliar with this spirit of community, honor, and appreciation. To us, these were rare and beautiful qualities, ones that we have, since that time, endeavored to remember and to cultivate in our own lives.

Memorial Day Flag Etiquette

"Off with your hat as the flag goes by!
And let the heart have its say;
You're man enough for a tear in your eye
That you will not wipe away."
—Henry Cuyler Bunner

On Memorial Day the flag should be flown at half-staff until noon to honor those who have given their lives for their country. After noon, the flag is to be raised to the peak until sundown, at which time it is removed.

Illuminated Fragments
Unintentional Miracles

"No seed shall perish which the soul hath sown."
—JOHN ADDINGTON SYMONDS

When I was ten years old, inspired by reading nearly every Louisa May Alcott book, I scribbled a poem about the sadness of a hunter's gun. This first endeavor at creative writing was stuffed into a school folder and promptly forgotten. A few weeks later, as we were tidying the house, my father handed me the sheet of notebook paper that bore my poem (it had slipped from my folder, as papers often do when you are ten). As I crumpled it into a ball to toss into the rubbish, my father asked me if I had written the poem. I sheepishly answered yes. Surprised, he told me he had enjoyed reading it—that I "had a gift" for words.

Nearly thirty years later, I can clearly see how my father's encouragement and kind words have subtly guided me—giving me a confidence I never would have felt otherwise. His words were a gift, a part of the whispering force behind my embarking on a writing career. The irony is that my father has no recollection of the incident.

The best things we ever do in our lives are often unintentional miracles. Most of us would be astonished if we were shown the great influence we exert on the lives of others. If you were to delve into your own past it is likely that you would find a similar incident—hopefully, words of praise or encouragement spoken to you years before—that have influenced your life. Yet the person who offered these cherished words would most likely not recall the incident at all, or at least find it difficult to remember the exact details of it.

Because such moments contain a mighty (and often miraculous) influence, would it not be wise to make a *habit* of cultivating and nurturing them—and *not* leaving them to the power of chance? With this thought in mind, let us train ourselves to consciously create *positive* words and experiences that will influence the future for the better, and help shape the destiny of ourselves and others. For your influence reaches far into the future and can affect the fate of individuals as well as nations.

Chapter 2

Spring Home Graces

~

"May the gods grant you all things which your heart desires,
And may they give you . . . a home and gracious concord,
For there is nothing greater and better than this."

—HOMER, *THE ODYSSEY*

Every Day's Most Quiet Need

"I love thee to the level of every day's
Most quiet need, by sun and candlelight."

—ELIZABETH BARRETT BROWNING

William James once noted that "the greatest discovery of my generation is that you can change your circumstances by changing your attitudes of mind." The attitudes you choose will define your life. Each of us lives *somewhere*—a specific place in this world that we call home. It is within your power to arrange and decorate this home of yours so that it satisfies something within you, regardless of how humble, grand, or temporary the spot may be.

It seems to me as if many people are always fantasizing about their dream home, yet rarely make the place in which they currently live attractive or satisfying to them. I was guilty of this negative way of thinking for many years. I constantly was dreaming of a rambling country cottage on the banks of a small tree-lined lake, while rarely appreciating or cultivating the positive attributes found within my very comfortable, but small, suburban home. I was reluctant to put much of myself into the place for the simple reason that we would be moving "someday." I developed the attitude of a visitor (although I had lived there for several years) and thought of the property as merely a place in which to mark time. I did not understand, then, that this way of thinking was causing a quiet frustration and discontent inside of me which, in turn, negatively affected others.

After much soul-searching, I made a conscious decision to stop waiting for that mythical dream home and began implementing the many ideas I had been collecting for so long. To my surprise, I found that—instead of being a hindrance—the limits of my time, talent, funds, and location actually *generated* artful solutions that I would never have dared to try (or even *thought* of) otherwise.

Are you living in the realm of "someday"? If so, choose now to surround yourself with things that echo your tastes and interests. Express yourself, not only with the things you purchase for your home, but also in what you care to create for it. Keep in mind that the element of caring is made visible in little touches. Caring is that sacred ingredient that must be added to walls and furnishings before a house can become a home. The intangible becomes animated via the process of organizing, decorating, and running a home with thought, planning, frugality, and artfulness, regardless of your dwelling's size, cost, or location.

Poetry in Ordinary Things

*"Poetry lifts the veil from the hidden beauty of the world,
and makes familiar objects be as if they were not familiar."*
—Percy Bysshe Shelley

We live in a disposable society. When something breaks, quite often it is not mended or repaired but thrown out and replaced by another, newer version. I lament this philosophy. Items that show visible evidence of use by past generations fascinate me.

I enjoy the imperfect quality found in old things. The finish on the door of my favorite antique armoire has been worn away from being opened and shut a multitude of times over the past century. And the wooden seats on our pair of seventy-year-old carved walnut chairs have been worn to an almost velvety softness, due to decades of faithful service. These beautiful patinas can only be authentically created by time and use; thus, they impart a priceless beauty that can never be successfully duplicated. Perhaps this is why vintage furniture and true antiques are so valued by collectors.

Firm believers in rescuing past treasures from benign neglect or underappreciation, Mike and I haunt flea markets, yard sales, and antiques stores. It has become an art for us to improvise ways in which to use ordinary things creatively, elegantly, and frugally. Even our garden is not immune to this recycler's philosophy. Plants are relocated, as opposed to being thrown out; miniature rosemary trees are transplanted into our own (or my father's) garden after enjoying them indoors during the holidays, as are seedling pines and paper-white narcissus.

Quite often we are able to find a new use for many of the objects we come into contact with, even after its first life has passed; my first book, *Frugal Luxuries,* tells you how to creatively recycle eggshells into planters, newspapers into gift tags, boxes into works of art, and nylon screens into mock–French ribbons. Outdoor furniture, such as garden benches, birdhouses, and iron planters find their way indoors, while outside, on the patio, you will find an old, six-sided, carved wooden table, painted to withstand wet weather. And before we buy *anything,* we look around the house to see if we can't improvise it first, such as copper pipe used as curtain rods, and brass coat hooks on which to mount them.

Even the simplest of belongings can be used to create a pleasant and attractive home atmosphere. The only guidelines are that they be attractive to you and/or echo personal meaning. For example, the antique, leather-topped drum table that was one of the very first pieces of furniture Mike and I purchased is very beautiful—the sight of it evokes pleasant memories of our newlywed days. And the two battered wicker children's chairs in which Clancy, Katie, and Rosie spent so much time when they were very young lend to our home a paradoxical air of past and future. I envision our (yet to be born) grandchildren sitting in these child-sized rockers while I spin tales of how their parents, seated in the same chairs, pretended to be airplane pilots, cowpokes, and Disneyland attendees, and hosted tea parties for their dolly's dolly.

The Taskmaster

"A small daily task, if it be really daily,
will beat the labors of a spasmodic Hercules."
—ANTHONY TROLLOPE

A few years ago, smitten with spring decorating fever, I drew up a master list of household projects that I wished to accomplish. However, because at the time I was writing a book, I was forced to put nearly all of them on hold. I promised myself that once my book had been published, I would spend the entire season tackling the many tasks on my master list. I painted all of our dark and dreary kitchen cabinets a gentle shade of cottage white; planted more herbs in the back garden; painted a shabby-looking armoire; sewed English-style cottage curtains for the kitchen and family room windows; and *finally* filled the lovely, picketed window boxes Mike had built for me earlier that year, with lettuces, herbs, and nasturtiums.

After completing these projects, I came to more fully appreciate how valuable a master task list can be. Such a list allows you to record all of the projects you *wish* you could accomplish, given the time and/or funds. There is a catharsis in list-making, a rebirth of optimism and enthusiasm. A list gives direction to actions, as well as carries the burden of remembering all of the things you wish to accomplish "someday."

Enrich your life by making a master list of all the projects you want to accomplish over the long term. In the future, whenever you have the urge to work on something, but cannot imagine where to begin or what to do, peruse your list. If your master list is at all like mine, you will always find one or two simple things to spark your enthusiasm. Furthermore, deleting completed projects gives you a lovely feeling of accomplishment.

Explore the Options

"We shall not cease from exploration
And the end of all our exploring
Will be to arrive where we started
And know the place for the first time."

—T. S. Eliot

Before I embark on any major home task I use the tool of research—not only to give my projects thought and direction, but to save time and money as well. Painting twenty-two large wooden kitchen cabinets was a massive endeavor. Quite obviously, I did not wish to embark on such a labor-intensive task without at least a small certainty of the attractiveness of the outcome. As an insurance policy of sorts I researched, by way of decorating books, magazines, and kitchen showrooms, to find precisely the look I wanted *before* I began the project. In the same manner, I researched colors, prints, textures, and patterns of curtains before investing the necessary money and energy into that project. Should you be planning a major task, remember to have an end in mind, and do not neglect to research the subject beforehand.

The Miracle of Discovered Objects

"Be still fed with fresh discoveries.
And kept alive by a new perpetual succession of miracles rising up to its view."
—JOSEPH ADDISON

One day, I noticed two tall, Shaker-style cabinets set outside of a small strip mall. I pulled in to investigate further and found them to be composed of a very heavy metal, and well constructed. A small, dark-haired woman came out of the store and asked me if I would like to take the cupboards—for free. She was remodeling the retail space into a beauty salon, and the cabinets had been left by a previous tenant. Delighted, I offered to pay her for them. She refused, telling me that I would be doing her a favor by taking them, as they were very heavy to move (her plan was to haul them to the dump). Gratefully, I thanked her and went home to tell Mike about my find. We returned to the store, where he and Clancy loaded the heavy cabinets onto the bed of the truck and drove them home.

At Grace Cottage, they were stored in our garage until I could wash and paint them a soft white, to match the kitchen cupboards. With the addition of two small, shell-shaped architectural ornaments boldly secured to their respective front panels, they impart a lovely, classically simple look to our dining room.

Recently, I transformed a large, carved wooden picture frame Rosie and I found at the curb one morning. After rubbing a whitewash of paint over its dark, rustic curves I was a bit puzzled as to what to do with it. I toyed with the time-honored idea of converting it to a mirror (this can be done for about twenty to forty dollars, depending on the size of the mirrored glass needed). Yet I longed to do something more creative. One morning, as I was deciding how to arrange the dining room furniture, it occurred to me to use this same carved frame above a chest-high, pine china cupboard that was tucked into the corner of the room. It fit perfectly! Inside the empty frame, I screwed a series of brass cup hooks into the wall, and hung my collection of new and vintage blue-and-white teacups in three neat rows of three. In autumn I will take down the delft cups and hang my collection of creamware in their place. During the winter holidays I will put up a combination of red and green transfer and chintz-ware teacups to reflect the mood of the season. The result is an absolutely unique and lovely way in which to display a varied collection of teacups (the gathering of these is a weakness that keeps me always on the lookout for creative, space-saving storage and display ideas). The cups also add much needed pattern and color to the dining room, and are an artful, frugal alternative to a wall-hung china cabinet . . . as well as a simple way to reflect the change of seasons.

Surrounded by Beautiful Thoughts

*"Surrounded by . . . the beautiful, and such reminders of history and art,
Children are constantly trained to correctness of taste and refinement of thought."*
—The Beecher sisters

Much of my adult life has been spent in the quest to master the skills that promote home graces. It is my wish to share with you my favorite secrets for cultivating quiet graces and beauty at home—simple, swift ways to implement the little touches that say so much to your family, and are the visible elements of your caring:

- The cluster of simple fresh ferns you place on the table

- The crusty loaf of home-baked bread or biscuits that enhance an otherwise ordinary meal

- The ice-cold milk at the dinner table, served in a chilled silver pitcher (acquired for a song at a tag sale, and polished by loving hands)

- Giving gifts you create yourself, in order to impart that "intimate quality of things made entirely by the human hand"

- The joy of surprising a family member by performing a household task that is their regular duty

- Allowing young children to "help" around the house and garden so that they may acquire a sense of self-worth—and share time with an adult who is important to them (Even when, ultimately, this means extra work for the adult.)

- Surprising a loved one with the simple treat of a breakfast lovingly prepared and served in bed

- Arranging a pot (or pitcher) of herb tea on a pretty tray to welcome your children home from school (to share while you unwind and discuss the events of the day)

Timeless pleasures such as these enhance and soothe the home atmosphere and will enrich your life and the lives of those you hold most dear. Your family will unconsciously save up these frugally luxurious graces and pull them forth to savor during life's more barren moments. Over time, they will grow to understand the deeper meaning of all of these little touches.

Egg Cups

". . . The vicar, having said grace, cut off the top of his egg.
'There,' he said, handing it to Philip, 'you can eat my top if you like.'"
—SOMERSET MAUGHAM

If the egg is the world's most ancient fast food, it stands to reason that the romantic object—the egg *cup*—is nearly as dated. While historians still have not pinpointed its origin, they do know that meals of roasted eggs were commonly enjoyed by the ancient Romans. Evidence found in the ruins of Pompeii indicates that egg cups were a popular way of serving this nutritious food. And until about a century ago, it was quite common for travelers (particularly those from Europe) to carry with them their own egg cup in order to enjoy a quick meal of a boiled egg while on a journey. During the reign of England's Queen Victoria, a traditional christening gift was a silver egg cup. My brother, who was born in England in the late 1950s, still keeps the silver egg cup that was one of his baptismal gifts.

In the earlier part of the twentieth century, egg cups were often manufactured and used as a form of advertising for restaurants, hotels, steamships, and train lines. In the 1950s, egg cups experienced a revival and were quite popular in America as well as in Europe. Some American companies even added novelty patterns, such as Mickey Mouse and Snow White. And as the century drew to a close, egg cups became a popular collectible—possibly due to the fact that they seemed to represent a slower-paced, more gracious and civilized lifestyle. As well, they are a lovely and sensible manner in which to serve an ordinary egg.

I must confess that the diminutive egg cup holds me fascinated. The odd fact of the matter is that I was not even aware of how much I was intrigued by these decorative, useful items until I was packing my china cabinet during our move into Grace Cottage. I then realized I had unwittingly amassed a mismatched collection of more than a dozen egg cups.

The traditional use of the egg cup (to hold and serve a boiled egg) has been in and out of fashion throughout the history of civilization. I have found a plethora of alternative, modern day uses for the *polcillum ovi* (Latin for egg cup). The happy news is that, should you wish to build a collection of your own, there are still an abundance of attractive, inexpensive egg cups available in a variety of styles and motifs.

How to Use an Egg Cup

"Though this be madness, yet there is method in 't."
—William Shakespeare

- In Jonathan Swift's classic tale *Gulliver's Travels,* wars are fought over which way to use an egg cup. In fact, according to etiquette expert Emily Post, the traditional and proper way to eat an egg served in a cup is to first remove the top of the shell (using a "decapitator"). The decision of whether to eat directly from the shell (as is the British custom) or to remove the egg from the shell and place it into a dish before consuming has been, in the past, a much discussed detail. It is likely that this is the reasoning behind single cups being manufactured for the British, while double cups were sold to Americans. If you desire to serve an ordinary egg in an elegant and extraordinary fashion, you might wish to serve it in an egg cup. (You may even have a bit of good luck getting your children to eat them if they are served this way.)

- The traditional shape of an egg cup also makes a lovely dessert dish for a rich mousse, a delicate sorbet, or an iced custard or cream.

- Your guests will certainly give a murmur of interest when you serve an after-dinner liqueur in beautiful china egg cups.

- You may also wish to use egg cups on your table to serve as unusual holders for smaller items such as nuts, sugar cubes, elegant chocolates, after-dinner mints, molded or small pats of butter, melted and drawn butter for crab or lobster, and—with the addition of a tiny spoon—as old-fashioned salt cellars.

- I have also discovered that egg cups make efficient catch-alls for small items such as rings (put a wooden cup near the sink to hold your rings), or to hold small earrings and necklaces on your dresser or vanity.

- Your craft pantry or sewing room can be enhanced by egg cups when they are used to hold small sewing notions, such as buttons, needles, beads, and pins.

- Enhance your bathroom with pretty egg cups filled with scented potpourri, tiny soaps, and bath beads.

- I always consider my egg cups to be valuable additions to our vase collection, as they are lovely holders for fairy-sized bouquets of dried and fresh flowers or greenery. Instead of using a large arrangement of flowers as a centerpiece at your next dinner party, perhaps line a row of flower-filled egg cups down the center of your table (or alternate these with similarly proportioned candles). Or tightly cluster several flower-filled egg cups atop a footed cake plate to simulate a larger bouquet.

- In the springtime you may find it useful as well as attractive to use humbler egg cups filled with potting soil to grow seedlings on a windowsill. Once the plants become established they may be transplanted into your garden or presented as gifts.

- Group a collection of your prettiest egg cups on an attractive tray and display them on top of a shelf or side table. At Easter, we enjoy using our cups to display decorated eggs!

Illuminated Fragments
Grace Cottage

"There are no mistakes, no coincidences. All events are blessings given to us to learn from."
—Dr. Elisabeth Kübler-Ross

Grace Cottage came to us in spring. "Fruit of the spirit," I called it, nurtured by a steady stream of prayers and accompanied by an unwavering faith in the miraculous.

Our little house, beloved as it was, was much too tiny a place to comfortably shelter and nurture three growing children and a home-based business. In retrospect, I am often amazed that I wrote my first book, *Frugal Luxuries,* in a cramped corner of my tiny living room, forcing myself to ignore the unruly mounds of paper and books that littered the floor for the better part of a year. There was no door on that living room, so the children flowed in and out of my "office." They interrupted my streams of inspiration much like the constant, periodic ringing of an alarm clock that has been set on the snooze mode.

&

It was only fair to inform the realtors we spoke with (and there were many) that we were asking for the impossible: a large house (at least two thousand square feet) in a safe and attractive neighborhood—at a *very* low price. The fact that they were polite and helpful was a wonder in its own right. For those of you uninitiated to the southern California real estate market, my house requirements might not appear so very unreasonable. However (even at recessed values) we knew, and they knew, that what we were asking for was no less than a miracle.

We began our search in our own area with little success. Expanding out, we explored other nearby cities and then neighboring counties. We drove up hillsides and down into valleys. The only places we avoided were the notoriously expensive beach areas.

Each new person I came into contact with was told of our quest: the friendly clerk at the grocery store, the nice gentleman in front of me in line for the bank, the grandmother in the waiting room at the doctor's office, the parents of my children's school friends. The answers were all nearly the same: The only houses available in the style, size, and price I desired were in unsafe neighborhoods or, possibly, out of state.

One morning I followed a tip from a good friend (who, thanks to her loyal nature, had faith in my mad endeavor) and explored a charming area in a nearby city that I had overlooked. After driving past two Realtors who were placing open house signs outside a large attractive town home, I impulsively decided to go inside. Suddenly, as I started up the pathway to the front door, I changed my mind. But as I turned to leave,

the friendly real estate agent invited me in. So, changing my mind yet again, I walked inside.

Graciously, she did not laugh when I told her and her partner about the home I was searching for. There was, however, a split second of silence before the Realtor told me the name of a gated complex of town homes in an affluent area within a few blocks of the beach, in which a bank-owned property was available that perfectly fit our description. She offered me the address and her business card.

That afternoon, Mike and I visited the property and were delighted. The grounds of this small private community were charming and impeccably maintained—the steeply pitched roofs of its buildings strongly hinted at New England architecture. The houses had precisely the square footage and character that we were looking for. The area and neighborhood were excellent and (because it was bank owned) the price met our criterion. I left a message for Carole, telling her we wished to make an offer for the property.

She returned my call the next morning, sadly informing me that the house had been sold the previous afternoon. (It seems that other people had recognized the property as a bargain as well—there had been *eight* other offers for it.) Not giving in to disappointment, we asked if there were any other units available in this desirable community. This was a rare, one-of-a-kind deal, she informed us, and no other units were for sale, at any price.

Trying to cheer me (and knowing my passion for yard sales) Mike half-jokingly mentioned that he had noticed a sign posted within the complex announcing a "first-ever community rummage sale." It wasn't scheduled until the following month but perhaps we could find some consolation bargains. We noted the date on our calendar and went about the business of living.

❧

The following month, the morning of the sale found me in my writing chair, engrossed in transferring some scribbled notes onto the computer. Dressed and ready to leave, Mike reminded me that it was time to visit the community garage sale. Not in the mood for bargain hunting, I absentmindedly told him I didn't want to go. Responding out of character, he gently persisted. He said he had a feeling we might find something unique.

The sale signs were posted. The security gates, usually closed to nonresidents, were propped open. We walked through the crowded entrance, six-year-old Rosie between us. We meandered from house to house, purchasing new candy molds, a beautifully made birch bark basket, and a small collection of stemware for the children to drink their milk from. As we prepared to leave, Mike noticed that the garage door of an especially beautiful home that had been closed earlier was now open.

I found myself admiring an immaculately arranged garage—its finished, painted walls and ceiling added to the sense of orderliness. The friendly-looking couple nearby smiled in appreciation when I commented on the tidiness and beauty of their property. They laughingly told us that it was because they no longer lived there. Impulsively, I inquired if they planned to put the house up for sale. The owners exchanged a glance between them and promptly asked us if we would like to buy it. After assuring us that they were quite serious, we were given a thorough tour of the vacant (but very lovely) home.

Large glass doors in both the living and dining rooms opened to a generous private patio lined with brick planters. The kitchen enthralled us with its gentle natural light—the illusion of spaciousness was greatly aided by an endless view of green from the adjacent golf course. From the window above the sink, I found myself gazing out over a wide strip of lush green lawn. The view was dotted with clusters of mature trees of pine, ficus, and eucalyptus. Upstairs, I discovered the same scene could be viewed from one of the mullioned windows in the large master bedroom. And *two* balconies offered me tremendous scope for the imagination.

Standing in the cool shade of the generous front porch, the kindly owners told us they had purchased a new home several months ago, in another city about eighty miles away. This property had become a bit of a burden to them. We were, they so graciously informed us, an answer to *their* prayers.

Within the week, we made arrangements to purchase the house at their very reasonable asking price—almost exactly the amount we had set to spend when we started our search. Twenty-four days later we closed escrow. Today we are enjoying our new cottagelike home—basking in its simple charm (and extra space).

&

Quite by accident, I discovered another benefit to living in Grace Cottage. This was revealed to me as I experienced one of those temporary moments of barrenness (the all-too-human occasions during which any kind of miracle seems far away). Looking up at the steeply pitched ceiling of our living room, I was sharply reminded of how close quiet graces are . . . even when we don't recognize them. Issuing a prayer of gratitude, I marveled at the many gifts available to those who have faith enough to see them. Silently, I sent out a wish that they be discovered and used by all people of goodwill.

Chapter 3

Home Rites of Spring

∽

"In this dance there are fulfilled the most ancient rites."

—Pablo Neruda

The Beauty of Everyday Domestic Life

". . . from the highest to the humblest tasks,
All are of equal honor; all have their part to play."

—Sir Winston Churchill

The first fresh and sparkling glimmer of spring sweeps in on the wings of a rushing March wind . . . bringing with it a renewed sense of the joy of life . . . a tingle of excitement that is as old as the earth itself. Spring is the season in which anything and everything seems possible. Why? Perhaps because this—the traditional season of renewal and rebirth—often represents new beginnings. In truth, spring does usher in so many new things: a new gardening season, new fashions, and . . . a new season of home-keeping.

Spring is the season in which to grace your home with a first-class reappraisal. On the first pretty day you might wish to give your house a hard look . . . as your worst enemy would. This impartial inspection may reveal many shabby and unattractive things that you haven't noticed because you've become used to walking by them day after day. Does your upholstered furniture need to be cleaned or recovered—or replaced? Is the kitchen in need of a fresh layer of wallpaper; do the hallway walls need a light washing or a new coat of paint? Should the carpet be cleaned? Are the contents of the hall closet threatening to tumble out into the hallway?

Once you have given your surroundings an honest and thorough appraisal, take a walk outside (during daylight hours) and give a critical look to the outer areas of your home. Note the condition of the exterior paint. Is it faded and/or peeling? Does your siding look as if it needs replacing? What part of your garden is messy or barren? Is the outside of your home all that it should or could be, or does it just get by? Investing a small amount of attention in the spring will yield tremendous returns over the remainder of the year. You will find that getting your property in order now will allow you to easily enjoy the benefits of an attractive home and garden for months to come.

I feel that I would be remiss not to mention how the season of spring often kindles my nesting instinct, igniting the urge to make home and garden attractive, comfortable, smoothly run places to be in. There is an obvious drawback to this motivator—springtime only visits once a year. However, the happy truth is that each season offers a kindred motivating force: Summer brings the urge to lighten and pare down—autumn prompts the preparation for winter—winter holidays motivate me to tidy with joy.

A Seasonal Blessing

"It is the first mild day . . . each minute sweeter than before . . . there is a blessing in the air."
—William Wordsworth

The keeping of the house can become the mainstay of your life. As I discovered some years ago, it is possible for the mundane chores within a household (such as tidying and cleaning) to become rituals of the commonplace. When this happens something quite wonderful occurs. Ritual, by its very nature, contains within it a gravitylike power. It is this very specific energy that anchors the fragments of our existence. It is this cohesive force that creates a continuity that keeps family, and friends, and self from floating away in diverse directions.

The yearly ritual of a thorough housecleaning should be thought of less as work, and more as a healing rite given to us each spring—preserving the healthy balance of body and soul. Cultivating such an attitude transforms drudgery into an act of faith, stirs memories, and spawns hope.

Nesting Instincts

"A few strong instincts, and a few plain rules."
—William Wordsworth

There is a phenomenon that, it is said, is experienced by all women within a month of giving birth. When I was expecting my first child, I was told to anticipate this "nesting instinct." Broadly defined, it is an uncommon surge of spiritual drive and physical energy that urges an expectant mother to put her house in order before the arrival of a new baby.

Thinking it to be an old wives' tale, I was taken by surprise when a wonderful surge of energy drove me to clean out closets, rearrange drawers, organize menus, and thoroughly clean house. I had never before felt such joy when doing mundane tasks, and was taken aback at all I had accomplished in such a short amount of time . . . and with such *enthusiasm*. Once my son arrived I understood the grand design behind this valuable instinct. Young babies, as you may know, take up an enormous amount of time and attention, leaving little time for the necessary tasks of a household.

The golden memory of all that I had achieved when smitten with the nesting urge haunted me. Wouldn't it be a wondrous skill to be able to call up such an instinct at will? To be able to face the necessary tasks of housekeeping with eagerness and pleasure would indeed be a priceless gift. With this ideal in mind, I sought ways in which to naturally trigger such an urge—that did not require pregnancy. Over the years I have found a few methods that evoked this lovely response:

- On cleaning days I often browse through the pages of my favorite decorating books and magazines. Doing so almost always ignites my home-keeping sensibilities. I treat myself to a cup of my favorite tea or coffee and make a habit of setting my kitchen timer for one half hour (doing this keeps me from spending the entire day engrossed in reading). This strategy has actually evolved into a private game: When the timer rings, I reset it for one hour, then work around the house on the chores I have previously listed on my sheet of things to do. When the hour expires, I allow myself another fifteen to thirty minutes of relaxation, or fun time (I determine the length of fun time by how much work I have done in the previous hour—and by the number of projects remaining on my list of potential accomplishments). This process is repeated as many times as necessary until my daily tasks are completed. On those days that I simply want to be done with the cleaning, I often dangle the prospect of fun as my reward for finishing my work—

usually a movie I have been wanting to see or a book I have been longing to read, or a meeting, or a visit with a friend.

- My good friend Alexis Larson (the talented artist responsible for all of the lovely drawings inside this book) shared her secret to cultivating the nesting instinct. She takes one small area of her home, such as a table, desk, or dresser top, or a small shelf in her kitchen, and decides that she will decorate or rearrange *only* that shelf in a pretty, new, manner. Once this is done, she inevitably decides that the rest of the room or house must be tidied up as well (so that it will look as nice as the original project). I tried Alexis's idea in my bedroom. I was so pleased with the results of stacking two pieces of vintage leather luggage atop my cherry-finished armoire (in graduated sizes) that I went on to rearrange and tidy the entire bedroom.

- Another very good friend of mine, Nancy, uses a motivating strategy similar to my own, the only exception being the type of reading she does. Books on the subject of housecleaning itself are a prime motivating factor in keeping Nancy's charming home attractive and tidy. Some of my own favorite books on this subject are *How to Avoid Housework* by Paula Jhung, *Confessions of a Happily Organized Family* by Deniece Schofield, and *More Hours in My Day,* by Emilie Barnes.

- I have another strategy for drawing out the nesting urge, and that is to casually entertain. Oftentimes I will invite friends to dinner (a few weeks in advance). Using the dinner date as my goal, I find myself cleaning the entire house, and sometimes I even accomplish small home-improvement projects such as repapering a kitchen wall, or repainting bathroom cupboards, or planting a set of flowering annuals outside the entry of our house. This is a fun way to motivate yourself. A note of caution, however—you must not expect too much from yourself in too short a time, or you will become frustrated and feel pressured (thus losing the joy of your accomplishments). For this reason, plan *only* the type and amount of projects that you can reasonably expect to finish in the amount of time you have allowed.

Secrets of Home-Keeping

"Leisure is sweet when it follows work well done."
—Proverb

Just as you cannot hurry the advent of spring, neither can you rush properly done household tasks. Spring is the ideal season in which to accomplish those tasks that are not necessary to do every day. While we are blessed with miraculous machines that whisk away dirt and dust, and transform dirty laundry into clean, there are still some frugal and enjoyable time-honored tricks that will help you to care for your home.

- Simple, inexpensive chlorine bleach has a multitude of uses within the household. I dilute one part bleach in five parts water, and store the mixture in spray bottles. These containers are kept under the sink in the kitchen and bathrooms and are wonderful counter cleaners and disinfectants. I also use about one half cup of bleach in a sink filled with warm, soapy water, and soak my coffee- or teacups, teapots, and other items that have been stained brown, for about fifteen to thirty minutes (depending upon the strength of the stain). It is almost like magic to see how quickly the stains disappear. You may also add about one quarter of a cup of bleach to a sink full of water when washing dishes, as it seems to disinfect much more efficiently than ordinary soap and water (this is especially useful if you have a minor illness in the family). This is quite safe to use on dishes (in our city the government puts large quantities of chlorine in our drinking water). But note that a few brands of dishwashing liquid warn on their labels *not* to mix with bleach, so please check yours. I also spray this bleach and water mixture onto freshly washed cutting boards on which I have chopped raw meats or fish, to ensure that germs are killed. This mixture is also quite efficient in eliminating many household molds and mildews (such as in the shower, tub, and other porcelain bathroom fixtures). One note of caution, however: Bleach will take out color from most fabrics, so be careful how and where you spray it. If you are uncertain if it is safe to use on your surfaces at home, test a very small amount on a discreet area of the item you wish to clean. Wait overnight, then check to see if it has discolored or damaged the surface. (Keep this bleach mixture, and all bleach, out of reach of children. And never mix ammonia or lye products with chlorine bleach, as the combination creates toxic fumes.)
- Spring is the ideal season in which to clean all the glass in your home. Simple ammonia, diluted with water, is an excellent, inexpensive glass cleaner. Mix one part ammonia with five parts water and pour into a recycled window-cleaner bottle

with a spray nozzle. Spray mixture onto glass or windows and wipe with a crumpled newspaper for a lovely streak-free shine. (When spraying any ammonia products, be careful not to spray onto any woodwork or furniture, as it may discolor the finish.) I have also found ammonia to be a useful cleaner for most ceramic tile floors. And, once or twice a year, I remove the glass domes from our light fixtures and wash them in a sink filled with ammonia and water. (Keep ammonia out of reach of children, even when it is diluted—and never mix ammonia and chlorine bleach as the combination creates toxic fumes.) If you wish to use a more natural product, wash glass or crystal with white vinegar and water. And if you would like to impart an especially lustrous look to your decorative glassware, try plunging it in a towel-lined sink (the towel is to protect the glass from chipping) that has been filled with warm water and a tablespoon or two of liquid bluing (available at most grocery stores, near the cleaning products). Use bluing on decorative glass *only*.

- My good friend Debbie gave me a wondrously simple and easy technique that will remove stains from light-colored one-hundred-percent cotton (untreated): Fill a nonreactive bowl (or your bathroom sink) with about four cups of water, and add two tablespoons of chlorine bleach. Allow your cloth to soak in this mixture for five minutes. Rinse thoroughly. If stains persist soak again (in the same mixture) for *ten* minutes. Rinse thoroughly. If stains still remain, soak item for *fifteen* minutes (never soak your items for longer than fifteen minutes at a time, as this may cause the fabric to burn). Rinse thoroughly. I have successfully used this technique several times to remove mystery stains from a variety of vintage cloths and laces. (Another of Debbie's useful suggestions is to *not* bleach any white permanent-press items. Why? The bleach will react with the permanent-press treatment that has been applied to fabric, causing garments to turn dingy yellow or gray.) Sunlight is a time-honored way in which to remove stains from whites. Even Shakespeare noted, hundreds of years ago, "the white sheet bleaching on the hedge." Hanging light fabrics outside on a bright day allows the sunshine to bleach the material. When I first was told of this suggestion I very much doubted if it would actually work. After trying all of my other tricks on a favorite white cotton dress (to no avail) I resorted to hanging the dress in the May sunshine. Three days later the large, stubborn, tea stain had completely disappeared. (If it's a particularly stubborn stain, apply a bit of lemon juice to it before putting it out in the sunlight.)

- I often spruce up my antique wooden armoires, chairs, and tables with Howard's Oil. An antique dealer once recommended this product to me as a polish for older wood (especially those pieces that are on the verge of needing a new finish.) I tried the product and was thrilled with the results it achieved. The oil seemed to instantly impart the polished look that I desired. Needless to say, I am a huge advocate of Howard's Oil, and use it at least once a year on all my old pieces that need a bit of brightening up. You may find this product at most hardware stores, as well as in many antique shops.

- With children in the house it is inevitable that the walls will show fingerprints and smudges (and perhaps even harbor the vestiges of marking pens and other horrors). I used to go about fretting at the state of my painted walls, until I discovered the very simple, tried-and-true touch-up technique. It has become one of my favorite ways to brighten the walls of our house between paintings (as well as extend the life of a coat of paint). Touch-up paint is simply paint that matches the color of your walls. It is used to touch up stains, spots, and nicks. One of my favorite tricks is to take a bit of the leftover matching paint and place it into a quart-sized Mason jar (be certain to close it very tightly). Keep this with your cleaning products, where you may easily retrieve it. Once you have cleaned your walls, you may take this paint and go about brushing it onto the (dry) areas that were resistant to washing. The dried dabs of paint should blend perfectly with the existing walls and be undetectable. Water-based paint works best (and makes cleanup quite easy, even if you happen to spill a bit). This technique not only keeps walls looking newly painted and clean (with very little time, effort, and money), it also allows you to experiment with stenciling and other designer paint techniques. If you don't like the results, simply paint over them with your touch-up paint, and no one will be the wiser.

- Silver is one of my favorite metals, but beautiful though it is, it has the drawback of tarnishing easily. Silver polishes to remedy this are legion, and there are many formulas that work well. However, once your silver objects are polished, you can inhibit the appearance of tarnish by applying two coats of inexpensive butcher's wax (or any good grade of paste wax). Be certain to apply the second coat of wax only after the first has thoroughly dried. Buff well with a very clean, very soft cloth. If the wax yellows after several months, you may remove it simply by washing the object in hot, soapy water, or detergent. Apply fresh wax if desired. (This technique should be used only on silver objects *not* used for food.) When storing silver you may inhibit the formation of tarnish by keeping it in a resealable plastic bag (try to remove as much air as possible before sealing, as exposure to air contributes to the tarnishing process). A vacuum sealer machine works well to remove air from the bag.

- To clean bronze and brass that have not been lacquered requires little more than a warm, acidic material such as heated vinegar, tomato or citrus juice, buttermilk, or a blend of salt and vinegar. Rinse items with clean water and dry with a clean, soft cloth.

MASTERING TIME

"All my possessions for a moment of time."
—LAST WORDS OF ELIZABETH I OF ENGLAND (1533–1603)

· Identify specific goals and make a long-term plan to achieve them. The sheer act of writing goals on paper forces you to give them thought and helps to implement them in your conscious (as well as subconscious) mind.

· When planning your hours, be certain to include the necessary tasks that will take you toward your desired goals. Understand that great achievements are composed of accumulated smaller actions. This knowledge allows the thread of joy and achievement to penetrate each task you carry out, regardless of how tedious or dreary it may first appear.

· The old proverb noting that "a journey of ten thousand miles begins with a single step" is a wise one. Begin with one small action—write out a to-do list, organize the most cluttered drawer in your kitchen, make out a monthly budget for your finances, or plan a dinner menu for the coming week. It has been my experience that one small act will lead to others. Eventually an entire chain of events can result, and your goals will transform into your desired reality—born from the seed of one small action.

Harnessing the Hours

"The moments we forego
Eternity itself cannot retrieve."
—Schiller

It has often been said that time is money, but time is, in essence, life itself. Yet, as we savor and appreciate life we quite often think nothing of wasting time. Why is it, then, that, as John Burroughs noted, "Time does not become sacred to us until we have lived it"? Perhaps the answer to this question should be categorized among the secrets of the ages, along with most other aspects of human nature.

Please don't misunderstand, I am not suggesting that we should be bound to a drudgery-filled existence. Quite the opposite. Time spent in simple pleasures and healthy games is a wise investment—for it is these activities that lend a richness and a balance to life. Yet, in today's topsy-turvy world, many of us are finding it increasingly difficult to balance our lives and harness the (seemingly) shrinking hours of the day.

The most classic tactic used in harnessing time is to develop a basic system. A system will help you to plan your work and work your plan. It can teach you to take action in the present rather than delegate it to the future. Because the future is shaped by the actions we take in the present, to develop and implement such a system could change your life in a positive way.

Victor Hugo once noted that "he who every morning plans the transactions of the day, and follows out that plan, carries a thread that will guide him though the labyrinth of the most busy life. The orderly arrangement of his time is like a ray of light which darts itself through all of his occupations. But when no plan is laid, where the disposal of time is surrendered merely to the chance of incidents, chaos will soon reign."

Ironically, the supreme value of time is not to be found in *future* hours (the future is deceptive, always chanting "someday"). The *past*, on the other hand, offers us something of value. "History," noted the great Roman orator, Cicero, "is the witness that testifies to the passing of time; it illumines reality, vitalizes memory, provides guidance in daily life, and brings us tidings of antiquity." The *present* is precious as well—it is the material from which both the past and the future are made. The present is brimming with new hope, new ideas, and new opportunities—at our disposal—to be acted on.

Working with Method and Order

"The beauty of the house is order,
The blessing of the house is contentment,
The glory of the house is hospitality."
—ANONYMOUS

The American poet Robert Frost, in an interview shortly after his eightieth birthday, was asked how he managed to maneuver so very many interesting, unusual, and important things into his vital lifetime. His reply was simple: "Learn how to do the things you *have* to do more quickly and effortlessly—save minutes—and you will gain an extra hour or more every day to do the things you really *want* to do—see friends, listen to music, or look at pictures . . . help others in your community . . . and religious activities . . . make the projects for which you're always saving plans . . . read, or perhaps even write a little poetry."

It is good to have an orderly plan for work . . . any work. To plan is a clever and intelligent thing to do in any endeavor—it is the human gift. As with anything else you organize in life, you must first know your outcome. Plan your work and work according to that plan. And, regarding keeping house, the most obvious secret to tidiness within the home circle is to not make it untidy to begin with! I offer you a few simple suggestions and strategies that may be helpful in doing just that:

- To reduce extra work, arrange your work areas close together, and place all of the necessary tools, equipment, and supplies where they will be used (if possible).

- Tidy up as you work. For example, when cooking put ingredients away immediately after you have used them. When folding laundry immediately put clean clothes in their proper storage area to avoid making piles.

- Provide comfortable seating and proper working heights, with surfaces that are easily maintained. For example, we have several bar stools of the appropriate height positioned around our kitchen countertop, and use these to sit and pare vegetables, fold clothes, roll out cookies and pie crusts, create craft or sewing projects, and eat simple meals. This same large counter area is covered with white ceramic tiles so that a simple spritz from a bottle of bleach and water will easily disinfect (and remove discolorations in the grout) as we wipe up any messes with a clean cloth or sponge.

- Put away only clean items in the refrigerator. Wipe off all items before putting them either in the refrigerator or cupboard, and remember to cover items securely when placing them in the refrigerator, to help keep down spills and prevent stickiness from spreading.

- Wipe up spills immediately, especially on the stovetop, in the oven (microwave as well as conventional), and in the refrigerator. Doing so will keep them from becoming hardened and difficult to remove.

- Rinse a pan immediately after using it. Place a dishcloth beneath pans before scrubbing, in order to prevent the sink from becoming discolored or scratched.

- Try not to allow work to pile up. Leftover work is like a pair of rabbits; when left alone they multiply. Dishes become more difficult to clean because foodstuff has dried onto them. Amassed clutter causes counters, floors, tables, chairs, and the like to become piled snarls of mess (which, due to human nature, you will want to avoid at all cost).

- Do not allow yourself to become sidetracked from the job you are on. Focus on one specific job until it is completed or nothing will ever be completely tidy or clean.

- Try to teach yourself to dovetail your activities. Prepare two or more meals while cooking one, and freeze the second meal for a busy night next week. Bake double the amount you had planned and freeze the second half for a future dessert. When doing manual labor, such as washing dishes, gardening, scrubbing floors, or folding clothes, use your mind to plan ahead for parties, menus, and work. These hands-on duties also offer an excellent opportunity to gather your children near you for singing, telling stories, listening to their stories, or have them recite the ABC's and multiplication tables, count, or read to you from a favorite book. Or, use your hands-to-work time to converse on the telephone with a friend. One of my friends and I used to spend far too much time on the telephone, so we made a rule for ourselves: We could not speak on the telephone unless we were doing a productive task such as peeling vegetables, folding clothes, dusting furniture, or wiping walls. With the advent of cordless telephones, I would even speak to her from my garden while I was weeding! I am now a qualified expert at holding a telephone between my shoulder and ear, using no hands.

- Make a habit to work quickly and methodically. I always think of Agatha Christie's character Hercule Poirot when I find myself working in a haphazard manner; one of Hercule's favorite catchphrases is "method and order." An example of methodical cleaning is to vacuum the *entire* house, do *all* of the dusting, polish *all* of the glass and mirrors, peel *all* of the vegetables.

- Use a timer. As you may have gathered from earlier readings, I am a tremendous advocate of using a timer in many areas of my life. This habit began when the children were in preschool and I needed them to tidy their toys in a hurry. Making a game of it, I would set the timer for five minutes and watch as the children tried to beat the clock when picking up their toys. The person who put away the most items was allowed to choose the book I would read that day, or the flavor of ice cream we would serve for dessert. I found this was fun for me as well. Quite often I set the timer, allowing myself fifteen minutes to do the dishes, fold and put away a large load of laundry, or tidy the living room. It sounds a bit juvenile, but I find the timer method to be tremendously effective, so much so that I now use it to complete writing assignments and other business-oriented tasks. The positive side effect of using my timer method for cleaning is that it makes me realize how little time it actually takes to do a dreaded task.

- Implement daily rituals. Schedule routine tasks at the same time each day, week, or month. Borrow from the past when Monday was wash day, Tuesday was for cleaning the floors, Wednesday was baking day, and so on. Try to schedule these ritual tasks Monday through Friday so that you may reward yourself on weekends with relaxation and fun.

- Organize your errands geographically and you will save valuable time, as well as gasoline and wear and tear on your automobile. Also remember to cluster your errands (as well as your telephone calls).

- "A place for all and all in its place" is an old yet wise axiom. Assign permanent places to store items in your home and keep them there! Teach your children the assigned places for their own items as well. Delegate certain shelves to store books, assign drawers to hold scissors and office supplies, etc. You will find that this strategy helps with cleanup as well (don't many of us often put off tidying because we have no idea where to put the items cluttering our homes?).

- Take care of the minutes, and the hours will take care of themselves. Make use of your small moments of time. Put the toothpaste cap on after brushing, wipe shoes (or take them off) before entering the house, change into old clothing before working on a messy project, and clean messes as they occur.

- Save time by attaching a list of necessary ingredients to each recipe that you regularly prepare. When you are preparing your shopping list you will know at a glance what items you will need to purchase for that meal.

- Cluster appointments. We group our children's orthodontist appointments one after the other in order to save an extra trip. Book haircuts in the same manner. If you have several family members seeing the beautician or barber you may even qualify for a quantity discount!

- Learn to make use of your pockets of time. Every person has to spend his or her fair share of time waiting. The wait may be a line at the grocery store, at the drive-through window of a restaurant, on hold during a telephone call, or in the waiting room of a doctor's office. You may use these seeds of time to plan a menu for the week, write a quick letter to a friend, make out a shopping or grocery list, or write a to-do list. Do this at home as well (while you are waiting for the soup to boil, the biscuits to brown, or while you are on hold during a telephone call). Ten or fifteen minutes can be used to put away the clean dishes from the dishwasher, tidy the silverware drawer in the kitchen, clean the top shelf or inside door of the refrigerator, sort the laundry, put a roast in the oven or Crock-Pot. These small jobs add up to tremendous gains in time and effort. You will be astonished at the wondrous results, for the cumulative effect of such a habit is a clean and tidy house—while you will be left with the illusion that you have only puttered a bit.

- Establish a basket, bowl, or wall-mounted key rack near your door for automobile and house keys. Make it a habit to deliberately place your keys in the designated key area and you will rarely waste time hunting them down. This idea sounds almost too simple to express, yet you would be surprised how many sensible people do not bother with a plan such as this!

- Does your mail end up scattered about the house, thereby causing monthly bills to be paid late (garnering extra fees) or appointments to be missed? Again, I urge you to establish one place to deposit the day's mail. In our home we have trained everyone who gathers the mail to put it into our "bill basket." The basket does tend to get cluttered, yet we are confident that everything we need is in one area.

- Have *one* place (usually a tabletop near the front door) where children can find their lunch money. If your family brings a lunch from home, establish a place in the kitchen where lunch boxes are left for refilling.

- Did you know that Tuesday and Wednesday are the slowest days at the grocery store? Save time (and possibly money) doing your grocery shopping on these days. Hint: Avoid weekends and early evenings—these are the *busiest* times—also the day before any major holiday.

- Keep a large shopping bag handy to fill with errand items, such as packages or mail to send out, videos or library books to return, and don't forget that baking dish you borrowed from your sister two months ago. Establish a second bag exclusively for clothes that you are sending to the cleaners or laundry.

Illuminated Fragments
Creating an Atmosphere of Home Peace

"A cozy atmosphere of home peace prevailed."
—LOUISA MAY ALCOTT

Just as a gardener cultivates a plot of earth, growing the fruits and flowers that sustain and enhance existence, and keeping weeds at bay, so may you tend your home—creating a physical and intangible atmosphere of loveliness and peace. By pursuing this process you will eventually discover that *you* are the master-gardener of your own happiness, home, and family.

To make the much-needed transition from house to home, there must be a cultivator—someone who cares enough to orchestrate the members of a household (and the objects within) and create a sense of love and harmony. There must be someone who understands that it takes patience, time, hard work, unselfishness, and planning to create moments—and thus memories—of love, beauty, and unity; someone who can influence the future.

Home can be a powerful force. One home and one family can do wondrous things to positively affect the world, or devastating things to destroy it. You have the power to create a home into which your family can go to separate themselves from the outside world—and be welcome and loved.

Is your house a home? Decide now to become the cultivator of your dreams and ideals, the conductor of positive thoughts, deeds, and actions. Create a plan, reach out for the happiness and beauty you desire, and, in a spirit of gratitude, claim them as your own. Discover the multitude of treasures within your own life that, like Poe's purloined letter, are hidden in plain sight—only waiting to be recognized amongst the jumble of the mundane.

Chapter 4

Home Order

~

"Out of chaos she brings order and light,
A goddess in sensible shoes."

—ALFRED, LORD TENNYSON

Untangling the Maze of Earthly Phenomena

"Let us . . . expatiate free o'er all this scene of man; A mighty maze!
But not without a plan.

—ALEXANDER POPE

While I lament the losses that accompany a "disposable society," I cannot profess to be an advocate of useless clutter. I am in fact a proponent of the belief that clutter contains magical powers that give it the ability to breed and multiply. The word itself is derived from a medieval English word, and its actual definition is "to clot or coagulate." Accurately named, clutter makes you feel frustrated and disorganized. It makes you feel like a failure if you can't find the gift you bought for the birthday party or the keys to the car as you leave for work in the morning. Clutter is a congestion of things and should be dealt with, for clogged homes may cause depression and an out-of-control feeling. Clutter causes disharmony in the home. (Don't many family squabbles stem from disputes regarding the other person's clutter?)

In order to really express who you are and what you are supposed to do in life you must be orderly. The more you organize your possessions the more you will organize your life. The idea of order seems like such an unimportant, trivial thing, yet leaving behind a cluttered home affects how you face the world. Clutter in your thinking can manifest as clutter in your environment.

Why do so many people keep clutter? The most common response is "just in case—you never know when you might need something." To abandon an overabundance of clutter implies that you have faith that when a need for these things arises you will find them again from another source.

The ordering of your physical world begins in the world of ideas. Through noble and ordered thoughts and ideals you may create a home environment that is rich and diversified—endowing it with life, intelligence, and soul.

Decluttering

"Nothing is particularly hard if you divide it into small jobs."
—Henry Ford

Have you ever noticed how some homes are comforting, and a joy to go into? You have the power to give your own home these same wonderful qualities. You may create your own personal paradise by first understanding that there is no *right* way to order your home. The only proper path to home order (be it organizing your home office, clothes closet, or bathroom storage areas) is to do that which is right for your lifestyle. Set up a system that you will actually benefit from, and use. Keep in mind that the end result is not necessarily tidiness. Your goal should be to set up a functional system of living where you can effectively find and use what you have in your home. (Thus, the following suggestions are merely guidelines, not rigid rules.) Each life holds idiosyncrasies—some individuals prefer to live with lots of things around them, others find comfort in less.

Sometimes you will keep clutter simply because you are just too exhausted to do anything about it. The irony is that it is often the clutter itself that is inciting this feeling of fatigue. Here are some ideas to help you to create your own personal paradise:

- Before you put away or shift one item in your home, first understand *why* you are putting your house in order. Is it for efficiency? Are you discouraged each time you go to the kitchen to cook a meal and are unable to find the pan you need? Are your bills scattered in different drawers throughout the house, so that some are forgotten? Are there stacks of things peppered around your home because you have not yet designated a place in which to store them? If so, then your purpose for organizing is to simplify the running of your life and home, and to save time as well as money. The only rule in orderliness is that you be able to put your hands on what you need within a minute or two of when you need it. Keep this in mind as you begin setting up your own decluttering system.

- Many people believe that clutter carries a negative energy that interferes with anything you plan to do in life. Begin your home organizing by sorting out and ridding yourself of those useless items that make your heart sink. Do not wait for the perfect conditions to occur before you begin decluttering your space, even if you are living in temporary quarters. By taking action you are inviting wonderful, positive change into your life.

- One of the biggest mistakes most people make when ordering their homes is to focus on only the public areas of the house (such as the kitchen and living and dining rooms). It is the private areas of your home in which you truly live, and spend most of your time each day. Your bathroom, clothes closet, bedroom, private office, pantry, linen closet, and children's rooms are the spaces in which you should first begin untangling the maze of earthly possessions.

- When decluttering, the old riddle of "how do you eat an elephant" comes to mind. Borrow from the wisdom of the riddle's answer, "one bite at a time." Take your time going through closets, drawers, and sheds as you weed out the banes from the blessings. Refine what you keep to what you really love and/or use. When you start clearing clutter it will feel great, but be careful to pace yourself so that you will not use up your enthusiasm for this task. Set your timer for one hour per day. Begin with one small area and move on to another when that is completed.

- Make a pact with yourself, and with the other members of your household: *When something new comes in, something old goes out.*

- To keep your home running more efficiently, you might designate a large box or basket in your home in which to store nonclothing items (such as cups, saucers, ceramic goods, plastic toys, and the like) that are in need of mending. In my dining room, I keep a deep, lidded basket in which I store a multitude of items that require my attention, when time permits: These include a vintage plate (broken in the move), the left temple on Rosie's favorite sunglasses, and pieces of a salt and pepper shaker set that are too pretty to discard. In this basket you will also find a variety of adhesives, such as superglue, E-6000, and (for stubborn jobs) epoxy compounds. When time permits or the mood strikes me, I will pull out the basket and do a bit of mending while listening to music, or watching a favorite movie. You will be surprised at how well this simple tactic will eliminate clutter and mess throughout your home.

- Because of the composition of life, it will be necessary (once or twice a year) to go through your home and declutter it as needed.

SPRING CLEANING

"I have come home to look after my fences."

—JOHN SHERMAN

Spring is a season that traditionally inspires the urge to improve or to tidy the home—in essence, to look after our fences. Winter is ebbing away; the longer days and milder temperatures are whispering secrets about the warm summer months that lie ahead.

You may easily satisfy this impulse by implementing some of these simple, frugal strategies for enhancing your home and garden:

- If you are feeling a bit overwhelmed by your possessions you might enjoy doing a complete reassessment of your lifestyle. Roll up your throw rugs. Box the bric-a-brac that was comforting during the cold months but now seems a bit cloying. If you are truly in the mood for simplifying, hold a tag or yard sale to dispose of the items that are no longer necessary in your life. Your proceeds may serve as the genesis for a redecorating project, a summer vacation, to pay off a debt, or to finance the frugal luxury of hiring a cleaning crew to perform all the tasks you dread.

- Spring is the season in which you will need to look after your outdoor furniture—especially if you live in an area where there is a significant change of seasons. If your pieces are a bit shabby you can swiftly revive them with a coat of fresh paint. Every few years I exercise my creativity by painting our iron ice-cream chairs a different shade of green. And each spring the children and I spend an afternoon in the backyard (wearing old clothes) painting our wooden picnic tables and benches. The children look forward to this activity as it signals the arrival of our own season of alfresco family meals. On warm spring and summer evenings we indulge in the frugal luxury of taking our evening suppers on the patio.

- Now is a good time to garner furnishings for your outdoor rooms. Treasure hunt at flea markets and yard sales for well-built pieces with classic lines. Be selective; check wooden pieces to ensure that they have not been eaten by termites or rotted out by too much exposure to inclement weather. Peruse gardening catalogs in order to familiarize yourself with current as well as classic garden furniture design. Studying catalogues is a lovely pastime that may inspire you to savor the pleasures of gardening, however tiny your plot of land. If you have no terra firma, you may discover that windowsill or patio gardening is beautifully satisfying as well.

- If you have been blessed with an abundance of lovely finds while treasure hunting, you might enjoy using some of that overflow of garden furniture *inside* your home. Wrought-iron patio tables are finding their way into the dining room, while garden benches and Adirondack chairs are being warmly welcomed into the bedroom and family and living rooms. The only adjustment needed is the addition of soft, cozy cushions covered in a favorite floral chintz, a checkered gingham, or, perhaps, a sturdy denim.

ॐ

The Art of Practical Home Order

"Order is Heaven's first law."
—ALEXANDER POPE

When moving into Grace Cottage, I took advantage of the much-needed opportunity to declutter and organize our possessions and created a classification system for our family's storage needs. By organizing your possessions into storage centers, you will be able to find everything that you need in one area (and know where to put items away). Obviously, no two households have identical storage needs or space; thus, your classification system must conform to your own home's storage space, as well as your family's needs. It is my hope that by viewing the manner in which I classify and store our family's goods, you may be inspired to adopt a similar system that will meet your own needs and that of your family.

What We Have and How to Organize It

"A little neglect may breed great mischief . . .
for want of a nail the shoe was lost; for want of a shoe the horse was lost; and
for want of a horse the rider was lost."
—BENJAMIN FRANKLIN

- Clothing, adult: cold weather and warm weather
- Clothing, children: cold weather and warm weather

- Perfume and vanity items (adult and children)
- Cosmetics
- Brushes and hair supplies for adults and children
- Vitamins and Medicines
- Spices and seasonings
- Cake and cookie decorating supplies
- Special baking pans (miniature pans, such as Bundt, bread, and muffin pans, special candy molds, etc.)
- Baking dishes (separate into bake-and-serve and bake-only)
- Toys: special toys that the children have outgrown (to save for posterity—selectively weeded)
- Toys: to be currently played with
- Toys: to be used in the near future (within the next year)
- Books: one place for all books—section shelves per subject
- Compact discs and cassette tapes: organized alphabetically (ideally)
- Videocassettes: organized alphabetically (ideally)
- Board games, playing cards, and other game paraphernalia
- Crafts Pantry: glues and adhesives; ribbons; faux greenery; recyclable items; tools such as scissors, X-Acto knife, soldering iron with solder, hot glue gun, and so on; dried flowers and other of nature's goods; recyclable items such as wrapping papers (used), paper towel cylinders, older silver plate to use in crafting, nylon screens, odds and ends; sewing supplies such as fabrics, threads, and other notions; sewing machines, set up for easy access; projects-in-progress (crafts, sewing, and mending)
- Gift Pantry: gifts purchased in advance to be used at a later time; completed craft projects; vintage wares and antiques to be included in gift baskets and so forth
- Party pantry: Include all future party favors purchased at sales, or created in advance; small gift soaps, powder puffs, brooches, pins, sachets, small photograph frames, and the like; small decorative bags or miniature hat boxes and baskets in which to place gifts
- Wrapping center: a central place in which to set up all wrapping papers, tape, glue stick, paper scissors, gift cards, ribbons, and small dried or silk flowers to ornament gifts
- Letter writing: fine pens, colored inks, stationery, postcards, and attractive sticky notes (keep in the writing desk)

- Hostess pantry: teapots and sets, silver and silver plate, cake plates, chafing dishes, special baskets for breads, serving pieces, teacup collection
- Everyday dishes (odd lots of blue-and-white china and English ironstone, and spatterware)
- Blue onion china collection
- Linens (moth- and moisture-free environment)
- Office space: computer; personal and business stationery; compact and floppy disks; research files; computer books; pencils and pens; glue stick and tape; blank computer paper
- File cabinets for family business
- File cabinets for business ideas (filed by subject)
- Large, long-term calendar
- Sporting goods: balls, golf clubs, bicycles
- Household tools and hardware
- Food pantry
- Plastic goods for kitchen storage (Tupperware® and the like)
- Lids for plastic goods
- Everyday cups and mugs
- Everyday drinking glasses
- Drinking glasses for entertaining
- Tablecloths for entertaining: lace, crochet, and damask
- Everyday tablecloths: sturdy crochet and laces, ginghams, vintage prints, and runners
- Christmas decorations
- Christmas wrapping paper, bows, and tags (keep separate from everyday use)
- Other seasonal and holiday items: Saint Valentine's Day decorations; Saint Patrick's Day sachets; Easter eggs and holders; July 4 flag, wreaths, and miniature flags; ceramic pumpkin and wooden cutouts for Halloween; Thanksgiving dried Indian corn and ceramic turkey

Illuminated Fragments
The Invisible Intensity of Being

"Nothing great was ever achieved without enthusiasm."
—Ralph Waldo Emerson

Sometimes referred to as the fortune-teller of life, enthusiasm is a very real force. Born from the Latin word *enthusiasmus,* meaning "to be inspired by God," the quality of enthusiasm can be divine. And with the proper mixture of faith and works, the trait of enthusiasm may help an ordinary individual perform miracles.

Often closely associated with faith, enthusiasm is one of your most precious assets, so treasure it. George Sand understood this when she wrote that "faith is an excitement and an enthusiasm: It is a condition of intellectual magnificence to which we must cling as to a treasure, and not squander it in the small coin of empty words."

The ability to conjure enthusiasm, in yourself as well as others, is the power to guide destinies. For nothing great can be achieved without enthusiasm. Enthusiasm is that pulse that gets us through those mundane yet necessary tasks that must be accomplished in order to achieve a goal. In retrospect, I now understand that it was the power of enthusiasm that pushed me out of bed at four A.M. each morning when I was writing my first book. It is the power of enthusiasm that drives me to organize and tidy our home—to transform the peaches and berries from my father's garden into delicious jams and jellies for our food and gift pantries. In truth, it is the power of enthusiasm that makes *any* task—from home-keeping to running a business—enjoyable.

How does one go about cultivating this miraculously divine quality? The first and most important step in harnessing this power is to make a conscious decision to do so. Once you have made this important choice, *you must act on it.* Ask yourself *why* you want to generate enthusiasm. To what purpose will you use this power? What is it that you wish to accomplish? Once you have answered these questions, collect your plans and ideas and concentrate your efforts toward achieving your goals and ideals.

True enthusiasm does not procrastinate. Take one small action that will engage you in your necessary task. I often do this when writing, telling myself that I will pen only two or three paragraphs and "no more." More often than not, I find myself becoming so enthusiastic about what I am writing that two or three paragraphs become several pages. (On those very blessed days, an entire chapter, or newsletter, will appear.)

Keep in mind, however, that in "this whirlwind of passion," as Shakespeare calls it, "you must acquire and beget a temperance, that may give it smoothness." Because it is enthusiasm that leads any life of achievement, it is the wise who harness this sometimes wild force and direct it toward what is productive, right, and good. It is in this manner that you use your precious gift of free will, and control your destiny.

Chapter 5

The Spring Gift Pantry

*"Liberality consists less in giving much
than in giving
at the right moment."*

—JEAN DE LA BRUYÈRE

Working Ahead of Need:
Preparing for Christmas All Year Round

"Necessity never made a good bargain."
—BENJAMIN FRANKLIN

Most people begin preparing for Christmas in December, but, as you may have gathered, I prepare for Christmas all year round. My Gift and Craft Pantries are often bulging by the time winter arrives, which allows me to spend the bulk of my time during the holidays savoring the joy of organizing gift boxes and baskets, baking, and putting the finishing touches on the gifts that I make. Why do I do this? So that what I give will impart that unique (now rare) quality of things made by the human hand.

My desire to prepare for the holidays often begins with the first sunny day of spring (sometimes sooner) and continues through the sweltering summer months, matures during autumn's golden days, and comes to rest during the season of winter. The only antidote for such a passion is to bring out one of my idea books and record the new concepts that are suggested to me by the garden. In it I organize my thoughts and, basking in the spring sunshine, assign a theme to my winter holidays (and the family Gift Pantry) for the year.

I am renewed by the planting of herbs such as lavender, rose-scented geranium, and other crops that will make delicious dried teas and fragrant potpourris for gift-giving. When the warm summer sunshine arrives I will gather and dry roses, whole and in petal form, to be used for packaging Christmas gifts, woven into arrangements of dried flowers, or used in potpourris and jams. I find a questionable joy in devoting a day or two (during the sweltering August heat) to preparing lavender, peach, and rose-flavored jams and jellies. (You will find a recipe for simple lavender jelly on page 143.)

I am never more satisfied than when I have my pantry filled with small, jewel-colored jars of jelly and preserves. These, I am certain, will delight my family and friends on various occasions throughout the year. I am soothed for a time from the malady that periodically possesses me to go Christmas shopping in April, create tree ornaments in July (at poolside), and decorate Easter eggs in September. And I often find it difficult to wait until it is socially acceptable to put up our holiday tree, sparking an ongoing debate about how early is *too* early.

Fortunately, I have tempered this obsession by establishing the year-round Gift Pantry. The Gift Pantry keeps in check my kindled holiday spirit, and thus becomes guardian of all the tangible manifestations of the wondrous festivals that garland the year. A magnificent by-product of the Gift Pantry is that it is an enormously frugal concept; it can save untold amounts of money, as well as time. Thankfully, my seasonal passions are sated by the knowledge that each year the same wonderful holiday seasons will reappear for my full enjoyment.

GRACIOUS TOKENS

"Verily great grace may go with a little gift;
And precious are all things that come from friends."
—THEOCRITUS

The act of presenting a gift to another should express the emotions of appreciation, affection, and generosity. And while it is wise to be sensitive to the circumstances and attitudes of others when gift-giving, there are many occasions on which you may wish to extend a bit more than your verbal or written good wishes to those people who have positively touched your life. This can be done simply by offering a small *token* of your esteem. These token gifts needn't be expensive, nor should they be a burden to present. I often bake a loaf of fresh bread, a small bundt cake, a platter of cookies, or a round of shortbread, and present one of these as a token of my appreciation and friendship. I am also continually filling my Gift Pantry with other small items that are waiting for the perfect recipient, such as:

- A tiny handmade wreath composed of vines and greenery found in the garden
- A small, air-dried bouquet of herbs and flowers (found in the garden or purchased from the greengrocer or farmer's market—I enjoy using rosemary, miniature ivy, yarrow, roses, and air ferns)
- Unfinished, miniature wooden hat boxes (available at most craft stores for one or two dollars each—or less) in which I will place homemade sachets, home-baked goodies, or purchased candy
- Attractive and inexpensive gift soaps, sponges, and wash mitts (homemade or purchased)
- Pretty teacups with saucers, or coffee mugs, in which I will place tea or coffee, sugar packets, flavored creamer, candies, an attractive silver-plated teaspoon, and a personal message written on a small piece of paper rolled into a scroll and tucked inside

These little touches will express your appreciation and affection in a much deeper manner than mere words or a card. Still, you should keep in mind that the most important aspect of a token gift is that it be small enough so that the receiver does not feel obligated to reciprocate.

This Cluster of Gifts

"Not what we give, but what we share—
For the gift without the giver is bare;
Who gives himself with his alms feeds three—
Himself, his hungering neighbor, and me."
—JAMES RUSSELL LOWELL

Some of my favorite gifts have been collections of goods and foods chosen especially for me—treats I would not normally get for myself. Yet the giver understood that I would savor these little luxuries for weeks after receiving them. It is simple, fun, and often very economical to assemble a custom-designed package that is aimed to suit the passions of the recipient. And, quite often, you may conduct a good portion of your gift-shopping during your next run to the supermarket.

Our gift baskets have become such a tradition with family and friends that we are always on the lookout for unique themes and topics for the gifts we put in them. Here are some suggestions for creating personal gifts in any season. You may wish to keep these in mind when stocking your Gift Pantry throughout the year.

Bibliophile—Favorite classic books; bookplates; bookmarks; books on tape; gift certificate to a bookstore

Athlete—Tickets to sporting events; sports hat or jersey; athletic bag for the gym; special clothing; sports videos; special equipment

Frugal Luxuries and Simple Pleasures—Gift certificate to a favorite restaurant; luxurious bath oils and bath salts; bottles of a favorite fragrance; gift certificate for baby-sitting; box of homemade or purchased chocolates; gift certificates for a movie or play

Coffee Lover—Special vintage cup or mug; small samples of flavored coffees; gift certificates for coffee shop; homemade gourmet coffee; gold (permanent) coffee filter; chocolate swizzles on a spoon (directions for making these on page 251.)

Every Day a Feast—Five-bean soup mix; flavored coffees and teas; muffin mix; curlicue pastas (all with keepsake recipe cards); mini-loaves of homemade bread; pretty sets of napkins (use vintage hankies, or make one-of-a-kind napkins by cutting and hemming fabric squares from the undamaged areas of dilapidated damask tablecloths)

Gracious Moments—Lovely hand towels (you can make these in the same way as the napkins above); fragrant guest soaps; a bottle of sparkling cider or wine; herbs; evergreens from your garden, wrapped in a hostess bouquet

The Children's Baking Basket—Child-size muffin tins with liners; muffin mix; child-size apron; a first cookbook; small whisks and wooden spoons; cinnamon sugar packaged in a pretty salt, pepper, or sugar shaker (wrap it in cellophane and tie a ribbon at the top, to keep the contents from shaking out into the basket)

Brunch Basket—Spiced waffle/pancake mix; clover honey; jars of preserves (homemade or store-bought); English breakfast tea (or home-dried herb or peppermint tea); tea strainer; vintage teacups and saucers

Oils and Vinegars—For the salad lover in your life you may wish to choose several small bottles of each (or make your own at home) in both savory and sweet flavors. These may easily be mixed and matched in a salad. Perhaps pair raspberry vinegar with almond or walnut oil, or rosemary or garlic oil with balsamic vinegar. Present these inside a salad spinner—or package simply, in a box or basket, with a set of salad tongs.

Champagne Taste—Is there anyone on your list who has a soda pocketbook and champagne taste? If so, treat these lovers of the good life to a sampling of the best: a small packet of Scottish smoked salmon, a tin of French pâté de foie gras, a small hunk of well-aged cheese, a tiny tin of caviar, and a very small box of the very best Swiss chocolates! Package these with rose-colored champagne flutes and you will be giving a ticket to the good life!

Thai—The particular flavors associated with Thai cooking include chili and sesame oils, satay and peanut sauces, cucumber salad dressing, and rice noodles. Package these in an inexpensive wok, or simply put them in a box, along with Oriental teacups and chopsticks.

Garlic Lover's Delight—For those on your list who consider garlic the staff of life, collect all of the accoutrements this lifestyle requires. A braid of fresh garlic (or, if this seems too difficult to find, simply buy a large package of garlic—usually less than four dollars—at your local warehouse store), a self-cleaning garlic press, a terra-cotta garlic baker. (A friend of mine made her own using two large inexpensive terra-cotta plant saucers purchased from her local nursery. She lined the bottom saucer with aluminum foil and inverted the other over it to create a lid. Together they made an enclosure deep enough to hold several bulbs of fresh garlic.) You might also want to add a garlic slicer and, need I mention it, breath mints.

Pasta Lovers—You can find sheaves of interesting pastas in a rainbow of colors. Include a chunk of well-aged Parmesan cheese (and perhaps an inexpensive grater) and jars of compatible sauces. Wrap the whole collection in a red-and-white-checkered dish towel—or present it tucked neatly into an interesting colander.

Tea Time—There are those of us who, on a daily basis, crave the comfort that only a nice cup of tea will give. For the tea enthusiast on your holiday list, choose an array of blends to present to them—perhaps add a tea infuser, a very thin china tea mug (usually made in England; vintage is quite acceptable) and a book for your enthusiast to enjoy with his or her tea.

Chocolate—Need I say more? For the chocolate lover in your life, compile samples of chocolate candy, sauces, coffees, and the like. Package this selection of sweetness with a good mystery novel. May I suggest *Dying for Chocolate*, by Diane Mott Davidson?

Wrapping and Bestowing Gifts

". . . wide enough to wrap a fairy in."
—William Shakespeare

Just as food that is attractively presented seems to be more flavorful, gifts can become a feast for the eyes when they are attractively packaged. Even the smallest tokens become more precious when they are bestowed in thoughtful wrappings. Why? Artful packaging of a gift is visible proof of caring.

Consequently, one of the loveliest qualities of creating a Gift Pantry is that it gives us the opportunity to collect and surround ourselves with delightful things. I find such pleasure in the accoutrements used in the creation of elegant and artfully wrapped gifts. Throughout the year I collect fine old silk ribbons and tassels at tag sales, flea markets, and thrift shops. I stock up on humble raffia, and cut and dry bundles of lavender from my tiny garden to embellish packages. Thick, embossed papers (purchased at last season's post-holiday sales) are an ultimate frugal luxury and mingle well with inexpensive, rustic sheets of brown craft paper and fragile wisps of white and ecru tissue papers. All of these combine to create the alchemy that transforms the ordinary into the exquisite.

Still, when the hour arrives in which you must bundle and bow your gifts, time and money are often in short supply, yet a mountain of gifts—some in very odd shapes—await your attention. However, there is no need to despair. This dilemma may be solved elegantly, easily, and economically. Simply by implementing a few basic strategies—and exercising your imagination—you will see how easy it is to transform household castoffs and ordinary gift wraps into frugally luxurious packages that will delight those special people in your life.

Signature Wrap   To simplify all of your packaging you may wish to create a signature wrapping style that people will automatically recognize as yours. I have taken to using raffia and white tulle (separately or together) as a signature bow on many of the gifts I give, as well as a sprig of dried lavender and/or a dried herb bundle. A friend of mine is known for her gingham ribbons, and another for her rustic birch bark cards and gift tie-ons. To find your own signature packaging style simply look for items that express your taste and that are easily and inexpensively available.

Rustic Paper Lace   Make "rustic" lace paper by spraying recycled brown paper bags (or craft paper) with white, gold, or silver spray paint. To achieve the lacy effect, simply place large doilies over your paper (rectangular or square shapes work well) before painting. These doilies become templates which may be reused numerous times if cared for. I store my (dry) doilies in a folder inside the Craft Pantry. Rustic paper lace may be used as attractive wrapping paper in any season.

Fabric Wraps   I have recycled inexpensive lace curtain panels (found at a tag sale for two dollars each) to give a romantic look to gifts for all seasons. You may also use fabric rounds you cut from scraps of new and vintage laces and other attractive fabrics. Simply gather fabric around the gift and tie at the top with ribbon to create a bundle. You may also enjoy using odd lengths of slender lace crochet instead of ribbon. Look for quality fabrics at yard sales and thrift shops—lacy prom dresses, chiffon bridesmaid dresses, and the like, are especially suitable (and good bargains, yardage-wise). Fabric stores sell white tulle (also known as netting) and scrim fabrics quite inexpensively (for about one dollar per yard). These are lovely fabric wraps as well.

Leafing Tissue Paper Elegantly embellish layers of white or ecru tissue paper by gluing *fresh* leaves directly onto wrapped packages (you may keep the leaves natural or paint them gold, copper, or silver). Adhere leaves to paper using a simple glue stick or rubber cement. I enjoy using silver-dollar eucalyptus, citrus, and ivy leaves because they are easily available to me. However, the technique works well with other sturdy, fresh foliage (experiment with the fresh leaves that are available within your area). I have observed that the paint acts as a temporary preservative, keeping the leaves from crumbling for several months or longer (depending, of course, on the amount of handling they receive). While you have the spray paint out, you may wish to paint extra leaves, and small stalks, to use as package tie-ons, to embellish your holiday tables and tree, or for other decorating projects.

Simple Freezer Paper Simple white freezer paper (also known as butcher's paper) makes a lovely palette for all sorts of gift wrap, including Christmas gift paper. You may wish to leave it plain—or embellish it with gold-inked stamps of angels, stars, or circles. You may purchase this paper at warehouse stores and restaurant supply stores (where you will get the best price per yard, although you will need to buy a larger quantity of it). You may also find it, more expensively, at grocery stores and teachers' supply stores.

Camouflage Wrap If you are trying to camouflage a fishing pole or golf club, try using a mailing tube to wrap it in or, even more frugally, recycle wide cardboard wrapping paper tubes (you may need to use two tubes taped together for longer items). Or, simply use an inexpensive plastic plumbing pipe cut to the length you need.

Copied Memories For unique wrapping paper, you may wish to photocopy a collage of old family photographs onto sheets of eleven-by-seventeen-inch paper. These may be made in color copies or black-and-white. You may also use this concept to duplicate an antique book of sheet music, a lovely handwritten letter in French, or perhaps a collection of one-hundred-year-old postcards that you think are beautiful. Simply take these to a copy center and have them reproduced. The results can be quite attractive, inexpensive, and most unique.

Painted Boxes   I have taken to spray-painting the white (or pink) bakery boxes that carry the goodies my mother-in-law often contributes to our family celebrations. Once the pies or cakes have been removed, the box is often like new (any messy boxes I discard). When these are not available for recycling I will purchase them from a cake supply store (for about forty cents each) and use them for the same purpose. I spray-paint the boxes until they are a lovely gold, silver, chrome, white, sage green, or pale blue. (The paint may impart an unpleasant odor to foods, so spray only the *outside* of the boxes in which you will be packaging food products.)

Cookie Tins   Recycle humble, unattractive cookie tins using, once again, that wonderful alchemist . . . spray paint. My favorite colors for this project are gold and white. These tins hide gifts such as compact discs, books, gift certificates, and other hard-to-wrap or obvious shapes. You may also use them in the time-honored manner of putting freshly baked cookies or candies inside of them (atop a paper doily). Glue or tape a large bow in the center of the the tin's lid; attach a small wreath to the lid; or wrap the tin with paper or cellophane so that it resembles an oversized hard candy.

Frugal Luxury Liners   Before placing gifts inside the bakery boxes or tins, I first line them with vintage linens I have garnered from tag sales or flea markets throughout the year. If these are not available, you may use men's white handkerchiefs (about fifty cents each when you buy a package of four) or use homemade or purchased paper doilies as liners. Once your gift box is filled, wrap it with ribbon and glue a large bow onto the outside top of the box, using a glue gun, to complete your presentation.

Creative Recycling   If you are at a loss for boxes, save time as well as money by recycling boxes from your kitchen. I have been known to spray-paint the most humble of boxes (cereal, cheese, tea, cake mix, and the like) with gold, silver, or white spray paint. One can of spray paint will often cover dozens of boxes (depending on their sizes). Even more economical, use up those small amounts of leftover spray paint for this project (the ones currently cluttering your garage or basement). To paint with minimal mess, I spray my smaller boxes inside a very deep, larger box in a well-ventilated garage, or outdoors. The boxes dry quickly (often within a half hour). They usually look so attractive when painted, I forgo the wrapping paper altogether. We simply tie attractive ribbons and bows around them, and they are ready for presentation. A set of three of these boxes painted the same color, in graduated sizes, make a lovely gift tower.

Restaurant Boxing When recycling boxes for gift-giving, do not neglect the options from fast-food establishments. Clean, nongreasy containers from Chinese takeout restaurants are lovely for giving gifts of baked goods. If your recycled boxes don't clean up well, ask the proprietor if you may have an unused container—or purchase these at restaurant supply stores. You may also paint and use recycled french fry containers from fast-food restaurants—simply punch a hole at the top and thread a sturdy ribbon or raffia through it. This will gently pull the high curved back over the low front and close the box. Wrap the ribbon around the entire box a few times, then tie securely.

Illuminated Fragments
Touching the Intangible

"God blesses still the generous thought,
And still the fitting word He speeds,
And Truth, at His requiring taught,
He quickens into deeds."

—JOHN GREENLEAF WHITTIER

Traditionally, a gift is a tangible expression of the intangible riches of friendship, love, and honor. Still, gifts can convey much more than their physical presence may outwardly indicate. As a child of twelve, I was given a set of three leather-bound books, each nearly identical in outward appearance. The first volume was a treasury of the world's best-loved poems. The second contained poems of childhood. However, the third volume was (for one fleeting moment) a riddle. No gold lettering was stamped on the book's face proclaiming title or author (as were on the other two covers) and the pages were . . . amazingly . . . *empty.*

Once I recovered from my initial puzzlement, I understood that these gifts were communicating very firm, yet subtle, messages. By way of these three volumes, the giver (my best friend's mother) was informing me—in the silent language of giving—that she thought me intelligent enough to understand adult poetry; paradoxically, at the same time she granted me much-needed permission to relish the few remaining years of my childhood. The blank volume rang with the strongest of her silent gifts: Each snowy-white page echoed her belief that my childish words had *value.*

The art of frugally luxurious gift-giving lies in understanding the people on your list. Do they appreciate handmade and/or home-cooked items—and treasure the time and effort put forth to create them? Perhaps they care for less artful objects, enjoying useful, practical gifts instead? Do they collect unusual teapots, antique fishing or golf equipment, or books on cooking?

The challenge of gift-giving is to keep ear and heart trained throughout the year, so that you will catch ideas and hints as they come from family and friends. The spirit behind the well-thought-out gift will reflect not only the mind and heart of the recipient—but what the *giver* thinks of the recipient. As well, giving items that will enrich lives, lighten work loads, and/or delight the recipient is rewarding for the giver.

GIFT PROFILES

Name:

Birthday:

Birthstone:

Scent:

School/Sport/Team:

Wine/Liquor:

SIZES

Belt:_____

Blouse or Shirt:_____

Coat or Jacket:_____

Dress or Suit:_____

Gloves:_____

Hat:_____

Pajamas or other Nightclothes:_____

Ring:_____

Shoes:_____

Sweater:_____

FAVORITE THINGS

Author:

Book :

Genre:

Candy:

Colors:

Flowers:

Hobby:

Collections:

Music:

Singer:

WISH LIST

THE GIFT PANTRY INVENTORY LIST FOR SPRING		
GIFT RECIPIENT & DATE OF ENTRY INTO GIFT PANTRY	GIFT ITEM(S) PURCHASED OR CREATED	WHEN TO PRESENT THE GIFT & PACKAGING IDEAS

Part II
Enchanted Summer

~

"And it was summer—
Warm, beautiful summer."
—Hans Christian Andersen

Chapter 6

Festivals of Summer

~

"When, at long intervals, the altars to patriotism, to friendship,
To the ties of kindred, are reared . . .
Then the fires glow, the flames come up
As if from the inexhaustible burning heart of the earth;
The primal fires break through the granite dust
In which our souls are set. Each heart is warm and
Every face shines with the ancient light."

—SARAH ORNE JEWETT

Flag Day: June 14

"I pledge allegiance to the flag of the United States of America
and to the republic for which it stands,
one nation, under God, indivisible, with liberty and justice for all."

—FRANCIS BELLAMY

"**A** thoughtful mind, when it sees a nation's flag sees not the flag only, but the nation itself," noted Henry Ward Beecher. A similar sentiment prompted, on June 14, 1777, the formal adoption of the official flag of the United States of America. Even so, it wasn't until 146 years later that a uniform code of etiquette was drafted regarding the United States flag.

In my humble opinion the flag of the United States is a lovely symbol of the original God-given freedoms that the founders of this nation helped to establish for themselves, as well as their posterity. However, aside from its intangible charm, I find that flying the flag enhances a building's visual character, adding an attractive, classic beauty that can be acquired in no other manner.

Flag Etiquette

*"It's the emblem of the land I love,
The home of the free and the brave."*
—GEORGE M. COHAN

"Everything we do to bring the Flag [of the United States] into proper consideration by the citizenship of the Republic is highly commendable and deserves to be cordially endorsed. Every salutation to the Flag makes my consecration to the Country and the Flag a little more secure," remarked President Warren G. Harding. It was for reasons such as these that an official Flag Code, prescribing correct ways of displaying and respecting the United States Flag, was adopted at the National Flag Conference on June 14, 1923.

Special Days   The flag may be displayed on any day, but especially on legal holidays and other special occasions. It is customary to display the flag outside only from sunrise to sunset. However, it may be displayed, on special occasions, at night—preferably lighted.

If you don't wish to fly the flag daily, perhaps you would like to honor occasions such as Flag Day, Independence Day, Columbus Day, Veteran's Day (November 11), Inauguration Day, Lincoln's and Washington's birthdays, Memorial Day, and state holidays, with a display of the stars and stripes.

How to Fly the Flag   The flag should be briskly raised, and ceremoniously lowered. It should never be allowed to touch the ground or floor. If hung over a sidewalk, the flag should not touch the building. When the flag is displayed horizontally or vertically against a wall, the stars should be uppermost and at the observers' left.

How to Dispose of a Worn Flag   When the flag is in such a condition that it is no longer a fitting emblem for display, it should be destroyed in a dignified manner such as respectful burning or burying.

When to Salute the Flag   All persons should face the flag and/or salute it when it is passing in a parade or in a review; during a ceremony of hoisting or lowering; when the National Anthem is played; and during the Pledge of Allegiance. A uniformed man or woman should render the military salute. A man not in uniform should remove his hat with the right hand holding it at the left shoulder, the hand being over the heart; men without hats should salute by placing the right hand over the heart. Women should salute by placing the right hand over the heart. Noncitizens should stand at attention.

Father's Day

"With my father, life became an adventure."
—Victoria Secunda

The only known historical precedent for honoring the paternal parent was in ancient Rome. Every year, in February, Romans would give honor to their deceased fathers. In the twentieth century, the idea for an official Father's Day celebration came to Mrs. Sonora Smart Dodd, of Spokane, Washington, on Mother's Day in 1910. Mrs. Dodd was attending church when, during a sermon extolling the sacrifices mothers often make for their children, she realized that in her own family it had been her father (William Jackson Dodd, a Civil War veteran) who had sacrificed so much to raise her and her five brothers after the early death of his wife in childbirth.

Mrs. Dodd's proposal of a local Father's Day celebration was well received by Spokane officials. The date of June 5 was suggested for the festivities because it was Mrs. Dodd's father's birthday. However, as it allowed only three weeks for the ministers to prepare sermons on such a novel subject, it was changed to the third Sunday in June, which fell on June 19. In 1972, sixty-two years after it was proposed, the third Sunday in June was officially established as the annual Father's Day.

Mrs. Dodd's story reminds me of my own father. After my mother was stricken with multiple sclerosis, he took over her family responsibilities, and made (and continues to do so) many sacrifices for the family. Still, he did his best to create happy moments for us, regardless of the difficulty of the circumstances.

Although he would sincerely deny the fact, my father is a creative soul. Out of necessity, he did much of the cooking when I was growing up, and the kitchen eventually became an outlet for his artfulness. Cleaning his notoriously large cooking messes was another matter entirely (that task usually fell to us children) but, oh, the delicious and *fun* meals he created have never been rivaled in all my years of eating.

On many weekends he would spend entire days in the kitchen preparing meals. Manicotti was a particular favorite. He would create the marinara sauce early in the morning. Quite often I would awaken to the aromas of sautéed garlic and onions wafting through the house and smile, knowing the day would be a delicious one. He then would patiently spend his afternoon continually tasting his sauce, tearing off small pieces of fresh Italian bread and dipping them into the bubbling tomato concoction, adding a pinch of oregano, a dash of sugar, or a touch of basil. And blending the precise combination of cheeses for the filling was another interesting endeavor that required many samplings, to ensure that its flavor was just how my father imagined it should be.

When early evening arrived, he would bring out a small bottle of inexpensive Chianti, pour a few inches of wine into a juice glass, and announce that it was time to make the pasta. As he sipped the wine, Papa would pour a thin concoction of beaten eggs and flour into a small, well-seasoned frying pan. This was carefully watched as it transformed into a thin, crepelike disk. After creating several of these pasta rounds, he would fill them with the ricotta cheese blend and place them into a large, deep baking pan. Once the pan was filled with cheese-stuffed pasta shells, Papa would ladle the tomato sauce over them and generously sprinkle the top with a layer of Parmesan cheese. The manicotti was baked for approximately thirty minutes (after it was allowed to sit for ten minutes so that it "settled") and served with homemade garlic bread and a lettuce and tomato salad (usually prepared by me).

After the first taste, he would pronounce the meal delicious, and proclaim quite seriously that it reminded him so much of "the old country." We children would laugh loudly . . . we all knew that there was not a drop of Italian blood in our father. So I'm particularly pleased to share his authentic recipe.

Papa's Weekend Manicotti with Homemade Pasta

"Just like from the old country!"

This recipe, adapted from one Papa found about thirty years ago in a *Better Homes and Gardens* magazine, is a tremendous amount of work but quite delicious. If you desire, however, you may substitute purchased marinara sauce (in a jar) and buy premade pasta shells. If fat content is a concern, you may want to substitute low-fat, small-curd cottage cheese for all or a portion of the ricotta cheese. I must warn you, however, the flavor will not begin to compare to the deliciousness of the original homemade version.

Papa's Tomato Sauce for Manicotti

⅓ cup olive oil or salad oil
1½ cups finely chopped onions
1 large clove fresh garlic, crushed
1 2-pound-3-ounce can Italian tomatoes, drained and mashed (you may also use
    chopped or whole tomatoes)
1 6-ounce can tomato paste
2 tablespoons chopped Italian parsley
1 tablespoon salt
1 tablespoon sugar
1 teaspoon dried, crushed oregano
1 teaspoon dried, crushed basil leaf
¼ teaspoon black pepper

Sauté onions and garlic in the oil, then add remaining ingredients plus 1½ cups water. Bring to a boil, then reduce heat and simmer until the sauce is cooked, at least 1 hour. Papa would prepare the sauce in the early morning and allow it to simmer over very low heat all day (checking and tasting it periodically). He claimed that doing this allowed the flavors more time to blend. Makes about 8 cups of sauce.

Cheese Filling

2 pounds ricotta cheese
1 8-ounce package mozzarella cheese, shredded
⅓ cup grated Parmesan cheese
2 eggs
1 teaspoon salt
¼ teaspoon black pepper
1 tablespoon chopped Italian parsley

Combine all filling ingredients in a large mixing bowl, blending well with a wooden spoon. Refrigerate until ready to fill pasta.

Homemade Pasta

6 eggs, room temperature
1½ cups unsifted all-purpose flour
¼ teaspoon salt

Combine all of the above ingredients in a bowl and beat with an electric mixer until just smooth (do not overmix). Allow mixture to stand at least ½ hour or longer before cooking.

To cook pasta:
Preheat a small, well-oiled but wiped-down skillet over medium heat (an 8-inch non-stick crepe pan works well). Make pasta shells one at a time by pouring 3 tablespoons of the batter into the hot, well-oiled pan, rotating the skillet so that your mixture will spread into an even circle about 6 inches across. Allow the pasta to cook over medium heat until the top is dry—the bottom should not be brown; do not overcook, or the pasta will become tough (pasta cooks very quickly). Use tongs or a fork to remove it from the pan, and allow it to cool on a wire rack, then stack, separating the pasta shells with pieces of waxed paper so that they do not stick to each other and/or tear. Repeat the process until you have used up all the batter. You should end up with about 12 to 16 shells.

To stuff manicotti:
In two empty 12 x 8-inch baking dishes (recipe should fill these to capacity), spoon in 1½ cups tomato sauce. Stuff pasta by spreading about ¼ cup filling down the center of each round and rolling each one like a crepe. Place eight rolled manicotti, seam side down, in a single layer, in one of your pans. Place 5 more filled manicotti (seam side down) in the second pan. Cover each pan of manicotti with 1 cup of sauce. Sprinkle generously with Parmesan cheese. Bake uncovered at 350° for ½ hour or until bubbly.

Note: If you would like to freeze one pan for a later meal, line the baking dish with foil before filling. Cook as directed, cover completely with foil, and place in the freezer.

Feasting Italian Style: Italian Sausage Sandwiches

Being sometimes governed by his palate, Papa would often create manicotti regardless of how high the summer temperatures soared. However, for those days in which time and weather inhibited our enthusiasm for a complex, heavy meal, Papa often put together a simple feast of Italian sausage sandwiches. Serve with a tangy cole slaw and a bowl of fresh fruit for a simple family meal. Delicious!

> 4 to 6 ounces canned tomato sauce, marinara sauce, or canned tomatoes per sausage
> 2 large onions (yellow or white), trimmed, peeled, and thickly sliced
> 2 or 3 large sweet bell peppers (green, red, or yellow, or any combination), washed, cored, and thickly sliced into rings
> 1 to 2 tablespoons of a light-tasting olive oil
> 12 sweet and/or hot Italian sausages, 6 to 8 inches in length, or 2 sausages per serving
> Sandwich rolls made from crusty Italian or French bread, or 6- or 8-inch lengths of French bread, split in the center

First grill or fry the Italian sausages until they are just fully cooked. Do not burn or overcook the sausage. Set aside. Sauté the sliced onion and sweet bell peppers in olive oil, then set aside. Do not overcook. Pour the tomato sauce into a large, deep kettle, then add the sausage, green peppers, and onions. Cover and simmer over very low heat for about one hour. Crisp your sandwich rolls in a 350° oven for 5 minutes immediately before serving. Ladle several large tablespoons of sauce onto the inside of the roll, being generous with the chunks of onions and bell peppers. Place 1 sausage inside each roll. If you desire you may sprinkle the sandwich with shredded mozzarella cheese or grate on a bit of Parmesan or Romano.

Jack's Father's Day Cherry Pie

"Of all nature's gifts to the human race, what is sweeter to a man than his children?"
—Cicero

Our friends, Jack and Debbie, have a cabin and garden in the local mountains that is blessed with a Napoleon cherry tree, whose golden cherries with a pink blush have a flavor much like that of the Bing cherry. Each year for the past decade—on or around Father's Day—while visiting the cabin, Debbie and her two daughters, Chrissie and Jessica, have gathered cherries from the tree to create their traditional Father's Day pie.

One year, the birds and squirrels had beaten them to so much of the harvest that the only way they could maintain their Father's Day ritual was by blending a can of Bing cherries with the small amount of fresh cherries they had been able to gather from their tree. The result was a cherry pie so delicious and easy that it has become a permanent adaptation of their original pie recipe.

2 cups fresh Bing or Napoleon cherries
1 9-inch pie crust, prebaked or homemade (see recipe on page 252)
1 can Comstock (Debbie and Jack's favorite) Bing cherry pie filling with glaze

Wash and pit fresh cherries; set aside. Prepare and bake pie crust and set aside until ready to fill. In a large bowl, thoroughly combine the fresh and canned cherries. Pour the cherry mixture into the prepared pie crust. Bake at 350° until fresh cherries are just tender, about 45 minutes. The pie will fall apart when you serve it (sort of like an upside-down cobbler). Add a scoop of vanilla ice cream on the top of each piece of warm pie and you will discover a flavor (as Debbie declares) "to die for."

This pie is much like a fresh fruit cobbler and is made without an upper crust. You should expect the filling to be a bit runny, due to the fact that you are adding the fresh cherries. It is very easy to make, and the the taste is not too sweet, not too tart . . . but juuuust right! If you would like to make this recipe as a cobbler instead of a pie, simply prepare filling as instructed, place into a deep baking dish, and top with about 2 cups of dry white or yellow cake mix. Pour ½ cup of melted butter over the dry cake mix before baking in a 350° oven for about 20 minutes (or until the top has browned).

Note: Debbie often stocks up on fresh Bing cherries when they are in season, and well priced (usually under one dollar per pound). She freezes the pitted, washed cherries on a cookie sheet, and then stores them in plastic bags for later use.

Midsummer's Eve

"The golden eve is all astir; and tides of sunset flood on us—incredible, miraculous . . ."
—JAMES STEPHENS

Long ago, people believed that brownies and elves came out and mingled among mortals at midsummer night; this superstition inspired Shakespeare's beautiful tale of fairy folk in *A Midsummer Night's Dream*. Midsummer madness was a customary time for strange happenings as well as witty cavorting and dancing through the woods, and was associated in folklore with the fairy people.

Astronomy fixes the date of midsummer in June, particularly on the twenty-first, which is the summer solstice and the longest day of the year. This romantic holiday is more obscure today, but in northern European countries like Sweden and England, midsummer's eve has long been a festive occasion. Today, midsummer parties are the high point of the season in these countries, and guests often will wear wreathlike garlands in their hair, play games, and exchange token gifts that echo ancient traditions of the day.

You may create your own summer celebration—in the garden, on your front lawn, or in the park—quite elegantly, easily, and inexpensively. Serve simple foods, in season, that you present out of doors, and arrange them with artfulness and care. I have been known to have Mike and Clancy carry the large dining room table out to the back lawn, and celebrate the season outside.

Midsummer's Eve Lawn Party
&

Menu
Fresh Fruit in Season
Turkey Breast & Cheese Sandwiches on Miniature,
Pansy-Shaped Biscuits
Tray of Crudités
Fairy Cakes
Herbed Iced Tea
&

Fresh Fruit in Season

Use damask- or chintz-lined baskets to display fresh (washed) whole fruits such as apples, pears, oranges, and grapes. Select footed compotes or attractive bowls to hold sliced kiwi, melon balls or squares, blueberries, blackberries, and strawberries. Allow for ½ cup of sliced fruit per guest. Always keep plenty of washed and sliced fruit in reserve, so that you may replenish baskets and bowls as they are depleted. I wash and dry large amounts of whole fruit the day *before* the party. On the morning of the party I prepare any sliced fruits and keep my extra stock in resealable plastic bags in the refrigerator.

Turkey Breast & Cheese Sandwiches on Miniature, Pansy-Shaped Biscuits

Sliced turkey breast and cheese (or cheese only) on freshly baked refrigerator biscuits that have been cut into pansylike shapes are very attractive for this flower- and fairy-oriented party. To achieve the flower shape, cut purchased refrigerator biscuits with a clean pair of kitchen scissors, making 5 evenly spaced cuts (about one-half inch long) along the outside circle of the biscuit. Bake according to package directions, and allow to cool about 10 to 15 minutes. While biscuits are cooling, blend a teaspoon of mustard (yellow or spicy) into a cup of softened sweet butter. Carefully cut cooled biscuits at their centers. Gently spread the softened butter inside the cut biscuits and make sandwiches by adding thin slices of turkey breast and cheeses (such as Swiss, cheddar, and/or Monterey Jack) that have been cut to neatly fit inside the small biscuits. You may wish to add thin slices of fresh tomatoes and leaves of fresh lettuce or sorrel, or a sprinkling of fresh alfalfa sprouts, inside the sandwiches. I like to use these miniature sandwiches to build a pyramid shape (often atop a large silver tray or a footed cake plate). If you are expecting a large group, you may make a few dozen extra sandwiches and store them on trays or cookie sheets that have been tightly covered with plastic wrap or aluminum foil (hold off adding the fresh tomatoes and lettuce until immediately before serving, in order to keep the sandwiches from becoming soggy—sprouts may be added at the same time as the meat and cheeses). Allow for 5 sandwiches per adult guest, and 2 or 3 sandwiches for each child.

Tray of Crudités

I enjoy setting out a variety of crudités and dips for our guests to snack on. Add crushed ice to them throughout the day, to keep vegetables cool and moist. Carrot straws are always an easy and welcome addition. Simply wash, peel, and cut carrots into long strips and place them on your plate or tray. Add small radishes that have been cleaned and trimmed; rounds of crisp cucumber and zucchini; as well as fresh snap peas; celery; green, red, or yellow bell peppers (cut into long strips); and any other hearty vegetable that is in season. (Remember to prepare an abundance of these to replenish your crudité trays when needed. Store the extras in resealable plastic bags in the refrigerator.) You may also wish to offer a yogurt or sour cream dip nearby. Add Italian spices and pressed garlic, or finely diced fresh dill and shredded shallot or red onions (the small side on a cheese grater will do this well) to your cream base.

Fairy Cakes

I collect miniature baking pans at tag sales and the like. Thus, I am able to make dozens of fairy-sized cakes using miniature muffin tins and an inexpensive white cake mix. You might also enjoy the addition of 2 tablespoons of fresh, minced herbs (perhaps mint, lemon verbena, or rose-scented geraniums) to the batter before baking to add extra flavor and more romance. At one time I found it difficult to find paper liner cups that fit these tiny tins. This dilemma was solved by substituting paper candy cups (very inexpensive and available at most craft and candy-making stores) for the standard liners when baking my fairy cakes.

You may ice the fairy cakes with homemade or store-bought icing that has been colored in pastel hues and sprinkled with what I like to call "fairy dust"—which is nothing more than the colored granulated sugars found in the baking section of most food markets. You may bake the cakes up to one month beforehand and freeze them, uniced, until the day before, or morning of, your party.

Herbed Iced Tea

I enjoy setting out clear glass pitchers of iced tea so that my guests can help themselves throughout the afternoon. I often make a very good Ceylonese tea (adding only a touch of fresh mint to its already delicious flavor), and a lemon-flavored herb tea (often created from infused herbs, such as lemon, verbena, or lemon balm that I have grown in my garden), or you can add berry flavors. (See page 34 for recipe.) With the addition of premade herbed ice chunks, the tea remains chilled and refreshing. I prepare the ice about one week in advance, using ordinary muffin tins as molds, adding small amounts of lemon verbena and rose geranium to the water before freezing.

Fairy Rings to Wreathe Fair Heads

"I sent thee . . . a rosy wreath."
—BEN JONSON

In Shakespeare's play *A Midsummer Night's Dream*, the fairies leave a ring in the grass where they have danced. I have adapted the concept to fit our party, and have created simple wreaths for each of our guests to wear in honor of the day. (These are to be taken home as a party favor when the party has ended.) If the younger girls who attend bring their favorite dolls, they will find doll-sized wreaths for these mute guests as well.

Wire, to use as a base—sturdy enough to keep its shape, yet flexible enough to bend into a circle and fasten
Wire cutters
Pliers, to close the wire wreath
Florist tape (available for only a few dollars at craft and floral supply stores)
Greenery—I use whatever abounds in our garden; eucalyptus leaves from the trees and rosemary from the herb garden are my favorites. Flowers are also lovely, but remember, these will be worn atop the head, so be certain to remove all thorns
Raffia strands, or thin satin ribbons— we use whatever ribbons and streamers are easily and inexpensively available

To make wreaths, cut wire into strips about twenty inches in length (eight inches for the doll-size wreath) and form into a circle. Using pliers, twist the ends tightly together—be sure to press down any protruding wire pieces so that they will not scrape the wearer. Wrap the entire wire circle with floral tape to disguise the wire. Gather a small portion of your greenery and create a tiny bouquet, attach this miniature bouquet to the wire, using floral tape. Repeat the process several times, until the entire wire ring is covered with greenery. Thread your ribbons and/or raffia around the wreaths and use it as needed to cover any gaps or messy areas, leaving several strands about 18 inches long to stream down the back of the wreath. You may make these the day before. Keep them fresh by refrigerating them overnight. If you omit flowers, using only sturdy greenery such as eucalyptus leaves, rosemary, small pine and cedar branches, or other evergreens, these may be made two or three days in advance. The girls and I often sit and watch our favorite videos while creating lovely tokens such as these. The day of the party I line a basket with a floral-printed cloth and stack the green circles inside; we use a similar, smaller basket for the doll-size wreaths. As the guests arrive, the girls and I extend a wreath as we welcome our guests.

Independence Day

" . . .This country remains to preserve and restore light and liberty . . .
The flames kindled on the 4th of July, 1776,
Have spread over too much of the globe to be extinguished . . ."
—Thomas Jefferson

John Quincy Adams, during his July 4, 1821, address, observed that "America, with the same voice which spoke herself into existence as a nation, proclaimed to mankind the inextinguishable rights of human nature, and the only lawful foundations of government." Maybe it is for this often unspoken reason that on the anniversary of the day of independence the American people celebrate so heartily.

I imagine that it is due to a similar (perhaps inherited) strain of independence that so many members of modern families often go their separate ways in adulthood. Yet, there is something magnetic about the season of summer that once again draws together families that have scattered. During this warm season such reunions most often occur. Members wander back from the four quarters of the earth to tell of their various experiences, to laugh at past pleasures, and to celebrate the private and public festivals of the season. Such homecomings keep green the memories of youth and happy days, keep hearts tender, and remind hands to be helpful to those of their number who are in need. As well, they serve to remind the faithful that there are a multitude of (often overlooked) blessings in every life, and offer a renewed opportunity to recognize and appreciate them.

A Family Gathering

"We were no more a . . . family celebrating its own existence and simple progress;
We carried the tokens and inheritance of all such households
From which this had descended, and were only the latest of our line."

—SARAH ORNE JEWETT

Games are a minor passion in our family. I attribute this love of fun to the fact that when we were newly married Mike and I did not own a television set. For entertainment we often would play marathon sets of card games such as cribbage, hearts, and double solitaire. Whenever family and friends came to visit we would expand our fun and play board games as well—Tripoli and the time-honored Scrabble were huge favorites and, when larger groups gathered, serious games ensued, often lasting well into the night.

On July 4, we hosted a family gathering at Grace Cottage. In honor of the holiday I put out a traditional two-flag swag, and set up tables throughout the house that harbored a selection of games. The back patio, amidst miniature white twinkle-lights and soft strains of John Philip Sousa, held the main table where family gathered, talked, ate, and played until the small hours of the morning.

The Blessing of an Outdoor Grill

In warm weather, our propane-powered outdoor grill is a tremendous blessing. Quite often I cook entire dinners on it, thus keeping the house at a comfortably cool temperature. The outdoor grill has become an incredibly useful and beloved tool in our household and so easy to use that it seems the ideal instrument in which to prepare delicious feasts to share with family and friends.

The Simplest Barbecued Chicken

My father introduced me to this incredibly easy mode of cooking whole or halved chickens and large roasts on the grill. I have dubbed it my summer slow-cooker. The results produce delicious, tender, juicy meats with a hint of smoky flavor.

A gas barbecue grill with double burners
4 large whole chickens (you may also use cut-up chicken pieces)
4 large garlic cloves, peeled and cut into thin slices
Fresh basil leaves (enough for 6 to 8 whole leaves per chicken), washed, stemmed, and patted dry
4 tablespoons olive oil (or another type of vegetable oil)

To prepare chickens for cooking:
Wash and pat dry whole chickens (be sure to remove innards from the chest cavity) or chicken pieces. With clean hands, use your forefinger to loosen skin. Take pieces of sliced fresh garlic and tuck them, one by one, between the loosened skin and the meat. Repeat the process with the fresh basil leaves (about 6 to 8 pieces per whole bird). Try to space the basil and garlic so that the flavoring will disperse evenly when cooking. Rub the skin with olive oil. If you like, you may truss the birds, or simply keep them natural.

To cook the chickens:
Light both burners of your gas grill, and allow them to warm up for about 10 minutes over low heat. *Turn the heat off on one side only.* Place all of your poultry on the cold side of the grill (keep pieces from touching). Depending upon the size and amount of chicken, allow it to cook (with the cover down) for about 1½ hours (or until cooked thoroughly). Carefully remove the cooked chicken from the grill and place it on a serving platter. If serving whole, garnish the cavities with large bunches of fresh parsley, or split the chickens in half before serving. The results are an exquisitely tender and savory entree that your guests will remember with pleasure.

Note: If you do not have a gas grill, you may adapt this recipe to your inside oven. Prepare the chicken or chickens as instructed, tent with aluminum foil, and cook in a pre-heated 325° oven for about 1¼ hours (or until thoroughly cooked). The results are delicious (although the poultry will be sans that trace of smoky flavor).

Grilled (Baked) Potatoes

If space permits, you may want to bake your potatoes at the same time as your chicken. Scrub and pierce large russet potatoes, and wrap them tightly in foil. Place these on the *off side* of the grill, with the chickens. (They should be ready at about the same time as the chickens.) Cut an X in the center of each cooked potato before serving with whipped butter and sour cream (I usually put crocks of these out so that guests may help themselves).

Diced Cucumber and Tomato Salad

This delicious and unique salad is best made the day, or several hours, before serving, and will keep well for two days in the refrigerator. Should you have family or guests who don't care for one of the prime ingredients, you may easily adapt it to become a cucumber-only salad, or a tomato-only salad.

> 3 or 4 pounds ripe tomatoes (we prefer Roma, but other varieties also work well) washed, cored, seeded, and diced (sometimes we leave the seeds in, for a more watery dressing)
> 4 to 6 large firm cucumbers, peeled, seeded, and diced
> 1 large clove fresh garlic, pressed (you may substitute finely diced shallots or red onions for the garlic if you wish)
> ¼ cup seasoned rice vinegar (as of late, we have taken to substituting Newman's Own Caesar salad dressing in this salad, or premade Italian dressing)
> ¼ cup chopped fresh parsley, oregano, and/or garlic chives
> Salt and pepper to taste
> 1 large, clear glass bowl

Place tomatoes and cucumbers in large glass bowl. Press fresh garlic directly over bowl of cucumbers and tomatoes (or add diced shallot or red onion). Add the vinegar (or salad dressing), herbs, and salt and pepper. Mix thoroughly. Cover bowl tightly with plastic wrap and set in the refrigerator overnight, or for several hours. Toss again before serving in small salad bowls.

Grandpa Mac's Garlic Bread

When Mike and I first met, he taught me how to make this delicious garlic bread that his father had created. It is now a worthy favorite at all family barbecues. If I am having a large gathering I will double the recipe. It may also be made ahead of time and frozen until ready to cook. Keep your freezer stocked with this delicious bread as an easy accompaniment to a light dinner of salad or soup.

> 1 large loaf fresh French or Italian bread, sliced
> ½ pound fresh butter
> 2 or 3 large cloves fresh garlic, pressed
> ½ teaspoon paprika
> Dash Tabasco sauce (or other hot pepper sauce)
> Pastry brush
> Aluminum foil (enough to entirely enclose the loaf of bread)

Place bread slices on a generous length of foil. Over low heat, in a small saucepan, melt butter. Add pressed garlic, paprika, and hot pepper sauce, stirring constantly. Once mixture has melted thoroughly, use the pastry brush to apply the butter and garlic mixture onto both sides of each bread slice (be certain to dip brush all the way to the bottom of the pan in order to evenly distribute the garlic). Once you have buttered each slice of bread, tightly cover the entire loaf of bread with foil. Heat in 350° oven for 10 to 15 minutes. You may also heat the bread on the warm side of your grill for about 5 to 7 minutes. Serve the bread warm.

Crushed Strawberries with White Cake

This adaptation of the classic American dessert, strawberry shortcake, is easy to prepare ahead of time, and may be assembled immediately before serving—or set out buffet style, so your guests may easily help themselves.

4 to 6 pints ripe fresh strawberries
¼ cup granulated sugar
¼ cup water
White cake mix (or use a store-bought or frozen pound cake)
Whipped cream

To prepare strawberries:
Several hours or the night before serving, wash and hull the fresh strawberries. Set aside 8 to 10 of the prettiest berries. With a potato masher, crush the strawberries until they are chunky (do not overmash them). Add sugar and water and allow the mixture to sit, covered, in the refrigerator for several hours or overnight. Before serving, thinly slice the remaining strawberries that you have set aside, and add these to the crushed mixture. Allow strawberries to come to room temperature and spoon the mixture generously onto slices of white cake.

To prepare the white cake:
(Prepare this several hours before serving, or the day before you plan to serve it.)
Grease and flour two standard loaf pans. Prepare your cake mix according to package directions. Pour half of the batter into each prepared loaf pan and bake at 325° or until the top springs back when touched. Allow cakes to cool for 10 minutes, then invert them onto a wire rack and allow to cool thoroughly for several hours. You can make these several weeks beforehand and freeze them (well wrapped) until the morning of your party. When you are ready to serve, use a serrated knife to carefully cut cakes into ½-inch slices. Arrange slices on an attractive plate so that your guests may help themselves, or put 1 slice onto each dessert plate and add strawberries and whipped cream.

Whipped Cream

Since my father refused to buy premade whipped cream, I learned, at an early age, how to use a hand mixer to whip heavy cream and sugar into a frothy concoction. Today, I continue to make my own whipped cream. Doing this often gives you more for your money, and the taste is always much better than the premade varieties. However, one of the worst aspects of making whipped cream is the fact that it stays fluffy for only a short while before turning back into its original, soupy liquid. Thankfully, I have found a way to store home-whipped cream that allows it to keep its volume for days in the refrigerator: Place it in a colander, with a plate directly beneath it. Why does this work? It is the excess moisture in whipped cream that causes it to collapse. By storing it in a colander, the deflating moisture drains through the holes and onto the plate beneath it, thus allowing the cream to keep its volume. I have been using this technique for years with excellent results. (And, by storing home-whipped cream in a colander, you may make it the day before, or morning of, your party—thus saving you that valuable commodity, time.)

Illuminated Fragments
Gracious Memories of Summer's Bounty

"How many loved your moments of glad grace . . ."
—William Butler Yeats

It fascinates me how many of our memories are linked to food. One of my most vivid memories is of a simple meal—prepared for us some six years ago—a sort of "end of vacation" dinner, hosted by my aunt and uncle at their lake cabin in the lovely north woods of Wisconsin.

It was dusk as we arrived at the gently lit cabin overlooking the lake. We heard rather than felt the patter of the rain on the treetops as we breathed in that timeless, musty smell of wet pine from the nearby forest. Inside, we were met by the soft aromas of the foods my aunt had so thoughtfully prepared and beautifully arranged for our benefit. The strains of Vivaldi's *Four Seasons* whispered in the background as Mike, the children, and I were made welcome. The menu, Aunt Jean confided, was "from the land."

While we grazed on crudités of raw jicama, carrots, and cucumbers that had been grown in the garden behind the cabin, we learned that the entrée was a breaded, baked fillet of rainbow trout, caught from the lake out front. Heaping bowls of steamed and buttered pole beans—green and yellow varieties—were accompanied by perfectly boiled whole new potatoes, and the most deliciously prepared zucchini I had ever tasted (also all from their garden). As we savored the food and enjoyed the atmosphere, I noticed that even the children were appreciating the meal.

After dinner we talked quietly while enjoying freshly brewed coffee and a luscious dessert of cheesecake topped with wild blueberries picked from the nearby woods. Driving home, Mike and I tried—with little success—to unravel the elements that had made the evening so magical.

The power of retrospection has helped to solve this little puzzle. The fact that the meal was from "from the land" lent a romance to it—as did the rain, the music, and the slight undertones of melancholy due to our vacation's coming to an end. Yet, the primary reason that this particular memory stands illuminated in my mind is the simple act of *hospitality*. That other people had thought enough of us to trouble themselves—preparing home, hearth, and sustenance "just for us"—was the sauce that made this dinner especially memorable.

Chapter 7

Summer Home Graces

~

"Eden is that old-fashioned House
We dwell in every day
Without suspecting our abode
Until we drive away."

—EMILY DICKINSON

Bending the Twig

"Just as the twig is bent, the tree's inclined."
—ALEXANDER POPE

Home is a powerful force. This is the place in which, as Robert Southwell tells us, "tender twigs are bent with ease." Within the magic circle of home the spirit is shaped, principles are implanted, and individual character is formed.

In my own youth (as the only girl and youngest of four children) we moved eight times before I had completed the fifth grade. I was nine years old when my mother began to seriously suffer from the debilitating effects of multiple sclerosis. Not long after, my father retired from the military and began caring for my mother as her disease progressed.

At an early age I understood that books were to be the great counselors of my life and thus were precious things. Between my schooling and domestic responsibilities, I retreated to the library, where authors such as Louisa May Alcott, Madeleine L'Engle, Jenny Lindquist, and Laura Ingalls Wilder became my closest friends.

Within the confines of this sometimes lonely childhood, I recognized that each person holds the power to choose how they will deal with the circumstances of life, and not merely *react* to them. I made a conscious decision to study and implement the seemingly elusive graces that create a happy and gracious home. I taught myself to recognize and celebrate each season of the year, and in so doing discovered that miracles are often hidden inside everyday occurrences. I also saw that many people do not recognize them for what they are.

These life lessons were not always learned easily. Oftentimes I empathized with the mythological Sisyphus who, over and over again, struggled up the high hill, heaving a huge, round stone—only to have it roll back down to the hill's base each time it reached the top. Yet, as discouraging as my circumstances sometimes were, I began to understand that it is often our most difficult moments that cause us to grow and become better, wiser people. There is power and catharsis in reaching for solutions—and in so doing we can defeat negative circumstance. This isn't to say we must seek adversity and disharmony—but when they are already in our lives we must look for ways to positively overcome and make use of them.

Through the course of the years it was also revealed to me that in the biography of a soul there are no such things as trifles. Happiness and graces are found in the study of *little things*. For isn't it by the study of little things that we attain the great art of happy living? Small things should not be looked down upon; isn't every lifetime composed of seconds? Little acts are the indicators and testers of character—and character determines the destiny of a soul.

Home is the magic circle in which we should find rest and refuge—yet it also holds the seeds of the future. Therefore, let us take special care to cultivate traits such as patience, faith, tolerance, love, appreciation, honesty, industry, and loyalty. Through our children, and our children's children, these noble qualities will be projected into the future, to unforeseen heights.

Summer Tokens for Home and Garden

"We have two lives about us, two worlds in which we dwell,
Within us and without us, alternate Heaven and Hell:
Without, the somber Real,
Within, our hearts of hearts, the beautiful Ideal."
—RICHARD HENRY STODDARD

"Nature is our widest home," noted Henry David Thoreau. I was inspired by this observation when pondering our decorating options for Grace Cottage. This little home, within walking distance to the beach, prompted me to envision a seaside garden with wild blueberry, blackberry, and raspberry patches hidden beneath a pale summer sky—

kindred with a neighboring strawberry patch that has been cultivated next to a grove of lemon trees. The beige sand of the beach, endless blue skies over the water, bright (almost white) sunlight, the ever-changing blues and greens of the ocean, and the gold of sea grasses, inspired me to choose the palest blue for the walls and ceilings of our downstairs rooms (the sort of color that deepens or fades with the changing light); and for the floors, a natural hardwood—almost identical to the color of sand at the beach. Ivory plates on the walls echo the subtle hues of the two large conch shells that rest on the mantel of the raised tiled fireplace. The berry colors are reflected in the floral and fruit motifs ornamenting the vintage and new fabrics peppered throughout the house, and are also found on the hand-painted china that dots the walls and shelves.

Although our decoration of Grace Cottage is still a work in progress, the results are taking on a sort of old-world quality. It takes only a bit of thought and planning to thread a comparable theme through the decorations in your own home. An English country-style cottage, a French-inspired kitchen, or a simple, modern city dwelling can be yours with only the (frugal) investment of imagination, time, and ingenuity. You will be astonished at what you can create.

- I enjoy collecting antique china and use my prettiest plates to add pattern, color, and texture to the walls of our home. I often rotate the plates on the walls of our dining room and kitchen to mirror the color of the seasons. In summer, I take down the vintage hand-painted saucers (with a rose motif) that I hung at the advent of spring—these are replaced with small ceramic platters, ornamented with colorful fruits and/or vegetables that idealize the warm season. In autumn, antique ivory dessert plates that have mellowed to a warm beige color take the place of the platters of summer. When winter arrives, out comes my cranberry-colored English transferware to ornament the walls. Thus, with very little effort, time, or money, I celebrate the change of seasons in a lovely, frugal, and unique manner—as well as add an ever-changing element of vibrancy and fun to our home. (Note: Plate hangers come in a multitude of sizes, and are quite inexpensive and readily available at many craft, hardware, and grocery stores.)

- "Every house should have a name, don't you think?" wrote Susan Vrh, a kindred spirit from northern California. At the top of her return address label was printed the name of her own home. The old-fashioned notion of naming an abode has appealed to me ever since I read *Rebecca* at age eleven; author Daphne de Maurier describes an enchanting English country estate named Manderley. In this era of nondescript, cookie-cutter-style tract homes, *courage* is required to implement

this notion. Our former house was named in a tongue-in-cheek manner; after we saw that the developers had labeled this particular model "Plan C," a little garden sign was painted and screwed onto a spare picket from an old fence, and the dwelling was christened "Planncee House." Our current home, however, acquired its name as a reminder that it came to us by way of a Providential gift. (I suppose I am too much like the title character of *Anne of Green Gables,* who found it very much her responsibility to embellish and rename ordinary things.) I am painting a garden sign that bears the name of "Grace Cottage," and have sent away for address labels with this designation as well. Does your home deserve a name? Naming your home is a lovely, easy, and frugal way to embellish the ordinary.

· During the warm months of summer our family often enjoys eating our meals out on the patio. In order to support this frugal luxury during the twilight hours, we maintain a small but constant supply of candles and alternative lighting (such as oil lamps and candle lanterns). The soft glow of natural light soothes the senses as well as the spirit after a long hot summer day.

· Summer is the season in which my herbs are most prolific. To preserve these for future use, I gather fresh herbs from the garden to dry in old-fashioned bundles (using rubber bands to hold them together). I have hung these attractive and fragrant bundles to dry on cup hooks and hat racks, and have even tucked them into the slotted sections of spoon racks. The result is a whimsical, yet useful, decorative vignette.

Summer in the Garden

"A Garden is a lovesome thing . . .
The veriest school of Peace."
—Thomas Edward Brown

- If spring is the season in which the bulk of gardening efforts are performed, then summer is the ideal month to enjoy the peace and prosperity of it. Now is the season in which to savor the garden atmosphere and harvest the fruits of your labors—while taking notice of, and appreciating, the many wonders and everyday miracles that abound within the secret life of the growing garden.

- To enhance the house in summer, I so enjoy arranging fresh cuttings from my herb garden. These are placed into a variety of vessels such as teacups (used for smaller cuttings); Mason jars in a selection of sizes and shapes; crocks; pitchers; and interesting-looking drinking glasses. In fact, because I have enjoyed sharing the abundance from past herb gardens, I have taken the habit of collecting such containers, in order that I might have several in my Gift Pantry at all times, to present

(filled with a bouquet of fresh herbs and tied with raffia) to friends and neighbors. One charming way to embellish this idea is to use an inexpensive crocheted doily as a sort of flower frog. How is this done? Set a doily across the top of a glass, cup, or jar (use a rubber band to hold it in place—disguise the rubber band with ribbon or raffia). The openings of the doily will hold your cuttings in place in much the same way a flower frog holds flower arrangements in more formal bouquets.

- You may transform a recycled wooden garden gate into an ideal display area for hanging garden tools, drying herbs, garden ornaments, small baskets, and dried flowers. To accomplish this you will need several wooden pegs (these are quite inexpensive, and may be found at most hardware or lumber stores, and some craft stores), a motorized drill, and wood glue. To make, simply drill holes at equal distances over the entire area of the gate (you may wish to make neat rows or use a random pattern). Dab a small amount of wood glue onto the bottom of the pegs and insert them, one at a time, into the holes. Leave the gate natural, or paint gate and pegs white, deep forest green, or another color that coordinates with your home. This display rack may be hung outdoors, against the wall of your garden or potting shed, or inside a sun or garden room.

- Keep fresh herbs for two weeks, or longer, by placing them (in bunches) in a water-filled glass or jar and refrigerating them (add water as needed). I keep mine in miniature, clear glass milk bottles that I discovered at a Wisconsin junk store years ago. These are lovely looking and are the perfect size for this task. To use the herbs, simply snip what you need for your recipe from the bunch, then return it to the refrigerator.

- Make herbal whipping cream by pouring fresh heavy cream over freshly cut herbs such as lemon, rose geraniums, lemon verbena, or flower blossoms such as lavender or rose petals (all must be washed, dried, and pesticide free). Allow to stand in the refrigerator overnight. Whip cream as usual. This delicious whipped cream makes an unusual topping for fruit salads and strawberry shortcake, or to ice a sponge cake.

- Remember to photograph or videotape your garden at the height of its glory! This is not only a joyful aid to memory; it is also practical in that it allows you to better and more easily plan next year's garden because it reminds you of what you already have and what areas look barren or inharmonious.

Flowery Language

If you are preparing a bouquet as a gift for family or friends (using a teapot, or another vessel), make your presentation even more memorable by keeping in mind the ancient, symbolic language associated with the botanicals you are presenting.

APPLE-BLOSSOM–Preference

BAY LEAF–Glory and Fame

BLUE VIOLET–Faithfulness

BUTTERCUP–Riches

CABBAGE–Prosperity

CAMELIA–Unpretentious excellence

DAFFODIL–Uncertainty

DAHLIA–Dignity and Elegance

GERANIUM–Gentility

HOLLYHOCK–Ambition

IVY–God

LAVENDER–Good Fortune

LEMON-BLOSSOM–Discretion

LILAC (PURPLE)–Fastidiousness

LILY (WHITE)–Purity

MINT–Cheerfulness

NASTURTIUM–Patriotism

OLIVE BRANCH–Peace

POPPY (WHITE)–Dreams

RED CLOVER–Industry

ROSE (RED)–Love

ROSE (WHITE)–Silence

ROSEMARY–Remembrance

SAGE–Wisdom

SNOWDROP–Consolation

SWEETBRIAR–Simplicity

THYME–Courage and Thriftiness

TULIP–Fame

VIOLET (WHITE)–Modesty

Fragrant Nourishment for the Soul

"Balm of hurt minds, great nature's second course, chief nourisher in life's feast."
—WILLIAM SHAKESPEARE

Enjoying the simple beauty of flowers in their season is a practical and frugal manner in which to feed the senses and comfort the soul. Here are lists of plentiful flowers in each season for you to enjoy.

Summer

"By the waters of Life we sat together, Hand in hand, in the golden days
Of the beautiful summer weather, When skies were purple and breath was praise."
—THOMAS NOEL

Summer offers you the wonderful frugal luxury of enjoying bouquets of fresh flowers in your home because, as you know, this is the season in which flowers are most plentiful, and often most reasonably priced.

It is also the season to begin drying or preserving flowers from your garden or florist. I have found that strawflowers and tansy dry beautifully in only a few weeks' time when placed upright in a vase or jar. I also enjoy hanging small bouquets of roses, upside down, on hooks inside my Craft Pantry. (Hint: You may keep roses from turning dark brown by allowing them to dry in a dark place.)

The following are a list of summer flowers:

- Baby's Breath
- Border Pinks
- Carnations
- Daisies
- Foxglove
- Geraniums
- Morning Glories
- Nasturtiums

- Pansy
- Queen Anne's Lace
- Roses
- Strawflowers
- Sunflowers
- Tansy
- Violets
- Wisteria

Autumn

"We thank thee then, O Father, for all things bright and good, the seed-time and the harvest,
our life, our health, our food."
—Nineteenth-century hymn

Autumn is the segment of the year in which warm days and cool nights bring on the golden glow that has long been associated with this tranquil season. There is an exhilaration in the air, and while fresh flowers are less abundant, you may make arrangements from stalks of burnished leaves taken from the trees that are turning colors in your area, and embellish these with miniature pumpkins and gourds for a truly autumnal feeding of the senses.

- Aster
- Calendula
- Chrysanthemums
- Cosmos

- Hawthorn
- Lily of the Valley
- Sweet Peas

Winter

"It is pleasant to think, just under the snow, that stretches so bleak and blank and cold, are
beauty and warmth that we cannot know, green fields and leaves
and blossoms of gold."
—Clara Hemsted

Winter has always been pictured with a double face, one looking backward at the old year, and the other looking forward into the future. During the season of winter, fresh flowers tend to be expensive. Still, if you combine cuttings from the balsam, pine, cedar, and box-wood that are already growing in your garden or neighborhood with a few well-chosen purchased flowers your eyes and senses may frugally feast on unusual, fresh bouquets all winter long.

- Snowdrops
- Primrose or violet
- Holly berries
- Rosemary (an evergreen)

- Branches from blooming trees such as apple and cherry (put these in water and they will often bloom within a few weeks' time)
- Paper-white narcissus

Spring

"How many million Aprils came before I ever knew how white a cherry bough could be
A bed of squills, how blue!"
—SARA TEASDALE

Spring speaks for itself. It is a season in which we may bask in the textures, scents, and vision of a multitude of beauteous blossoms.

- Tulips
- Daffodils
- Daisies
- Rosemary Blossoms
- Cherry Blossoms

- Sweet Peas
- Hawthorn
- Lily of the Valley
- Ivy (to add a bit of green to your arrangements)

ॐ

Illuminated Fragments
Mundane Magic

"As much of heaven is visible as we have eyes to see."
—WILLIAM WINTER

So many people believe that miraculous things are separated from real life. Yet when you give it thought, you may see that magical things happen every day. A mother may know instinctively when her child needs her, although many miles separate them. How many times have you dreamed of something and then have had it happen? Have you ever been thinking of someone whom you haven't seen in years and then accidentally met them in the market the next day? How many times, when visiting yard sales or thrift shops (where the merchandise is notoriously transient) have you discovered an unusual item that you had recently stated a desire or need for—at exactly the price you could afford to pay? Such occurrences happen to me quite frequently, and I look upon them as very special blessings—as answers to unconscious prayers. These are the every-day miracles that abound in the life of each person. Some people recognize them for what they are; others just shrug them off as coincidence.

☙

Nature offers us very tangible wonders on a daily basis. The miracle of the never-ending seasons is perhaps the most mysterious, as well as the most overlooked of these. Yet the four seasons are miracles of wisdom in that they supply the physical body with its needs, as well as revive and replenish the soul with each rhythmic sweep of the circle of the year.

The wind is an ideal metaphor for the many magnitudes of daily miracles that exist in our lives. It is an example of how powerful the unseen world can be (for, as Christina Rossetti asks, "Who has seen the wind?"). Isn't it true that sometimes—when preoccupied with the tasks of living—you take no notice of the wind at all, especially when it is a gentle one? Yet, on other days you awaken as if from a hypnotic trance and are acutely aware of its existence—when, in fact, it has *always* been visible to some degree or another. And, just as there are myriad types of winds—a little gypsy wind, gale force winds, hurricanes, and gentle breezes—there are degrees of wonders.

Magic is all around us in practical forms as well. Is not the airplane akin to a magic carpet, in that you sit on it and are flown to where you desire to go (of course, you must first purchase a ticket). The fact that its design allows the powers of thrust and lift to supersede the laws of gravity is a miracle! And what of the multitude of other modern wonders that we use daily and take utterly for granted? Consider the telephone (standard and cellular), the television, video recorders and players, compact discs, radios, computers, facsimiles, the Internet, the electricity that enables many of these things to function, as well as the miracle of modern medicine. All are wondrous creations that at one time seemed to belong only in the realm of fiction.

There are a multitude of quiet graces that thread through our lives daily. Often these are not visible until they are looked at with hindsight. Only then can that miraculous golden thread be seen—the same thread that has been beading each of your seemingly small decisions and accidental incidents into a patterned whole.

Chapter 8

Home Comforts

∿

"Ah, There is nothing like staying home for real comfort."

—JANE AUSTEN

An Elegant Sufficiency

"An elegant sufficiency, content, retirement, rural quiet, friendship, books."

—JAMES THOMSON

While many people consider it a great privilege to visit foreign lands and observe other cultures, I find it difficult to decide which is the better pleasure, enjoying the travels themselves or the sense of reunion felt when returning home to a familiar fireside, books, and friends. You may easily enrich your life, and raise the intangible value of your home, by cultivating a similar sense of appreciation on a daily basis. Appreciation is the bond that enables you to avoid fragmenting your life. Always surround yourself with what you enjoy and find beautiful as well as comforting. These tangible items can help you to live the sort of life you aspire to.

Just as you do when putting your house in order, pay attention to every aspect of your home when ornamenting it—from the laundry room to beneath the kitchen and bathroom sinks. Make certain that all the important things you love are represented in your home. Create an emotional affinity with every space and detail. Doing so will not only impart an intangible sort of beauty (objects seem to look more beautiful to us if they are loved, cared for, and appreciated), it will make home a place that beckons you to go inside and enjoy it—a favorite location in which to spend time.

Dry Dust and Stray Papers

"Fire in each eye and papers in each hand."
—ALEXANDER POPE

The wallpaper pattern in my kitchen with its tiny French-inspired print of blue, lavender, and pink flowers on a cream background, had pleased me for years. However, after electrical work was done, I found it necessary to replace the friendly, sprigged wallpaper, choosing a classic pinstriped pattern of blue and white to take its place.

Once the old wallpaper was removed (a tedious, time-consuming job), I found it difficult to throw out the larger strips that had remained intact. The years, and an abundance of California sunlight, had imparted an almost vintage quality to this pretty paper. It reminded me of a trio of very expensive antique hatboxes I had recently seen at one of my favorite home stores. So . . . instead of jamming these stray papers into the overfilled trash bag, I decided to tightly roll the larger, cleaner fragments (using a rubber band to hold the rolls in place) and stored them in my Craft Pantry. They take very little space—I store them upright in a wide-mouth Mason jar. Now, whenever the muse of artfulness strikes me, I will transform these papers into a variety of beautiful mysteries.

If you haven't stripped any walls of their paper in recent memory (and haven't any plans to do so in the near future) you may still easily implement the following strategies by using paper from discontinued wallpaper sample books. You may also purchase attractive wallpaper from the bargain bins at wallpaper, department, and home stores, for as little as a few dollars per roll. Wallpaper border also works well when used on smaller projects. And, of course, do not neglect to seek out odd rolls of wallpaper when shopping at thrift stores, tag sales, and flea markets, to use on these fun and fanciful projects.

- I've created dust jackets for some of my more tattered yet beloved books, which protects them from further disintegration while imparting a whimsical, decorative look to my bookcases. And, I am sure Katie and Rosie will wish to cover their school books with it as well.

- Use the larger pieces to line the walls behind bookshelves and china cabinets, or to line the walls of ordinary closets to make them *extraordinary*. You needn't apply wallpaper in the traditional manner when using it in this fashion. Simply purchase double-stick tape at your hardware store, applying it only to the edges of the cut-to-shape wallpaper. You may also line drawers in this same manner.

- I am saving the more vintage-looking pieces of wallpaper to use for covering hatboxes. Should I run low on my patterned paper, I will line the insides with newsprint, using a foreign-language newspaper. When using newsprint, I always paint an even layer of plain white glue over it. The layer of dried glue will protect the items you place inside the hatbox from the newsprint ink.

- I sometimes use fragments of wallpaper to line the mats inside of picture frames; these are pretty backgrounds when framing simple prints or postcards, fragments of antique lace, doilies, and the like. I used this strategy when framing my father's baby bib (hand-knitted by my grandmother) when Clancy was just an infant. If you wish to cover a mat with wallpaper, cut the paper to wrap around the mat neatly (much like wrapping a gift), and adhere the paper with rubber cement or a glue stick.

- Of course, you may recycle wallpaper in the time-honored manner . . . to wrap a gift. Or, line the wallpaper with plain writing paper—attach with rubber cement for best results—and cut, to create a unique set of note cards and gift tags. Use these to stock your Gift Pantry.

Displaying Your Beloved Treasures

". . . Architecture . . . presents so noble a field for the display of the grand and the beautiful, and which, at the same time, is so intimately connected with the essential comforts of life."
—WILLIAM HICKLING PRESCOTT

There are many rules that govern the display of objects and collections within a home, and most of them are quite sensible and useful. Basic recipes for decorating allow your rooms to look more polished and serene.

Graceful Groupings for Your Walls   There is a simple formula that allows you to easily arrange a group of pictures and/or objects for display on a wall. This strategy allows you to unify a variety of diverse objects and is ideal for displaying those beloved treasures you have garnered from a variety of sources, such as tag sales and flea markets. To begin you must group objects into a large *shape* (I do this on the floor) in much the same manner as you would fit pieces of a puzzle together. You may use a rectangular, square, triangular, diamond, or circular outline for your grouping. The foremost rule to remember is to decide upon your corners *before* filling in the remainder of the arrangement. Be aware that the pictures or objects (such as architectural fragments and mirrors) need not line up perfectly; what you are trying to achieve is the basic outline of the shape you have decided upon. It is important to fiddle with your grouping a bit before you begin putting holes in the wall. Perhaps leave them on the table or floor for a day or two, so that you may return to them with a fresh eye. Once you have made your final decisions, hang the corners first (again, akin to a puzzle), and then fill in the blanks. Keep your spackle and touch-up paint handy so that you may fix any miscalculations as they occur.

A Passion for Porcelain Art   I have long held a passion for beautiful porcelain plates, bowls, and teapots. Over the years I have found some very special pieces at flea markets, tag sales, and antique shops. Using the tried-and-true method of blending the humble with the grand, I use these pieces to ornament my walls. Doing so adds a subtle pattern and intricate texture to the rooms. To camouflage an unsightly (but highly useful) thermostat, I mounted underneath it an ornamental bracket I discovered at a yard sale for only one dollar. Using this as a centerpiece, I surrounded it with my favorite plates, arranged in a diamond pattern. The thermostat is neatly hidden behind a small mirror propped atop the bracket

The Noble Art of Childhood: Framed and "Lined"   For many years now I have exhibited my children's artwork by framing their Picasso-like abstracts. As the mother of three I have, over time, amassed quite a collection, and have displayed them, using the shape trick mentioned earlier, in a short hallway. You may wish to devote an entire wall to similarly framed children's art. And, for more transient creations (or to safely hang those still-damp paintings) you may wish to establish a special art-line in the kitchen or laundry room. I have done this quite easily by taking four yards of variegated ribbon, and four yards of tulle ribbon, and gently twisting them together. Tie a bow at each end and, using thumbtacks, stretch them across the wall in a loose line. Use painted wooden clothespins (I like to spray-paint them white, gold, and silver) to clip the noble works of childhood onto the art-line. You may change them as desired.

Remember to Look Up   The space above doorways and windows is often overlooked when thinking of artful ways to display our beloved objects. Try hanging a trio of miniature plates above a window, or a set of miniature paintings or prints above the doorjamb (this looks especially pretty in rooms with high ceilings). Doing so may add a subtle architectural element to an otherwise ordinary room.

Ornamenting the Walls of a Home Achieve the look of stenciling or hand-painting in a fraction of the time by using stencillike rubber stamps on your walls. Craft and stamp stores often carry (or you may order) kits that include stamps, instructions, and sometimes paint. Motifs will vary—hearts, roses, stars and moons, vines and flowers, cherubs, fleur de lis, or shells. These are quite easy to use. Moisten the stamps with paint (using an artist's brush) and press the stamp onto the wall, but practice on paper before stamping your walls to define the precise pressure and amount of paint you will need to use. (Keep in mind that, if you have touch-up paint for your walls, you may always paint over the stamped pattern if you make an error, or don't enjoy the final look.) To save even more time, mark your walls with a light pencil before you begin your project. These will guide you when stamping your designs. By stamping or stenciling a repeating pattern on a wall you can achieve the effect of wallpaper, without the expense and aggravation.

Artful Uses for a Teapot Collection

• A teapot, lidless or otherwise, makes a lovely, whimsical vase for roses, herbs, and ferns cut from my garden. (I often purchase teapots to add to my gift pantry for just such uses.) These make lovely table decorations, as well as charming one-of-a-kind hostess, thank you, or christening gifts. (Please see the box, "Flowery Language" on page 114.) You may also use them as vases for dried flower arrangements. I currently have a cream-colored, lidless teapot filled with a bouquet of home-dried hydrangeas. I keep them in place with a bit of Rosie's clay pressed to the inside bottom of the pot.

• Also, I have lined a sturdy teapot (sans lid) with an attractive napkin for use on a buffet table as a utensil holder (you may gather them all in one pot for a small

NOBLE VESSELS

"There is a great deal of poetry and fine sentiment in a chest of tea."
—RALPH WALDO EMERSON

There is an ancient story that tells us about the Chinese emperor Shen Nung noticing less sickness as a result of water being boiled before it was consumed. He therefore made it a practice to carefully boil all drinking water. One day, it is told, Emperor Nung (also referred to as the Divine Healer) was waiting for his water to boil when a few stray leaves from a branch in the fire beneath his pot floated into the hot water. The emperor drank the brew and enjoyed the taste. Emperor Nung made a note of the type of branch from which the leaves came and began cultivating these plants in his garden. This shrub is now thought to have been the wild tea plant.

Tea was introduced to the West in the sixteenth century, when it was touted in a variety of advertisements as being "for all persons of eminence and quality." With the arrival of teas from the Orient came small reddish-brown teapots, which inspired English and Dutch potters to make their own versions. The original teapot shape was round-bodied, with a large curving handle and a short, straight spout.

During the early 1700s, British potters reshaped the teapot to make the more elegant shapes we are familiar with today. These potters designed a pear-shaped body with a swan-neck spout, adding a strainer to the inner construction to weed out undesired tea leaves in the cup. The European-designed teapot also served to create a better balanced vessel, so that pouring the tea itself would be simpler.

During Victorian times the teapot became a familiar object, even in working-class homes, due to the advancing courses of world trade. This growing industry made tea (and its accoutrements) more readily available and much less expensive than they had been in the past.

In today's fast-paced world, I find myself drawn to this gentle symbol of nobility. In my mind, the teapot holds an aura of romance, comfort, and magic. For tea represents a very true alchemy—a shrub's simple leaves, mingled with the most basic of liquids, boiling water, metamorphoses into a warm, soothing, sometimes healing, liquid.

Perhaps this mysterious transformation is the reason I have collected a mismatched menagerie of these vessels—why they have cluttered my china cabinets, Gift and Craft Pantries, and adorned my tabletops, kitchen counters, vanity, and fireplace mantels for the past twenty years.

❧

party, or use separate teapots for forks, knives, and spoons). I am careful to bring out only my sturdiest pots for this use, as the more delicate ones may be accidentally chipped.

- We often use smaller, individual-size teapots as creamers. (Sometimes we even use creamers as teapots, as these are also the perfect size for our girls to use in their dolly tea parties.)

- A large teapot (with or without lid) may be used as an informal cookie jar (if desired, you may use an attractive saucer in lieu of a teapot lid).

- One of the more practical uses for the teapot is as a collection vessel for spent tea bags. (We use these to supplement the soil in our garden and window boxes.)

- A fine porcelain teapot will look lovely on a dressing table, hosting fresh cotton balls or cotton swabs.

- We have also used a pretty teapot on the powder room countertop to store linen hand towels or washcloths. Simply roll them lengthwise and insert inside the teapot. Their top halves extend out of the pot, making a lovely fabric "bouquet" for all to enjoy.

- Some of my more forlorn yet attractive teapots make a home within my Craft Pantry. I often use these to store glue sticks, scissors, or dried flowers for craft projects. They look pretty on the shelves—and, should I invite friends over for a crafting party, they look lovely and inviting at the worktable.

- If you haven't a jam pot (and wish to leave the commercial jam jar in the kitchen) simply fill a small or medium-size teapot with your favorite jam or jelly. Add a vintage silver serving spoon and place it at your table so that your family and guests may help themselves.

- Perched atop a vintage, lace-edged doily and accessorizing my desk, the teapot that sparked my collection now displays an assortment of favorite pens, pencils, and scissors. This is a lovely way to make use of charming, yet lidless, teapots—as well as those lovely vessels damaged by hairline cracks yet too beautiful to discard.

- And, of course, I use my collection of teapots in the traditional manner—for brewing and serving tea. Quite often we serve two or three different varieties at one time (darjeeling for the adults, cranberry and herb for the children) simply for fun and variety.

My teapot mania extends to the realm of the miniature as well. Each Christmas it is a tradition to present a tiny tea set to both of my daughters, Rosie and Katie. Needless to say, we have garnered quite a collection over the years. One of my favorite ways in which to display the prettiest doll-size teapots was devised years ago. I transformed several inexpensive wooden spice racks (purchased for one or two dollars at yard sales and thrift shops) into miniature china shelves. A few coats of white paint, a flower sprig strategically placed, and the tiniest of brass cup hooks was all the alchemy needed for them to become charming miniature tea cabinets.

Cultivating Home Peace

". . . Give nothing but the highest quality to your moments as they pass."
—WALTER PATER

How we view ourselves—our abilities, our purposes, our aspirations—makes us either rich in spirit or impoverished. Choose now to enrich your life and affect the future by consciously checking destructive habits—and cultivating positive moments.

- Begin each day by taking note of, and consciously *appreciating,* the blessings that are currently in your life.

- Be the guardian of your words. Words are powerful and can destroy in seconds what may have taken years to cultivate. In the legal field they have a saying: "You cannot unring a bell." Keep this in mind when you are tempted to utter unkind things to your children, partner, or friends.

- Make it a habit to look for and praise positive behavior and attitudes of your family members. I have discovered that by recognizing and building up the positive traits, they become stronger, leaving less room (and little time) for negative qualities to take root.

- When your partner and/or children are speaking to you, look up from what you are doing and offer your full attention to their words. If you are involved in a project that requires your undivided attention, allow a few moments for a brief intermission. If it appears that this is more than just a momentary interruption, politely ask if they can save the details for when you are finished (because you don't want to miss *any* of what they have to say). Explain that you cannot concentrate fully on *them* until this "chore" is finished; I always make an effort to let them know that my first choice is always to be with *them,* yet I am obligated to finish what I am doing before I can have "fun." Seek out the interrupter as soon as you are free. (I sometimes bring in tea, or a small treat of some kind, for us to share as we talk.) Give your undivided attention to their words. A note of caution: The secret to making this strategy successful is found in *following through.* Implement this strategy only if you are willing and able to follow through. If you do not live up to your promise you may increase hurt feelings and sow the seeds of mistrust.

- Make every effort to master a quick temper. Seek to consciously check anger and impatience in yourself, as these are the streams from which negative words flow. Do not be disappointed if you don't succeed the first dozen times. As with any habit, perseverance is required for a new trait to become absorbed into your character (in this case, patience). A good trick is to pause for a few seconds before you speak—easier said than done, I know, but not impossible.

- Keep in mind that bad moods are contagious. Try to differentiate between a sour mood and a true dilemma (your own as well as others'). This will take a bit of practice, but an awareness that there *is* a difference between the two is the beginning of mastery. On most occasions on which I find myself irritable and angry (often due to fatigue, stress, or hunger) I am aware that I am behaving (or am about to behave) unreasonably. Because I am conscious of this, I have formed the habit of retreating to a quiet corner to calm down. Sometimes, if I know hunger is the cause of my irritation, I ask the children to not ask me for anything until I've eaten something substantial. (There is a standing joke in our family about low blood sugar being the culprit for all grumpy behavior.) If someone else in our household is showing fits of temper, I have found the ancient Biblical advice of using a soft answer to turn away wrath tremendously effective (about seventy-five percent of the time, or more).

- Never underestimate the power of an apology. Be prepared to look at yourself with complete honesty and admit and apologize when you have snapped unnecessarily (due to illness, hunger, or simply from lack of self-control). Try not to let apologies take the place of better behavior. Certainly they are easier, but you will never master yourself if you depend on apologies to excuse you from the bad habits of irritability and snappishness.

- Pride and stubbornness are inhibitors to happiness and will negatively influence your life. Always accept a sincere apology, avoiding the habit of unforgiveness. Unforgiveness will lead you into a twisted maze of hurtful words and misunderstandings (deliberate and otherwise) and can completely destroy happiness, home, and family.

- The human family is a very precious thing. It is within the family circle that we conduct our apprenticeship to life and make our first social contract. And, as William Cowper wisely noted, "God gives to every [person] the virtue, temper, understanding [and] taste, that lifts him into life, and lets him fall just in the niche he was ordained to fill." Each of us is alive for a purpose. It is our responsibility to find the gifts that were bestowed upon us. Once found, it is our joy—as well as our obligation—to cultivate and make use of them. And, of course, we are doubly blessed when we are born into a family that recognizes and nurtures these positive traits.

Illuminated Fragments
Works of Wonder and Quiet Graces

"Angels and ministers of grace, defend us!"
—WILLIAM SHAKESPEARE

*T*haumaturgi was their ancient name, a name born from the marriage of two Greek words, *thauma,* meaning "wonder," and *ergos,* meaning "working." The Bible gives many examples of these saintly personages who performed miracles, Moses and Jesus being the best known. The world has also been home to a different type of wonder-worker: Human beings who, throughout civilization, have invoked awe by way of their achievements, inspiring generation after generation with their wondrous works.

The ancient Greek poet Homer authored what are thought to be the greatest works of Western literature, *The Iliad* and *The Odyssey.* The philosopher Socrates turned scientific method into the art of living, and profoundly influenced the future. All the great schools of philosophy that sprang up in the Greek and, later, Roman worlds were claimed to have descended from him. Today we are still living with the wondrous Socratic heritage.

Through the arts, Michelangelo exposed a great soul full of sublime visions and passions, in spite of his many human frailties. Through his paintings, sculptures, poetry, and architecture he accomplished a multitude of wonders that continue to influence Western culture today.

Four hundred years ago, a man of simple origins and education held a magnifying glass to the spirit of his age and spoke to the soul. His command of the English language was so precise that he could pack entire philosophies into single syllables. "To be or not to be" is a most profound question, condensed down to the simplest verbal form. His works have enabled readers throughout the centuries to better understand human nature—its awful frailties and noble strengths. It has been said that every age finds its reflection in William Shakespeare's universal mirror.

Wolfgang Amadeus Mozart, often considered a wonder child, composed graceful, precise, spirited music from the age of six. By the age of fifteen, he was the author of twenty symphonies and six short operas. Several decades after Mozart shared his genius with the world, Ludwig van Beethoven composed the magnificent ninth symphony. The wonder of this? At the time of its composition he was so deaf that he never heard one note of it.

These and numerous other wonder-workers have existed throughout the history of civilization and the world. What a blessing it is to have their gracious examples to learn and to grow from. Yet, many people do not realize that wonders continue to swirl around us. A multitude of quiet miracles abound in each life—simple, unstinting, often overlooked graces offered to mortals during this necessary tenure on terra firma.

Chapter 9

Clothed in Loveliness

~

"Clothing the palpable and familiar with
golden exhalations of the dawn."

—Samuel Coleridge

Preparing for School

"To tell tales out of school."
—John Heywood

Summer will be over in no time at all, and school will soon be starting once again. And with the advent of school come those inevitable back-to-school expenses. Therefore, now is the ideal time for parents to budget and set aside money for the needed clothing, supplies, and other necessities of school days.

Wise Tactics

". . . Wise men shun the mistakes of fools, but fools do not imitate the successes of the wise."
—Marcus Porcius Cato

- Establish a careful budget for back-to-school expenses. Planning ahead allows you the opportunity to teach children how to budget and also gives them a chance to make decisions regarding their own purchases. As well, planning ahead may enable parents to save enough cash to cover clothing expenses and thus avoid incurring credit card debt.

- Establish a spending limit for each child. List all expenses the child may have, including supplies, clothing, band or athletic uniforms and equipment, or instrument rentals. Do not forget some less obvious back-to-school expenses such as haircuts, immunizations, and annual physicals for school and/or sports activities. Summer is a convenient time for dental and eye examinations, so don't forget to include these expenses in your budget as well.

- Comparison shop for school supplies. Prices can vary tremendously from store to store. Look at office supply stores, volume discount warehouses, and large drug and grocery stores for the best values. Take advantage of advertised specials throughout the summer to stock up on items you will need. You could also share bulk purchases with other families.

- Start early and shop wisely. Many schools distribute lists at the end of the school year of the supplies required for the next grade level. Don't wait until the last minute to begin your back-to-school shopping. Spread school purchases over an extended period of time to keep from spending a large amount of money at any one time, and make an effort to always pay with cash.

- Have your children help when making the list and estimating costs of the items. Use this opportunity to instruct your children about money management. They may be surprised as to how quickly the dollar amounts add up. Including children in the planning and budgeting efforts teaches them to approach spending carefully.

- Allow your children to determine priorities. They must have school supplies, but not necessarily the latest fad in footwear. Allow them to learn to differentiate necessities from luxuries.

- Tell the children the dollar amount for their total expenditures. Let them discern what they can buy for that amount of money. They may realize that they can buy two pairs of regular jeans for the price of one pair of designer jeans. As your children grow older, allow them more responsibility by letting them take part in more of the financial decisions that concern them.

- Be a good example for your children through your own money management skills. While shopping for their school supplies, show them how to compare prices and quality. Resist the urge to spend impulsively, and explain why you are doing so. Point out the benefits of sales, discount stores, and volume buying.

With a bit of careful planning and shopping the beginning of the school year needn't be a financial burden. To learn more about budgeting, using credit, or to receive confidential money management counseling, contact The National Foundation for Consumer Credit (See Resources).

Strengthening Sales Resistance

"Strength and honor are her clothing."

—Proverbs 31:25

When purchasing clothing at retail establishments you may soothe your budget by familiarizing yourself with certain methods that salespeople sometimes implement to weaken the customer's sales resistance. Here are a few facts to consider:

- Most sales personnel who are paid on a commission basis aim for a multiple sale. Once you have purchased a basic garment, a savvy salesperson may suggest matching shirts, hats, and other accessories. If you have these things at home already, or have already spent your budgeted amount, walk away from these extras. Be aware of this sales strategy by looking for cue phrases such as "I know you aren't looking for an extra blouse for this outfit, but I have the perfect cream-colored silk . . ."

- When purchasing more expensive items (and also when purchasing automobiles) a "takeover" person is often called in. Once the initial salesperson has answered all of your questions (and your choices have been narrowed down) a supervisor, or possibly the store owner, will join the discussion and offer his or her opinion on your purchase. When this happens the dynamics have shifted to a two-against-one ratio, and the customer's sales resistance often evaporates at this point.

- Beware of the false hectic atmosphere. This is created by a salesperson urging the customer to buy an item *now* for fear of "losing it to someone else." This sort of stress-induced salesmanship is most effective on younger customers and, if you are not aware of it, you may find yourself dramatically overspending.

෴

Beware "the Look"

"Give me a look, give me a face, that makes simplicity a grace."
—BEN JONSON

It is true, most fashion-conscious individuals prefer to wear a "look." In and of itself the look is not a negative phenomenon; the problems arise when seeking to *reflect* it, because current looks are notoriously expensive and transient (changing like the wind). Current trends are reflected in fashion magazines and department stores and are, at minimum, changed seasonally. Because of this, fashion and trends can be dangerous to any budget and are especially harsh to a small one. The danger is built into the garment itself. Yet, as expensive as it is for those who strive to capture the current look, it is often more costly for the manufacturers who must produce these different styles from season to season.

A new fashion trend inevitably means that manufacturers must retool their equipment and redirect or even retrain their employees. What this means to consumers is a quickly made garment of questionable quality. Why? Because spending time on how well the garment is made would further increase manufacturing costs. Instead, the manufacturers often invest their time and money in creating that ever-changing, much-sought-after "look." This process often results in the production of lower-quality garments.

The happy news is that you can circumvent a portion of the cost of quality garments. How? By understanding that menswear is much less prone to change than garments made exclusively for women. Men's suits can remain current in the fashion world for years. Because of this stability, men's clothing manufacturers do not need to invest in the expense of retooling each season. It is for this reason that the manufacturers of menswear may use their money and time to produce well-made garments composed of higher-quality fabric.

While you are shopping for yourself, do not neglect to investigate the offerings from boys' wear manufacturers as well. In my pre-children days I often purchased larger (sizes 18 to 20), quality polo shirts, belts, and walking shorts in the boys' department (often during sales) at a fraction of the cost I would have paid if purchasing comparable items offered by womenswear manufacturers.

If you would like to add new, well-constructed garments such as blazers, classic button-down shirts, vests, and trousers to your wardrobe—and soothe your budget at the same time—you would be wise to investigate the menswear department at better stores (preferably during a sale). If you desire, you may easily embellish these classic designs with a few well-placed tucks, a flounced or lacy blouse, a satin or vintage handkerchief tucked into a pocket, and a strand of fine pearls. (I add a lace camisole beneath a linen dress shirt—culled from the menswear department—over a skirt, and cinched at the waist with a leather belt.)

Acquiring and building your wardrobe should not become a spiritual or financial burden. Instead, it should lift the spirit, ease your life, and consume very little of your time and budget.

Garmenting Wee Ones

"In shining robes and garments fair."
—GUSTAVE NADAUD

I have been shopping at better children's consignment stores for many years. These establishments are often brimming with like-new children's garments, and other items, at a fraction of their retail costs. I have discovered gently used classic Laura Ashley mother-daughter dresses for eighteen dollars each (retail cost for these is well over a hundred dollars each); quality children's party shoes for three dollars (these are almost always in mint condition as party shoes are often worn only once or twice before being outgrown); barely worn name-brand sneakers for five dollars (retail value sixty dollars); well-made, designer boys' blazers and suits; Lanz pajamas for four dollars (brand new, with tags still attached); plus a plethora of other items, ranging from video game stations to china tea sets.

&

I am constantly amazed at the versatility of the classic drop-waist jumper. On hot summer days my daughters may wear this style of jumper over a T-shirt. During winter I will slip a cozy turtleneck underneath the same jumper for a day of school. When dressing them for a party, I have embellished the same simple jumper with a romantic, flounced underblouse, a frilly petticoat that peaks out from beneath the hem, tights, party shoes, and a pretty hat or an oversized, matching hair bow. (I must confess, when I was expecting I often wore simple jumpers myself, and expanded my limited maternity wardrobe by implementing many of these same strategies on an adult level.)

&

If you enjoy seeing your children wear coordinating clothing (but find this strategy nearly impossible to achieve through consignment or thrift shopping) consider the classic nautical look. The nautical look consists of the color combination of navy blue, white, and red—and sometimes a traditional square sailor collar. This classic motif goes back hundreds of years and is still widely popular today. Many children's garments (dresses, shirts, shorts, and jackets) are designed in this style, thus allowing you to achieve a coordinated appearance, even when the clothing is derived from different sources. Another strategy for coordinating your children's clothing is to purchase gently used uniforms such as jumpers and skirts from local private schools. Garments made by uniform manufacturers are also quite practical; most are well constructed of quality fabric—and the patterns tend to be timeless classics that are immune to trends.

⚮

Another side of the consignment shopping spectrum is to sell your own children's outgrown clothing through these establishments. You can benefit most by delivering clean clothing in good condition that needs no ironing and, if possible, on hangers (you needn't leave the hangers at the store). Children's consignment stores are a wonderful way to recycle good-quality high chairs, cribs, and other baby paraphernalia that you no longer find necessary. Most store owners will take about fifty percent of the sales price of each garment, although this may vary with the store. Each consignment shop will furnish its own guidelines for suppliers. To receive a list of resale shops near you, write to the National Association of Resale and Thrift Shops, 157 Halsted Street, Chicago Heights, IL 60411.

The Art of Retail Bargaining

"Lest the bargain should catch cold and starve."
—WILLIAM SHAKESPEARE

The main obstacle most shoppers encounter when faced with the opportunity to bargain is the idea that nice people don't do it. Before you can negotiate successfully, you must overcome this fallacious attitude. The art of bargaining is a classic and useful skill that is as ancient as the art of selling. In this modern world in which we live, it is important to understand that intangible skills such as bargaining are again being openly recognized as having value.

Realize that all shopkeepers see when you walk in the door is dollar signs. If you are willing to spend, they will probably be willing to deal. Every individual who spends money has a right to bargain.

- Although department stores sometimes bargain (especially on large-ticket items such as appliances and furniture), your best chances of getting a lesser price at the retail level are from smaller, privately owned shops.

- Adapt your bargaining to the situation. For example, a true discount store has a low profit margin and depends on volume to make money. I wouldn't ask for more than five percent off in such a store. On the other hand, a boutique that charges whatever the market will bear has more bargaining leeway; therefore, begin negotiations by asking for about twenty-five percent off the marked price, and work from there.

- Make it clear to the shopkeeper that you are a serious shopper who intends to spend money. Select several definite articles as well as several tentative purchases. Ask the shopkeeper the total cost before writing the bill. Then, softly and politely, ask the merchant if she can make a better price. Be prepared to leave without any merchandise if you cannot garner a price you can afford (you can always return later if you wish).

- Be discreet when practicing the art of retail bargaining: Try to keep your negotiations private. If other customers can overhear your dickering, the shopkeeper must stay firm in his or her price. A shopkeeper won't reduce a price if he's worried that the special value will be made public. Therefore, when in the process of bargaining be certain to express the fact that you will keep the discount confidential.

- Be respectful of the merchandise as well as the salesperson. Do not mishandle the products you wish to purchase, and always address salespeople in a polite, friendly manner. Assume that they want to do their best for you.

- Look for unmarked merchandise. If there is no price tag, you are invited to bargain.

- Shop during off hours. You will have better luck garnering a retail bargain if business is slow.

- Shop at the end of the season, when new stock is being put out. Offer to buy the older goods at a discount.

- Ask the appliance or electronics dealers in your neighborhood if they will consider giving you a price break so that you can keep your business in the community— as opposed to getting a better price at a larger chain store out of town or in a different neighborhood.

- Always remember that friendliness and courtesy are essential in gaining the best prices, and do not become offended if you are unable to garner a discount every time you ask. Continue to seek a better price in your most courteous and respectful manner.

SEASONAL BARGAINS

*"Mere parsimony is not economy . . . expense, and
Great expense may be an essential part of true economy."*
—EDMUND BURKE

To be acquainted with the specific seasons in which retail merchandise is often offered for sale is an essential piece of knowledge that enters into the art of frugality. Those individuals who anticipate need, before the need is felt, are counted among the wise. As Benjamin Franklin rightly noted, "Necessity never made a good bargain."

Summer

- Air conditioners—late summer
- Bathing suits—mid- to late summer
- Bedding
- Blankets—early summer
- Building materials
- Children's clothing—early summer
- Christmas gifts
- Clothing (spring styles)—early summer
- Coats (women's, men's, and children's)—early summer
- Coats (winter)—early summer
- Curtains and draperies
- Fans—late summer
- Frozen foods
- Fuel oil
- Furniture
- Furs
- Gardening equipment—late summer
- Handbags
- Home appliances
- Home furnishings
- Housewares—late summer
- Paints (household)—late summer
- Rugs and carpets
- Shoes
- Summer clothes and fabrics—late summer
- Summer sports equipment—late summer
- Tires—late summer
- Towels—late summer

Autumn

- Automobile batteries and mufflers
- Bicycles
- Camping equipment
- Children's clothing—late autumn
- China
- Dresses—late autumn
- Fishing equipment
- Gardening equipment
- Glassware
- Hosiery
- Housewares—early autumn
- Lamps—early autumn
- Ranges and cooktops
- Rugs and carpets
- School clothes—late autumn
- Silverware
- Suits (men's and boys')—late autumn
- Water heaters

ℰℓ

Winter

- Air conditioning
- Appliances
- Art supplies
- Bedding
- Bicycles
- Blankets—late winter
- Books—late winter
- Cars
- China—late winter
- Curtains—late winter
- Drapes—late winter
- Dresses—mid- and late winter
- Electronic equipment (home)—mid- and late winter
- Furniture—late winter
- Furs—late winter
- Glassware—mid- and late winter
- Handbags—mid- and late winter
- Home furnishings—late winter
- Housewares—mid- and late winter
- Infant's wear—late winter
- Linens
- Luggage—late winter
- Men's clothing—mid- and late winter
- Party goods—late winter
- Ranges and cooktops—late winter
- Shoes (women's, men's, and children's)
- Silverware—mid- and late winter
- Sportswear
- Suits (men's and boys')—late winter
- Table linens—mid- and late winter
- Toiletries—mid- and late winter
- Towels—mid- and late winter
- Toys—mid- and late winter
- Water heaters—mid- and late winter

❧

Spring

- Blankets—late spring
- Christmas gifts
- Clothes dryers
- Clothing (spring styles)—late spring
- Clothing (winter styles)
- Coats (children's and women's)—late spring
- Coats (men's winter coats)
- Infants' clothing
- Linens—late spring
- Shoes (children's)—late spring
- Skates and skis (and other winter sporting equipment)
- Storm windows—late spring
- Stoves (those used for cooking as well as heating)
- Suits (men's and boys)
- Table linens—late spring
- Tires (for automobiles)—late spring
- Washing machines

Illuminated Fragments

A Quest for the Best

"The best in this kind are but shadows."
—WILLIAM SHAKESPEARE

Some people quest for the best of *everything*. They are satisfied only with the *best* ingredients for cooking; live only in the *best* cities, the *best* neighborhoods, the *best* houses; and settle for nothing less than the *best* furniture; the *finest* china and silver; the *best* linens; the most expensive towels; the *best* handmade soaps. They wear only the *best* clothes, and drive the *best* automobiles.

Quite obviously, there are occasions on which a desire for the *best* is worth the price and effort involved in obtaining it. To work and try your *best* when taking on any job or challenge is part of achieving a successful outcome. As well, it is vital that you carefully choose the *best* life mate. And, if your child were ill you would, of course, want only the *best* physician. A true *best* friend is a precious gift. And it is also important to treasure and to cultivate the *best* of times, the *best* life lessons, the *best* memories, and the *best* thoughts.

Like all imperfect creatures, I have been tempted by desires for the finer *things* that life has to offer. Still, when caught up in my own search for the *best* I was continually haunted by a simple question. Why? What could questing for the best *things* do to improve the quality of my soul and character?

At the end of each life's journey, what remains that is of value? I would venture to guess that what becomes most precious is the knowledge and wisdom acquired throughout a lifetime. The memories of positive deeds you have done, the seeds of faith, love, appreciation, patience, strength, and kindness that you have sown (along with the hope that, by the grace of God, you have left the world in a *little* better condition than you found it) can be nothing less than comforting.

There is, however, no way to avoid the silent question that is put to each earthbound mortal: Should we waste our most precious commodity, time (and money earned by the use of it), to hunt out and consume a multitude of tangible *bests*? Each individual must answer that question for him- or herself. As for me, I will continue to look for my favorite luxuries among other . . . less tangible . . . *best* things.

Chapter 10

The Summer Gift Pantry

*"Earth was bountiful, and we were surrounded with the
blessings of the great mystery."*

—Luther Standing Bear

Summer's Dispensations and Bountiful Gifts

"Fortune reigns in gifts of the world . . ."
—William Shakespeare

I was born with an instinct for putting things by. Although neither of my parents
brought us up to learn the skills of food preservation, I am attracted to the idea of self-
sufficiency. I enjoy stories about how the early pioneers prepared and stored available
food during the warm seasons so that they would have enough to eat during the long,
cold winter months. This, to me, was a wise course of action. Thus inspired, I try to
find time and energy to stock my food larder. Once this is filled, it seems only natural
to turn my passion for putting things by to the Gift Pantry.

My pioneer spirit is aroused when I have a garden filled with luscious herbs and vegetables and a refrigerator filled with summer fruits from my father's trees and bushes. There is always so much more than we can eat on our own. After offering samples to neighbors and friends, I take pleasure in preserving summer's bounty *now*, while it tastes its best and is least expensive. I begin by using the fruits and herbs to create simple jams and jellies. The lavender and rosemary bushes in our garden generously provide fragrant bundles that I dry and use for gift-giving. And the roses (cut from our Cecile Brunner rosebush) are air-dried and fill our extra-large antique English apothecary jars. These roses are used to enhance special gifts and are made into unique tree decorations for use during the winter holidays.

Kitchen Miracles

When preserving foods for your Gift Pantry, remember that summer offers us a bounty of fresh fruits and (hopefully) a kitchen garden brimming with delights. However, if you are too busy to garden or have no earth to till, you may wish to make use of the gifts of the season via roadside stands, farmers' markets, and "pick-your-own" orchards.

Simple Lavender Jelly

3½ cups granulated sugar
1¾ cups lavender infusion
½ teaspoon butter or margarine
2 tablespoons fresh lemon juice (you may substitute white vinegar for lemon juice; however, I find that vinegar imparts a bit of a sour taste to the jelly)
Several drops blue or violet food coloring
1 pouch liquid fruit pectin (you may choose from several brands on the market)

To make lavender infusion:
Wash about 1½ cups firmly packed lavender leaves and stems. With clean scissors, snip the lavender leaves and stems into small pieces and place them into a saucepan with 2¼ cups of water. Bring the mixture to a boil. Remove it from the heat and allow the infusion to stand for 10 minutes, before straining.

To prepare jelly:
Prepare your glass canning jars, lids, and seals according to manufacturer's and USDA

guidelines (be certain the jars are free of chips and cracks, and are very clean—contaminates may cause spoilage).

Measure the sugar carefully. Stir the sugar into the lavender infusion, adding the lemon juice and food coloring. Add ½ teaspoon margarine or butter to prevent foaming during cooking. Bring the mixture to *a full rolling boil* on high heat, stirring constantly.

Open your pouch of liquid fruit pectin and quickly stir contents into lavender and sugar mixture. Return to a full rolling boil and boil *exactly 1 minute, stirring constantly*. Remove from heat. Skim off any foam. Immediately fill jars, and seal as directed by the manufacturer.

Note: Other herbs—mint, verbena, lemon balm, even rose petals—may be substituted for the lavender (be certain they are all pesticide-free).

How to Sterilize Jars and Glasses for Preserving

Wash the jars in very hot soapy water and rinse thoroughly with scalding water. Place the jars in a large clean kettle and fully cover them with hot water. Cover and bring the contents of the kettle to a full boil. Continue boiling for fifteen minutes after the initial boiling point (at which time steam should be emanating from the kettle). Turn off the heat under the kettle and allow the jars to stay in the kettle of hot water until immediately before filling. When you are ready to use the jars, invert them onto a clean towel and allow them to drip dry. While the jars are still hot, fill them with your cooked jelly or jam.

Secret Sauce

Last summer, one small batch of the peach jam I prepared did not jell. My frugal nature, of course, would not allow me to discard these jars. Therefore, instead of labeling them as "Peach Jam," I pasted on a label that read "Peach Sauce." This watery jam was used as a sauce to embellish simple desserts of unfrosted spice cake or vanilla ice cream (and sometimes it became the main ingredient for peach shortcake topped with whipped cream). I even put a jar of this sauce in a damask-lined basket, along with a homemade pound cake and a vintage silver cake server, and presented it as a holiday gift to a neighbor.

Collecting Ribbons

Throughout the year, and especially during the summer tag sale season, I collect interesting ribbons and fabrics for our Gift and Craft Pantries. These are culled from my usual sources (flea markets, tag sales, and thrift shops). I have also been known to recycle ribbon rosebuds, silk tassels, lacy decorations, and odd bits of dressmakers' braids as embellishments.

Create your own ribbons for pennies by cutting pretty fabrics into strips (we often use fine netting, fine-patterned gingham or floral prints, stiff brocades, plush velvets, and heavy satins, as well as metallic-look fabrics such as lamé). Leave the edges fringed for a homespun look, or use a product called Fray Check to keep the edges from unraveling—or cut them with pinking sheers. Use discarded clothing from your closets or garments culled from yard sales specifically for this purpose. We have recycled some of the more worn, yet sentimental, garments the children have outgrown and converted them into ribbons. These special ribbons are stored in a lidded basket and are reused from year to year.

Alternatives to the Traditional Gift Basket

"All the peace that springs from the large aggregate of little things."
—HANNAH MORE

Sometimes the best gift baskets are not baskets at all. Along with the classic gift basket, in our household, we also use soup tureens, old wooden tool holders, colanders, spatterware pots and pans, and more. Keep similar alternatives in mind when you are shopping the summer tag sales and flea markets; they are lovely additions to the Craft and Gift Pantries. Here are a few more of our favorite alternative packaging suggestions:

- Pie tins (glass or aluminum) with ingredients for pie or apple crumble
- Homemade or purchased Christmas stockings filled to the brim with goodies from your Gift Pantry

- Pretty paper gift bags
- Pretty serving trays are pleasant hosts for a variety of gifts. (Quite often I find inexpensive metal trays at yard sales and rejuvenate these with a coat of gold or silver spray paint for this purpose.)
- Large terra-cotta flowerpots (We use these to package small garden tools and seed packets.)
- Terra-cotta pot saucers (These are charming when used as rustic plates for presenting baked goods—line first with a homemade paper doily.)
- Serving platters or large dinner plates (often available for under a dollar at thrift shops and garage sales, and even at certain discount shops—we collect these during the year and add them to our Gift Pantry for use in any season)
- Wooden produce crates (For whimsically practical last-minute gifts, line these with a tablecloth or kitchen towels, and add fresh fruit and produce such as cabbages, root vegetables—rutabagas and turnips—as well as oranges, tangerines, and apples. To obtain the crates, simply inquire at the produce department of your local grocery store. I have found the employees there to be exceptionally helpful and generous.)
- Attractively decorated hatboxes (You can purchase these, or create them from recycled cylindrical cereal containers or shoe and boot boxes—use Modpodge and pretty recycled wrapping or tissue papers to cover.)

Illuminated Fragments
The Land of Eternal Summer

"But thy eternal summer shall not fade."
—WILLIAM SHAKESPEARE

When I was a very small child, I lived on a tiny, working farm in southern Ohio. Although my actual memories of those years are not conscious, I like to think that I possess somewhere deep within me mistlike wordless memories of that time. Is it these elusive vapors, I wonder, that sometimes take hold of me when I find myself directing my life to complement the age-old rhythm of the seasons from my southern California home?

May I blame *them* then, when I am overtaken with the sudden urge to serve summer suppers on the porch, to collect and display crumbling brown leaves found on the sidewalk during an otherwise green and glorious autumn? Can I make *them* the driving force behind my impossible cravings to see snow at the beach (happily settling for a spot of fog and a bit of rain instead) during the Christmas and winter holidays?

If these vapors are blameless, what, then, is the cause of this quarterly urge that I inevitably experience to view tangible evidence of the change of seasons? Living as I do in the land of eternal summer, I find it almost necessary to acknowledge and celebrate the joy and richness of the year's circle.

Still, the reason may be less mysterious than I imagine. For is it not a primal instinct, a human need, to be a valuable (albeit small) part of something larger, better ordered, and more disciplined than oneself?

THE GIFT PANTRY INVENTORY LIST FOR SUMMER		
GIFT RECIPIENT & DATE OF ENTRY INTO GIFT PANTRY	GIFT ITEM(S) PURCHASED OR CREATED	WHEN TO PRESENT THE GIFT & PACKAGING IDEAS

Part III
The Still Small Voice
of Autumn

~

*"Thus out of small beginnings
greater things have been produced
by His hand that made all things of nothing,
and gives being to all things that are; and,
as one small candle may light a thousand, so
the light here kindled hath shone unto many,
yea in some sort to our whole nation."*
—William Bradford
(speaking of Plymouth Plantation)

Chapter 11

Festivals of Autumn

～

"The Autumn seems to cry for thee,
Best lover of the Autumn-days!"
—SARAH CHAUNCEY WOOLSEY (SUSAN COOLIDGE)

Labor Day

"In all labor there is profit . . ."
—PROVERBS 14:23

The noblest thing in the world is wise and honest labor. Labor is the powerful magician that brings order out of chaos, transforms barren deserts into thriving cities, and produces works of genius from all fields of endeavor, be it the creation of grand architecture, powerful prose, tilled and cultivated soil, a clean cottage, or a home-cooked meal.

In ancient times all, including the wealthy, labored in their own kitchens and fields. In the Bible, Abraham and his wife Sarah are early examples of the dignity found in toil. And during the infancy of the United States, George and Martha Washington, although they were quite well off financially, set fine examples for industry *and* frugality.

There is a dignity in all honest labor that makes it beautiful and mighty. And if we remember that all true luxuries and achievements are the result of labor, we understand that nothing great can ever be accomplished without it. Thus, the first Monday in the month of September (in the United States and Canada) has been established as a special day on which to remember and honor this worthy quality, and those souls (past, present, and future) who exemplify it.

Leisurely Garlic-and-Rosemary Roast Beef

This recipe is especially easy and delicious. If the weather is still quite warm you may wish to roast the beef on top of the grill (in the same manner that the grilled chicken recipe offers on page 101).

1 roast beef (allow for 1 to 2 pounds per guest), trimmed of excess fat
3 or 4 large garlic cloves, peeled and sliced into about 4 slivers each
1 small branch fresh rosemary, washed and dried
1 tablespoon light vegetable oil (such as corn or very light olive oil)
Salt and pepper to taste

Preheat oven to 325°. Wash and pat dry the beef and place it onto a rack inside a roasting pan. Using a small paring knife, make tiny cuts (equivalent to the amount of garlic slivers you have) evenly across the top of the uncooked beef. Tuck 1 sliver of garlic and 2 or 3 rosemary needles inside each of the cuts, continuing until you have used them all. Rub the top of the roast with oil and salt and pepper. Bake for about 1 to 1½ hours (depending upon how rare you like it).

Note: You may make leg of lamb or pork roasts in this manner as well. The process of tucking garlic and rosemary throughout the roast before it is cooked distributes their flavors more thoroughly throughout the meat, and by cooking it over a slow heat you are able to enjoy a tender, moist, and tasty entrée, which has a deliciously haunting flavor.

Very Simple Italian Pasta Salad

This dish is best made at least two hours before serving so the pasta has a chance to absorb the flavors of the dressing.

> 4 to 6 cups bow tie pasta (or any shape of pasta that you have on hand), cooked and well drained
> 2 cups Italian salad dressing, store-bought or homemade
> 1 or 2 fresh tomatoes, diced small
> 1 fresh sweet bell pepper (green, red, or yellow), diced small
> 1 clove fresh garlic, pressed
> ¼ cup fresh Parmesan cheese, finely grated
> Salt and pepper to taste

Toss cooked pasta with 2 cups of dressing, and add diced fresh tomatoes, pepper, and garlic. Toss with cheese. Cover tightly and refrigerate for several hours. Serve as a side dish to accompany your chicken entrée (may be served cold or at room temperature). Salt and pepper to taste. This serves 12.

Note: If you have quite a lot of pasta salad remaining, you may serve it a few days later with diced bits of leftover beef or chicken added to it (as well as a bit more dressing to coat the meat). Combined with a loaf of fresh garlic bread, and a tossed green salad, you will have a frugal fast-food feast!

Fresh Fruit Salad

On Labor Day, the late fruits of summer are often still abundant (and usually quite reasonably priced). Take this opportunity to combine these luscious flavors into a delicious fresh fruit salad to savor on this day of rest. You may prepare this the night before, or the morning of, your meal. Hint: This salad is a wonderful way to make use of *slightly* overripe fruits.

Melons such as cantaloupe, watermelon, and honeydew, without the rind and cut into chunks (If the melons are very juicy, I often set a small cutting board inside of a clean jelly roll pan in order to capture the juices from the fruit as I am cutting. Doing this saves cleanup time, and allows you to pour the delicious fruit juices back into the salad bowl if you desire.)

Strawberries, sliced (You can add a handful of blueberries, raspberries, and/or blackberries if they are available.)

Optional: Kiwi, sliced

Any other diced fresh fruits that you enjoy and that are easily available to you

I have used as few as two fruits for this salad (watermelon and blueberries) and as many as ten. It is very forgiving and flexible. You may even try this salad in winter with a mixture of frozen, canned, and fresh fruit, with tasty results.

For Lemon Dressing you will need:
¼ cup fresh lemon juice
¼ cup honey, or ⅓ cup granulated sugar
2 tablespoons mild-tasting vegetable oil
½ teaspoon salt
Optional: ¼ cup finely diced fresh mint leaves

To make salad:
Combine fruit in a large bowl (I like to use clear glass so that you may see the beauty of the fresh fruit). In a separate, small mixing bowl combine all ingredients for the lemon dressing and blend well. Pour dressing over salad and mix gently with a wooden spoon or rubber spatula (be careful not to crush the fruit). You may serve it immediately, or allow the salad to rest, refrigerated, until ready to serve.

Columbus Day

"In 1492, Columbus sailed the ocean blue."
—Old childhood rhyme

This day on which we celebrate the discovery of America by that Italian seaman Christopher Columbus was traditionally October 12, but today this holiday is observed the Monday falling closest to that date.

To honor the courage and perseverance of Christopher Columbus, and in remembrance of his perilous journey, you might like to serve a special dinner to your family and friends (or perhaps they may wish to help you prepare it). If you have the time and energy, perhaps retell a bit of history regarding the discovery of North America. If your children are older, make a game of having *them* tell *you* at least one piece of knowledge about this holiday and/or the person it is named for.

Sailor's Delight

This simple dish is so named because its main ingredient is derived from the sea, and we serve it on this day as a tongue-in-cheek nod to the noble Columbus.

½ cup chopped onion
1 cup diced sweet green peppers (you may substitute frozen green peas or small broccoli florets)
1½ tablespoons melted butter or margarine
2 cans cream of mushroom soup or other cream soup
2 cups cooked tuna, flaked (canned tuna works very well in this recipe)
1 cup of cubed, cooked ham
1 can (about 8 ounces) crushed pineapple, drained
⅓ cup slivered, toasted almonds
4 cups hot, cooked rice

Sauté onions and vegetables in butter. Blend in soup, meats, and pineapple. Mix well and heat thoroughly. Sprinkle with almonds. Serve over hot rice. A delicious, fast, and fun meal that easily serves 4 to 6 people.

The Autumnal Equinox

"The day becomes more solemn and serene
When noon is passed; there is harmony
In autumn, and a lustre in the sky,
Which through the summer is not heard or seen,
As if it could not be, as if it had not been!"

—PERCY BYSSHE SHELLEY

Astronomically, the equinoxes occur at opposite points in the calendar where the sun crosses the celestial equator, when the duration of night and day is equal in all parts of the world (twelve hours each). These crossings occur about March 21 (usually on or near the Easter and Passover festivals) and September 23, marking the beginnings of the northern hemisphere spring and autumn, respectively.

In ancient Greece and Egypt the greatest festivals were marked at the equinoxes and solstices. Today we take minor note of the change of the seasons and, if we think of them at all, view them only as events that influence nature and our physical world.

Savoring Lake Ahmeek Stew
on an Autumn Evening

"Hospitality consists in a little fire, a little food, and immense quiet."
—RALPH WALDO EMERSON

When my father returned home from his much-needed vacation last September, he brought with him wonderful descriptions of the miracle of autumn. Green leaves were metamorphosing into bronze-colored wisps, generously cloaking the tree branches that lined the roads leading up to the great wooded landscape of northern Wisconsin, where my father had spent his youth.

He arrived at his destination at dusk. Walking toward the warm lights of his sister and brother-in-law's snug cabin home, his senses were awakened by the familiar fragrance of pine, and the faint musty aroma of the surrounding forest. Upon entering the cabin he found the table gracefully set, and a delicious meal of rich savory stew awaiting him.

Lake Ahmeek stew has since become a favorite meal in my father's house, as well as our own. It is not only delicious but simple to prepare. We serve it with generously buttered, piping hot dinner rolls, and a fresh salad composed of whatever vegetables may be in season, and savor it along with the happy memories it evokes.

Aunt Jean's Lake Ahmeek Stew

1½ pounds lean stew beef, diced (we dice a boneless chuck roast for this recipe; there is no need to brown beef)
3 or 4 potatoes, cut into large squares
2 medium onions, diced
4 to 5 stalks fresh celery, chopped
Any other fresh vegetables you desire
1 or 2 cans golden mushroom soup, plus ½ can of water for each can of soup
1 teaspoon salt
¼ teaspoon black pepper
Crock-Pot or slow-cooker

Put all ingredients into a slow-cooker in the order that they are listed above. Cook for 8 hours on low heat. (If you prefer, you may use a 2-quart casserole dish and bake the stew, covered, in a 200° oven for about 5 hours. My father says this is the way the pioneers cooked a similar stew, using a Dutch oven.) As a variation on this recipe I often place a generous sprig of fresh rosemary on top of all the ingredients before cooking (remove the whole sprig before serving). Makes about 6 ample portions.

Allhallows' Eve

"By fairy hands their knell is rung;
By forms unseen their dirge is sung . . ."
—William Collins

Before the dawn of the Christian era, in the days of the Druids, the ancient Celts celebrated the last evening of October as a festival of harvest. At the end of these celebrations great bonfires were built on hilltops in honor of their god, the sun. This night—which we call Halloween—remained for many centuries a night of superstition and mystery. Supernatural beings and fairies were believed to come out at this time, and their powers were thought to be more powerful than those of earthly mortals.

In today's more practical world, we allow no fairies or spirits to interfere with our busy lives. Halloween has evolved into a night of costumes, trick-or-treating, and merriment. Coming as it does in the busy season of autumn, this holiday often finds us occupied with a new school year, as well as preparing for the approaching winter holidays. Thus we are left with little time and/or energy to focus on celebration. Still, to highlight the occasion, I sometimes bake oversize pumpkin-shaped sugar cookies for the children (using the sugar cookie recipe that follows), iced with a quick orange-tinted butter-cream frosting. These cookies are displayed on small doilies or saucers, and set out for the children as a surprise to enjoy when they return home from a busy day at school. The cookies are served with a tall glass of cold milk as the children carve silly faces onto the shells of pumpkins in the late afternoon sunlight.

It is even more fun, if time permits, to have your children help you bake and decorate the cookies. They each can draw a pumpkin shape onto wax, parchment, or craft paper and cut it out, then use it as a template for your cut-out cookies. What a thrill to see their art become edible!

Faerie Sugar Cookies

I named these "Faerie Sugar Cookies" because they taste as if they were made by the light hands of sprites. This recipe makes two dozen cookies, but I recommend making double batches of these, as they disappear so quickly. In our home their rapid disappearance is often *blamed* on the faeries!

½ cup salted butter
1 cup sifted confectioners' sugar
2 small eggs, well beaten
1½ tablespoons vanilla
3 to 4 cups sifted all-purpose flour
White icing

Cream butter until very fluffy, then beat in confectioners' sugar. Add vanilla and eggs and mix well. Add flour gradually until you have a dough you can roll out without sticking.

Separate the dough into thirds, working with one third at a time. Using plastic and/or wooden cutting boards (generously floured) roll out the dough as thin as you dare—about ⅛ inch thick if you can. Press your favorite cookie cutters (or trace a template) into dough. Use a thin spatula to lift the cut dough onto an ungreased cookie sheet. Reroll any scraps of dough and cut again. If these cookies aren't going to be iced, sprinkle the tops with granulated sugar before baking them at 350° for about 12 minutes or until they are slightly browned at the edges.

Note: This recipe lends itself to the home version of "slice and bake" cookie dough. The dough freezes beautifully when stored in a recycled juice can or rolled and sealed in plastic wrap or waxed paper. You may wish to use this recipe to prepare cookies for other holidays as well. (For icing recipe see page 19.)

Toasted Pumpkin Seeds

When you and/or your children are cleaning out the pumpkins to carve jack-o'-lanterns, be sure to save the seeds. Wash the pumpkin seeds well (I use a colander) and pick out any remaining pulp. Drain well and dry with paper towels. Fry the seeds in a large skillet, adding a teaspoon or two of butter, until they are heated all the way through and have lightly browned. Salt generously and serve immediately!

Another method for cooking pumpkin seeds is to place cleaned, drained, and dried seeds onto a cookie sheet and bake in a 350° oven for about 20 minutes. If you are baking them do not allow the seeds to brown, and do not add butter.

To eat, crack the seeds open in the same manner as you would sunflower seeds, and eat the kernel. Discard the hulls. Toasted pumpkin seeds will keep very well in a covered mason jar for several months.

Homemade Pumpkin Puree Made From a Jack-o'-Lantern

The frugality in my soul finds it difficult to throw away perfectly good fresh pumpkins (especially when the innards of carved jack-o'-lanterns are so obviously at hand). Thus, each November 1 you will very likely find me inside my kitchen making homemade pumpkin pack. Here's how:

1. Thoroughly wash your carved pumpkins. Cut away and discard any wax that has dripped onto the inside of your pumpkins from Halloween candles.
2. Cut the pumpkin into large chunks, using a serrated cutter that was designed for the specific purpose of carving jack-o'-lanterns. I find these much easier to work with than ordinary knives, if you don't have a special cutter, you may find a small serrated knife will work in its place.
3. Place the pumpkin chunks into a very large pot and fill it with enough water to cover.
4. Bring the water and pumpkin to a full boil, then reduce the heat and allow the mixture to simmer uncovered on low for about 1 to 2 hours. Check on your simmering pumpkin periodically to ensure that the pot does not go dry. If necessary, add more water.
5. When the pumpkin is tender (the consistency should be soft, like that of fully boiled potatoes) carefully pour the entire contents into a large strainer inside the sink. Allow to drain and cool thoroughly.
6. Once the pumpkin has cooled enough for you to safely handle, remove the

peels from each chunk (this is very easy, peels should just slip off with the help of a butter knife). Place peeled pumpkin into a large bowl.

7. Mash the peeled pumpkin with a potato masher.
8. Store in freezer bags (I like to store it in 2-cup increments) and use as you would canned pumpkin. A pound of pumpkin will yield about 1 cup of puree.

Another method for making pumpkin puree is to split the pumpkin in half, and place the halves, cut side down, onto a deep baking pan, along with about 1 cup of water, and bake in a 350° oven for about an hour and a half. Remove from oven, scoop the pulp from each piece, and puree in a food processor.

The color and consistency of homemade pumpkin puree is lighter than that of the commercial product; the taste is much more delicate and, in my opinion, quite superior to the store-bought variety. I have used homemade pumpkin to create traditional pumpkin pies; added it to cake mix (along with spices such as nutmeg and cinnamon) to create deliciously easy pumpkin muffins; and used it in homemade pumpkin breads and cookies. You will be surprised at the delicious freshness this simple and economical ingredient will give to your time-honored recipes.

Rosh Hashanah (New Year)

"Sublimity is Hebrew by birth."
—SAMUEL TAYLOR COLERIDGE

The Jewish calendar is the controlling force in the observance of Jewish holidays and festivals. Instead of being solar (sun-based), like the Julian or Gregorian calendars, it is reckoned according to the phases of the moon. A Jewish month is either twenty-nine or thirty days long, as in the Moslem calendar. But unlike the Moslem calendar, which follows the cycles of the moon completely, the Jewish calendar has sought to bring the length of its year into some accordance with the seasons. Thus, in Judaism, a thirteenth month is added seven times in nineteen years. This allows Rosh Hashanah (New Year) to fall approximately at the time of the autumn equinox.

Rosh Hashanah (literally translated as "head of the year" is observed on the first and second days of the Hebrew month Tishri, and is a time of meditation, commentary on the passage of time, prayer, penitence, and high resolution. The ram's horn (shofar) is blown as a signal to repent, special melodies are chanted, and special prayers—such as "Unetaneh Tokef," with its wise utterance: "Prayer, repentance, and charity avert the evil decree"—are recited.

Reform Jews often observe only one day of the New Year, while Conservative and Orthodox Jews observe two days. The customary greeting for the New Year is "Leshanah tovah tikatevu," meaning "May you be inscribed [in the book of life] for a good year!" After returning home from the New Year's Eve service it is traditional to eat apples and honey, signifying a blessing for a "good and sweet year."

A charming folk custom that is associated with Rosh Hashanah is the Tashlikh ceremony, which is performed the afternoon of the first day (or the second day, should Sabbath commence the festival). This requires the forming of processions at the banks of a running stream or river (in large cities the site is often a reservoir). Under the leadership of a rabbi or respected layman, prayers are recited, chiefly the passage found in Micah 7:8–20, from which the name of the ceremony is derived. Crumbled bread, representing promises made to God that have not been kept (and thus are symbols of sin), is flung into the water.

Fresh Challah for Rosh Hashanah

You may shape this bread into rounds, which are symbolic of the cycle of a year and/or braid the dough and shape the braids into loaves. Apply an egg yolk wash, for a glorious sheen, and bake.

> 2 cups water, hot but not boiling, since you don't want to kill the yeast
> 1 tablespoon salt
> 1 tablespoon sugar
> 1½ tablespoons vegetable oil
> 1 package active dry yeast
> ¼ cup warm water
> 2 beaten eggs
> 8 cups flour

In a mixing bowl combine hot water, salt, sugar, and oil. Allow this to sit while you dissolve the yeast in the ¼ cup of warm water. Once the hot water mixture has cooled to lukewarm, add the dissolved yeast and the eggs, and gradually mix in the flour. Knead dough until it is smooth and elastic. Cover with a clean cloth and set aside. Allow dough to double in bulk, then punch down the dough and divide it into half. Place one half on a lightly floured board, and cut into four equal parts. Roll each part into a strand about 1½ inches thick. Twist three strands of dough into a braid (in the same manner that you would braid your hair). Pinch ends closed and place braided dough into a floured bread pan. Cut remaining dough into three parts and roll into ½-inch-thick strands. Braid these dough strands and lay the smaller braid atop the larger braid in the pan. Allow to rise until dough has doubled in bulk. Form the remaining dough into a large round circle and set it atop a floured baking sheet. Allow it to double in bulk.

Once dough from either loaf has doubled, brush the top with beaten egg yolk and sprinkle with poppy seeds (optional). Bake loaves in a hot (400°) oven for about 15 minutes, then be sure to reduce the heat to 350° and bake for another 45 minutes. This delicious, traditional bread makes a tasty addition to a celebratory meal, as well as a lovely hostess gift. Perhaps you might also enjoy preparing and baking this bread with the help of your children as a yearly family tradition.

Sukkoth (Tabernacles)

"How goodly are thy tent and thy tabernacles, O Israel!"
—The Fourth Book of Moses, called Numbers

On the fifteenth day of Tishri (falling two weeks after Rosh Hashanah) begins the Pilgrimage Festival of Sukkoth (translated as "tabernacles," or "booths"). This enchanting, eight-day festival is a time of thanksgiving for the autumn harvest and for the fruits of the vineyards and orchards. The American holiday of Thanksgiving was inspired by this festival, as was the British celebration of the Harvest Festival (during which grains, fruits, and vegetables are offered to, and adorn, the churches).

During this festival, a tabernacle, decorated with fruits, vegetables, flowers, greenery, and tree branches, is erected on the roof or in the courtyard of a home. In many Reform synagogues the Sukkoth is built upon the temple altar. Branches of palm, myrtle, and willow trees, together with the citron fruit, are the chief emblems of the Sukkoth festival. Gifts of foods, fruits, and charity-money are given, and plays and oratories are performed to commemorate the festival, in accordance with biblical precedents.

The origins of the Sukkoth festival may be found in the very ancient agricultural celebrations of Canaan. The architects of the Jewish faith retained the harvest principle, but changed its associations with the historical memories of the Jewish people. Thus the Festival of the Tabernacles is actually a blend of two traditions, the celebration of appreciation and thanksgiving for the harvest, and the chronicle of the departure from Egypt. The dwellings built to celebrate this festival are symbolic of those in which the forefathers once dwelt in the wilderness and, paradoxically, they are suggestive of the colorful and bounteous life of Canaan, the promised land.

Veterans Day

"The mystic chords of memory, stretching from every battlefield and patriots grave
to every living heart and hearthstone all over this broad land . . ."

—Abraham Lincoln

Established in 1919, Veterans Day was originally called Armistice Day, to celebrate the armistice of World War I. In 1954, this holiday was renamed Veterans Day and was designated as a day on which to honor all veterans who have fought for the United States.

Because this holiday falls in the season of autumn, on November 11, I find it fitting to try to serve an apple-cranberry pie in honor of the occasion. The apple is, next to the native North American cranberry, thought of as the most American of all fruits. The first recorded apple orchard was, after all, planted in 1625 on what is now Beacon Hill, in Boston. The early settlers set a high priority on planting and raising apple trees. It seems they appreciated the fruit itself, as well as the fermented and hard ciders it eventually yielded. There appears to be a true love between the apple and America. And by including cranberries, the following recipe is even more American than plain old apple pie.

American-Flag-Shaped Apple-Cranberry Pie

For dough, use pie crust recipe on page 252, with the addition of ½ teaspoon cinnamon and ½ teaspoon ginger.

> About 3 pounds fresh apples (5 or 6 large apples); Jonathan, Fuji, Golden
>   Delicious work well
> 1 can whole-berry cranberry sauce thoroughly mashed by hand

Peel and core apples, then cut them *lengthwise* into ¼-inch slices. Roll your dough, on a lightly floured surface, until it resembles a small flaglike rectangle (about 12 x 16 inches). Place rolled dough onto a large, ungreased cookie sheet. Crimp the edges of the dough into a 1-inch lip (similar to a pizza crust) all around the edges of the rectangle; doing this will keep your filling from sliding off. Spread the cranberry sauce evenly over the inside of the crust (avoid the lip area). Cut 8 to 10 smaller apple slices into a star shape (use a sharp cookie cutter or paring knife); place these at the top left-hand corner of the crust (where the stars in the American flag would normally be). Use the remaining apples to arrange long lines (to resemble the stripes on the flag) underneath and next to the "stars." Be certain that you overlap each apple slice onto the other as you lay out your line, as the apples will shrink with cooking. Brush the entire edge of the pastry with cream or water, and sprinkle the entire pie (including crust) generously with granulated sugar. Place tart in the freezer, uncovered, for 5 to 7 minutes. Bake for about 45 minutes in a preheated 400° oven, or until apples are tender and pastry is golden. Allow it to cool on a rack. If you like, you may melt about ½ cup of apple jelly in a saucepan and spread it over the warm tart as a glaze before serving. Serve with a scoop of vanilla ice cream and a prayer of gratitude.

Thanksgiving

"I do, therefore, invite my fellow citizens in every part of the United States, and also those who are at sea and those who are sojourning in foreign lands, to set apart and observe the last Thursday of November next as a day of thanksgiving and praise to our beneficent Father who dwelleth in the heavens."

—ABRAHAM LINCOLN

Thanksgiving is the quintessential American holiday. And while we primarily associate the origins of this festival with the Pilgrims of North America, the traditions of this celebration reach back into the ancient past—and have been observed, in one form or another, for as long as humankind has cultivated the earth. As just described, the Hebrews, in biblical times, celebrated the Feast of the Tabernacles (Sukkoth); the ancient Greeks annually celebrated the bounty of autumn by giving Demeter, goddess of the harvest, honor and thanks. The Romans (borrowing from the Greeks) celebrated Ceres, the goddess of grain, in a festive ceremony called Cerealia (our modern word *cereal* is derived from these ancient roots). The Middle Ages found the French celebrating the autumnal season, in the Feast of Saint Martin of Tours, also known as Martinmas, during which a great goose was the featured entrée.

Thus the three-day festival of thanks celebrated by the Pilgrims in 1621 had a long, rich, and varied history. Still, the Pilgrims were grateful—and not only for the abundance of the harvest, they were grateful for their very survival. This first Thanksgiving (as proclaimed by the governor of the colony, William Bradford) officially commemorated the survival of the colony itself during its first, very difficult, year. For of the original 102 settlers who arrived at Plymouth in the winter of 1620, only 55 remained alive by the following spring.

It is believed that the entire colony would have perished, had it not been for the help of the Wampanoag Indians, who graciously taught the colonists how to hunt and fish in the new land. As well, they showed them how to cultivate corn and other native vegetables. It was these specifically American crops that kept the Pilgrims alive.

The first Thanksgiving celebration featured game birds (including wild turkey), venison, and the bounty of the Pilgrims' newly cultivated gardens, such as corn, pumpkins, and squash. There was merriment and games, a display of arms, and an overall feeling of goodwill and kinship between the Indians and the colonists.

Over the next two hundred years, Thanksgiving was celebrated in a haphazard manner, with individual states eventually instituting regular observances. There was, however, no national Thanksgiving holiday until Sarah Josepha Hale (editor of Godey's *Lady's Book* and author of "Mary Had a Little Lamb") made it her mission. Mrs. Hale spent seventeen years of her life devoted to having Thanksgiving Day officially instituted as a nationally recognized holiday, on the last Thursday in November. Finally, on October 3, 1863, her tireless efforts were rewarded, when President Abraham Lincoln declared Thanksgiving Day a national holiday.

Today, for many people, Thanksgiving Day is the one time of year when family and friends assemble to celebrate, feast, and give thanks for the many blessings they are privileged to enjoy. Aside from the entertaining, eating, and parade and ball-game watching, Thanksgiving is the perfect opportunity to focus on life's positive aspects—and to practice the sometimes forgotten art of appreciation.

Thanksgiving Dinner

"All-cheering Plenty, with her flowing horn, led yellow Autumn, wreath'd with nodding corn."
—ROBERT BURNS

For some this day is the one occasion of the year when they entertain on a large scale, so it is important to do some preplanning. If you are to enjoy the holiday along with your guests, it is important that you start well in advance; do not wait until the day before to begin. First write out a guest list, so you will know how much food to prepare and how many people you will be seating (always make enough food for one or two surprise guests). Select the dishes you will be making. Write out a menu and a corresponding shopping list, and give advance thought to the table settings, serving dishes, flowers, tables, chairs, and timing. Write out a new list of all the things you will need to do, and establish a budget. Estimate how much money you will need to spend on food and other purchases, and note the estimated completion date for each project. Be sure to break up the tasks well beforehand, so you are not overwhelmed.

Serving a Crowd

Avoid being unfaithful to your holiday food budget by buying too much food. Here are some ratios to help you determine exactly how much you will need:

- *Whole poultry with bones:* Allow 1 pound per person; for example, 8 pounds serves eight; 12 pounds serves twelve; 16 pounds serves sixteen.
- *Roast beef, ham, beefsteaks—with bones:* 2⅔ pounds serves eight; 4 pounds serves twelve; 5½ pounds serves sixteen.
- *Roast beef, ham, brisket, steaks—no bones:* 2 pounds serves eight; 3 pounds serves twelve; 4 pounds serves sixteen.
- *Broccoli, cabbage, carrots, cauliflower:* 2 pounds serves eight; 3 pounds serves twelve; 4 pounds serves sixteen.
- *Spinach, kale, collards, and other cooked, leafy vegetables:* 4 pounds serves eight; 6 pounds serves twelve; 8 pounds serves sixteen.
- *Shelled vegetables such as peas and beans:* 4 pounds serves eight; 6 pounds serves twelve; 8 pounds serves sixteen.
- *Potatoes, corn on the cob, yams, sweet potatoes, and the like:* Prepare at least one piece for each guest (I often make several extra, for those who may want seconds, or for that extra unexpected guest). This estimate also works when determining how many potatoes to prepare for mashed potatoes.
- *Stuffing:* I allow for 2 cups per person.

Golden Roast Turkey

Many people are intimidated at the prospect of roasting a turkey. There is a fallacy circulating that this is a difficult and tricky job that can only be performed by a specially qualified few. However, if the truth be known, roast turkey is one of the easiest entrées to prepare. A roast turkey is quite easy on the budget as well, and usually there's an abundance of leftover meat for many delicious future feasts.

Preheat oven to 350°. Bring out a roasting pan in the appropriate size. (If you do not have a pan large enough to accommodate your turkey, a disposable aluminum roasting pan can be purchased from your grocery store, at minimal cost.) Wash out your fresh or thoroughly thawed turkey in the sink with cold water, including the cavity (first remove the giblet bag inside the bird).

Rub the outside of the turkey thoroughly with room-temperature butter (my first choice) or a mild vegetable oil. Next rub a salt and pepper mixture (about 1 tablespoon of salt mixed with ½ teaspoon of black pepper) over the bird. Stuff the cavity carefully with the stuffing of your choice.

We always use our clean hands when stuffing turkey (if it is a large bird, Mike or my father will hold it while I fill the cavity with stuffing). I stuff the turkey lightly to allow room for the dressing to expand and the cooking heat to penetrate fully. Truss the bird if you desire, or simply tuck the wings under a bit before cooking.

For decades we have cooked our Thanksgiving turkey in a large, covered roasting pan that once belonged to my grandmother, always with very good results. Last year, however, my father wanted to try the new roasting bags available in the markets. We placed the bag-covered turkey in the bottom of the family roaster and cooked it uncovered, according to manufacturers' directions. The results were spectacular. The entire family proclaimed it the best-tasting turkey in memory. And the cleanup time was cut in half, thanks to the bag. It was well worth the investment of a few dollars in terms of taste enhancement, and time saved in preparation as well as cleanup.

The usual cooking time for turkey is 20 minutes per pound for birds under 12 pounds, and 15 to 18 minutes per pound for larger birds. You may test for doneness by pressing a meat thermometer in the densest part. Be careful not to touch a bone or you may get an erroneous reading. The thermometer should read between 170° and 180° if the turkey is done. If you do not have a thermometer, simply use the old-fashioned method of pressing a drumstick. If the turkey is done, the drumstick should twist out of its joint easily, the meat should be soft to the touch, and the juices should run clear or light yellow—never pink. Remove the roasted turkey from the oven and allow it to sit for at least 20 minutes before carving. Doing this will allow you to carve more easily, and give the juices time to settle.

While the turkey is roasting, turn your attention to the bag of giblets that was enclosed in the inner cavity. Place the contents of this packet into a medium saucepan with plenty of water to cover (if you wish, you may add a clove of garlic, a few chunks of celery, and an onion, to enhance the flavor). Simmer this for about ½ hour, or until it is well cooked. Remove the meat from the pan and discard the vegetables. Remove the small bits of meat from the neck bone and reserve for the dressing, gravy, or another recipe. (I must confess that we always save this meat to feed to the animals as a special Thanksgiving treat.) My father also keeps the cooked giblets, which he likes to puree with the back of a spoon, and adds them to the gravy for a rich flavor. Reserve the cooking water; it will be mixed with the drippings in the roasting pan, and used to make gravy.

The Doctored-Up Stuffing

The stuffing that dresses the Thanksgiving turkey has long been a source of pride, friendly banter, and, on occasion, family squabbles. In our own home we long ago adapted a generic boxed corn-bread stuffing mix that we have "doctored-up" (to use my father's term) to fit our personal expectations of a delicious stuffing.

To stuff a 12- to 14-pound turkey you will need:
  14 ounces (about 10 cups) cubed stuffing mix—please note that I am not
    referring to the instant type of stuffing mix, but the seasoned cubes (we prefer
    Mrs. Cubbison's or Pepperidge Farm)

Note: You may extend the quantity of your store-bought stuffing mix by adding 2 or 3 cups of dried bread crumbs or crumbled, dried corn bread to each packet of the purchased variety. Doing this will add three servings to the original package.

  2 tablespoons finely chopped fresh sage, or 1 teaspoon dried, ground sage
  8 tablespoons melted butter or margarine
  1½ cups chopped celery
  1½ cups chopped yellow onion
  2½ cups chicken broth or water. (You may wish to use the strained broth from
    the simmered giblets, if you won't be using it to season the gravy. Or you can
    substitute chicken bouillon to create the amount of broth you need.)

Place all of the stuffing mix into a very large mixing bowl along with the sage. In a frying pan melt the butter or margarine and sauté the celery and onion (be careful not to burn the butter, or a bitter flavor will result). Place the sautéed celery and onion into a very large mixing bowl. Pour the liquid (broth or water) over the other ingredients in your mixing bowl and toss well. When stuffing the turkey allow no more than ¾ cup of prepared stuffing for each pound of poultry. If you have excess stuffing place it into a ceramic casserole or soufflé dish, cover with aluminum foil, and set it in the oven to warm during the turkey's final 30 minutes of cooking time.

Rich and Easy Gravy

After you have removed the bird from the roaster, scoop out any pieces of stuffing that may have dropped out during cooking, and discard. Place the roaster over a burner on the stove (if yours is as large as ours you may need to use two burners). Over medium heat, pour the strained giblet broth into the roasting plan, and allow it to simmer for a moment or two as you stir it with a sturdy wire whisk. Be sure to scrape the bottom of the pan as you stir; this will deglaze the roasting pan and give your gravy a rich golden color. Bring the broth to a slow boil, stirring all the time, and then thicken the gravy by *slowly* dribbling and stirring in cornstarch or flour that you have made into a thinnish paste beforehand, using cold water. For an almost no-fail gravy, try using Wondra® flour. It is specially processed to decrease the possibility of lumpy gravy. You will need about 2 tablespoons of thickener for each cup of broth. Continue cooking and stirring for at least 1 minute after broth has come to a boil. The gravy needs a few minutes to thicken, and it takes at least 1 minute for the starch in the thickener to cook thoroughly. Add giblets or diced meat if desired. Taste. Add salt and pepper to taste.

Classic Pumpkin Pie

Mike's favorite dessert is pumpkin pie. But, as he can tell you, not all pumpkin pies are created equal. He enjoys a classic, dense pie, with lots of fragrant spices.

Pie crust (see the recipe on page 252, or use premade pie crust from the market)
2 cups canned pumpkin pack or fresh pumpkin puree (see page 160 to make your own pumpkin puree)
3 large eggs
1½ cups heavy cream (you may substitute condensed milk if you prefer)
1⅓ cups granulated sugar
1 teaspoon vanilla extract
1 tablespoon ground cinnamon
1 teaspoon powdered ginger
½ teaspoon ground allspice
½ teaspoon cloves
½ teaspoon grated nutmeg

Prepare your crust and place in a 9-inch pie pan, unbaked, in the refrigerator until ready to fill. Preheat oven to 400°. In a large mixing bowl, combine pumpkin, eggs, cream, and sugar. Add vanilla and spices and combine thoroughly. Remove the prepared pie shell from the refrigerator and place directly onto a cookie sheet. Pour filling into pie shell and bake at 400° for 15 minutes. (This is a very important step as it will keep your crust from becoming soggy—please resist the temptation to bypass it.) Immediately reduce the oven heat to 350° and bake for about 45 minutes more. The pie is done when a knife tip, inserted into the pie's center, comes out clean. Cool on a wire rack. Makes one pie, which serves 8 to 12. Serve with whipped cream.

Remains of a Thanksgiving Feast

When I was a child the meals served at our table on the days following Thanksgiving dinner were often turkey-based. I still find it amazing that something so ordinary as turkey can be magically transformed into something so completely different and delicious.

Arroz con Turkey

This adaptation of the classic Spanish recipe Arroz con pollo (rice with chicken) was one of my favorite childhood meals. The fun was found in the fact that my parents would triple the recipe and bake it in the bottom half of the turkey roaster! You may wish to double this recipe (if leftover quantities permit) and freeze half of it for a future meal.

6 tablespoons butter or margarine
4 small cloves fresh garlic, pressed
2 medium onions, diced
3 or 4 cups of diced cooked turkey
1 tablespoon minced fresh oregano (or 2 teaspoons dried)
2 tablespoons minced fresh Italian parsley (or 1 tablespoon dried)
1 teaspoon minced fresh thyme (or ½ teaspoon dried)
1 cup frozen peas and carrots (you may substitute small broccoli florets)
Salt and pepper to taste
1¼ cups long-grain white rice
1 can or 2 cups chicken or turkey broth, plus ¼ cup water
Optional: ½ cup leftover stuffing

Melt 4 tablespoons of the butter in a 4-quart oven-proof casserole. Sauté garlic and onions for about 5 minutes, or until translucent. Add the diced turkey, herbs, vegetables, and salt and pepper. Mix well. In a small saucepan, melt remaining 2 tablespoons of butter and add uncooked rice. Sauté over medium heat for about 2 minutes (do not burn). Add the sautéed rice to the casserole and mix well. In the same saucepan, bring the broth and water to a full boil and pour it over the mixture in the casserole. Add ½ cup leftover stuffing, and mix well. Cover tightly and bake in a preheated, 375° oven for about 25 minutes, or until rice has cooked tender. Uncover and bake for another 10 to 15 minutes. Serve with a winter fruit salad and fresh French bread.

Turkey Soup

A delicious and frugal way in which to make use of *all* of the remaining turkey is to simmer it, along with other ingredients, to create a stock. You may use the recipe for chicken stock on page 189. Substitute the turkey carcass for the chicken pieces (break it in half, if necessary, so that it will fit in your stock pot). You may also wish to add any amount of leftover turkey gravy to the stock as it simmers. Skim and discard fat (this will have hardened and is easily removed with a spoon).

> 1½ or 2 quarts turkey or chicken stock
> 2 or 3 cups leftover turkey meat, diced small
> 1 large onion, peeled and diced small
> 1 cup diced celery
> 2 cups carrots, peeled and cut into ½ inch pieces
> 3 tablespoons fresh parsley, chopped
> 1 small bunch of fresh sorrel, chopped (optional)
> 4 to 6 cups cooked egg noodles, drained and cooled
> Salt and pepper to taste

Bring the skimmed stock to a gentle boil. Add meat, onion, celery, carrots, parsley, and sorrel. Simmer over low heat until vegetables are tender but not mushy (about 30 minutes). Remove from heat and add cooked noodles. Cover for about 10 minutes; keep off heat. Serve as a meal in itself with homemade corn bread and crudités.

More Tips for Using the Remains of the Thanksgiving Feast

- If you reheat leftover turkey, but feel that the taste is not as fresh the second day, simply add ¼ cup of milk to the meat as you warm it in a saucepan. Heat over a low flame and do not allow the milk to come to a boil. This seems to neutralize any staleness, and remoistens the meat.

- If you have leftover pumpkin filling, you may bake it in lined muffin tins as you bake the pie, or refrigerate it, and bake these the next day. Sprinkle the tops with cinnamon and powdered sugar before serving.

Illuminated Fragments
Blessings Among the Banes

"Thus have the gods spun the threads . . .
two jars stand on the floor . . . of the gifts which he gives . . .
one of evils and another of blessings."
—Homer

Knowledge, even of seemingly less romantic subjects such as cookery, can contribute immensely to the qualities of self-sufficiency, independence, and luxury. For, as Milton asks, "Who would suppose, from Adam's simple ration, that cookery could have call'd forth such resources . . . from the commonest demands of nature?"

The art of food preparation has proven to be a subject of such importance as to inspire the passions and pens of history's finest poets. Quite simply, the enjoyment of creative cookery and artful serving are among the finest instincts of the human race. And—if we are to believe Milton—even Eve enhanced humble foods: In Milton's literary epic, *Paradise Lost,* the angel Raphael made his visit to the Garden of Eden just in time for dinner. He notes that although Eve had prepared only a "little dinner," she had taken the trouble to embellish her simple garden feast with roses and sweet cream.

The material world of which we are a part requires that we eat—and thus prepare—food in order to sustain life. And *successful* cooking requires a dose of forethought. The process of taking raw and/or simple ingredients and transforming them into delicious meals involves several steps: planning a nutritionally sound menu that is within the confines of your tastes, as well as your income; acquiring the basic ingredients needed for these meals; and cooking or processing these same ingredients properly, and with at least a small amount of skill.

Perhaps the most deceptively simple element in the magic of becoming an excellent cook is *experience.* Unfortunately, in today's world we are not always permitted the luxury of sufficient time in which to properly experiment and learn the blessed skill of cookery. You may happily overcome this dilemma, however, by understanding that you can easily borrow from the experience and knowledge of others.

While our modern world presents its share of anxiety-producing banes, it also offers blessings. The willing pupil may now learn (via books, magazines, newsletters, television, videos, and the Internet) from the life experiences and wisdoms of those who have already benefited from the charm of action.

Chapter 12

Autumnal Home Graces

~

"That most sacred flame, the fire of domestic love."

—Harriet Beecher Stowe

Guardians of Home

"Necessity is . . . the guardian of nature."

—Leonardo da Vinci

Harriet Beecher Stowe and her older sister Catherine wished to elevate the keeping of a home to a "profession offering influence, respectability, and independence." In 1869, they published *The American Woman's Home,* an instant best-seller that spread their philosophy of kindhearted child-rearing; establishing and running an efficient yet attractive abode; and, above all, respect for the keeper of the home. Taking their cue from the Bible, the Beecher sisters defined domestic wisdom. And perhaps no one was more fitted to this task than Mrs. Stowe, mother of seven children and wife to Calvin Stowe, a noted biblical scholar.

Their timeless philosophy regarding home ornaments echoes my own. Calling for simplicity, suitability, and "harmony of color," the Beecher sisters heartily believed that a charming decor could be achieved on the most limited of budgets. Pretentious furniture and "wallpaper swearing at the carpet, and the carpet swearing at the wallpaper" were to be banished and replaced by a home that emphasized simple charm and beauty, as well as function.

Harriet's own "pretty cottage," located in Hartford, Connecticut, and restored in

1964, was her last home. It stands as a charming example of her decorating precepts. Doorways open into gardens, walls are decorated with paintings, as well as prints and copies of the works of Old Masters that would provide an "educating influence" on her children.

Artful Uses for Ordinary Things
Simple Salvage

"The ancient and the honorable."
ISAIAH 9:15

More and more people are salvaging fragments from the past. Philosophies are often resurrected and adopted (or adapted); ancient architectural embellishments, rescued from buildings, impart a unique charm and character to modern homes. I find delight in the fact that others, like myself, recognize that history offers people today an abundance of tangible as well as intangible gifts.

Salvage has long been *treasurable* to me. I have used carved wooden brackets, salvaged from a torn-down home, to add architectural interest above a mundane window frame. I have added a salvaged plaster relief (in the shape of a shell) to embellish an ordinary wall. And if you look closely at the window swag in our dining room you will see that I have used antique silver forks as lovely, ornate tiebacks.

I have even salvaged trim from cast-off furniture to glue onto my *very* plain fireplace mantel. Painted the same color as the mantel, these pieces impart a classic look of carved wood. One of our most treasured finds is a set of wonderfully weathered wooden pilasters—a fine layer of peeling paint offers precisely the right amount of decay that is currently *most* fashionable. (Mike and I purchased these at a garage sale, and paid only five dollars for each.) We are still searching for the perfect location for them.

What a joy it is to discover that the current fashion in home furnishings and decor is to use these bits of the past in new ways. What a pleasure it is to know that these often inexpensive yet elegant pieces of old are now being legitimately recognized as having value and beauty—and not looked upon (as they once were) as mere trash or junk.

Do not be misled into thinking you must be artistic or creative to give new uses to old or ordinary things. It is quite easy to do. You begin by acquiring pieces that touch you emotionally. My own salvage mentality took root years ago, when I bought pieces of carved wood and broken china at flea markets, simply because I thought they were beautiful; the prices were very low as well. At the time of my purchases I often have only a whisper of an idea of where I will put these things, or what they will metamorphose into. Yet, if I love a piece enough, I often find a perfect use for it once I get it in our home. The trick is to not overaccumulate (or you will have a house and/or garden filled with junk). Begin by looking around your home for such salvageable treasures you may already own. Once you have successfully transformed a few "saved" items, you will acquire the necessary confidence that will turn this hobby into a useful skill or—if you are at all like me—a passion.

How to Metamorphose the Ordinary

"Everything is in a state of metamorphosis. Thou thyself art in everlasting change . . . So is the whole universe."
—MARCUS AURELIUS

- A piece of ornate wrought iron, salvaged from an old-fashioned window guard, can be transformed into a fire screen, to place in front of a fireplace opening.

- Hang antique wrought-iron window guards or garden gates above the fireplace as art. Hung on the wall behind your bed they create an attractive headboard. Don't be afraid to use these pieces in the garden as well—a piece of ornate metal may be pressed into service as a trellis, for climbing roses and vines. Or hang a set of them along a plain block wall to add architectural interest.

- Old maps, with their lovely, faded colors, antique or foreign currency, stock certificates, letters, sheet music, antique book covers or dust jackets, fans, lace, linens, and vintage children's clothing (especially well-made christening gowns) are all framable, and make a statement about what you value.

- Timeworn kitchen items look lovely on your dressing table. An old salt or sugar shaker can hold talcum powder or bath salts (be certain the perforations are large enough for the salts to shake loose). Sugar bowls are lovely when placed on your vanity to hold attractive guest soaps or glistening bath beads in jewel tones. Vinegar cruets are lovely containers in which to store homemade scented bath oils or astringents. And, of course, cut-glass jam pots and classic apothecary jars can house necessary ear swabs and cotton balls.

WARM UP TO AUTUMN

"That I am here afore thy sight, For gifts and grace;
A burning and a shining light
To a' this place."

—ROBERT BURNS

- Warm up to autumn. Once the first cold snap sends you to the cedar trunk to embrace the warm woolen blankets, you will know that the time has arrived to seasonally adjust your home.

- Add warm layers to sofas and chairs by way of paisley or plaid throws; add attractive runners to visually warm tabletops; and layer hooked or Oriental-style rugs on the wooden floors.

- Now is the time to store your summery china and glasswares and replace them with the holiday stoneware or china you have collected throughout the year.

- Slipcover your down comforter in a warming cotton flannel, and add colorful panels of fabric to the windows, over your sheers.

- Remember to rearrange your furniture away from drafts and cold window areas, drawing the sofa or table up to the hearth. Now is also the season in which to stack the books you've been meaning to read on the coffee or side table. If you like, cluster your easy chairs around the dining room table, and/or pull a small side table in front of the hearth for cozy games of chess or cribbage, or perhaps a small supper in front of a gently warming blaze.

- Cluster candles on a plant stand or stack in a fireplace to add visual warmth to a room. Place small votive candles in salvaged martini glasses all around your kitchen (add a bit of water to the bottom so the glass won't crack). This seems to help dissipate unwanted cooking odors.

- Borrow from nature and gather bouquets of fall leaves, and fill wooden bowls with pinecones, colorful gourds, Indian corn, or a combination of all of these.

Horns of Plenty

"The harvest truly is plentious."
—Matthew 9:37

Cornucopias are charming symbols of the bounty of the harvest, and have long been associated with the autumn season. Their classic motif has the ability to enhance everyday as well as special occasions, which is why we form our own, from heavy paper or light cardboard.

Cut paper into a 4- to 6-inch square, and lay on a flat surface, facedown. Use a compass to draw an arc pattern on your paper: Place the point of the compass at one corner of your square, then extend the arm of the compass to an adjacent corner. Drag your pencil across the square to form an arc, and cut along the line using scissors. This will transform your square into a fan-shaped piece of paper.

Form a cone from the arced paper by gluing the side edges together with a glue stick. Use paper clips to hold the edges together until the glue has dried completely. Make holes (to attach your handles), using a small-sized hole-punch, on opposite sides of the rim of your cone. Cover or paint cardboard. String wired ribbon, raffia, sturdy cotton string, or silken cord through the holes. (Secure the ends with large knots or sturdy, attractive stickers. If you aren't going to hang these you may omit the handles.)

These small cornucopias may be used as holders for party favors; as place markers at the dinner table (perhaps for Thanksgiving); or arranged attractively on a tray filled with candies, popcorn, fresh nuts, and so forth. You may also use these horns of plenty to hold small token gifts such as fresh or dried flowers, herbs, home-baked cookies, or candies. You may even wish to make several extra paper cornucopias, and stock them in your Gift Pantry.

The Power of Fragrance

*"I wish that life should be not cheap, but sacred.
I wish the days to be as centuries, loaded, fragrant."*
—RALPH WALDO EMERSON

Fragrance carries the power to evoke memory and provoke emotion. The great sixteenth-century playwright William Shakespeare understood this well, and often referred to scents in his prose. In his dramatization of the famous love story between Antony and Cleopatra he tells of Antony's first glimpse of Cleopatra and "the barge she sat in, like a burnish'd throne . . . Purple the sails, and so perfumed, that the winds were love-sick with them . . ." In *A Midsummer Night's Dream*, Oberon recalls the place where the lovely Titania is lulled to slumber by the beauty of nature: "I know a [river] bank where the wild thyme blows. . . ."

In today's more sophisticated world, we need not wait for warmer seasons to transport ourselves through the power of scent. Fragrances are easily available through homemade and commercial potpourris, sachets, colognes, perfumes, and air fresheners. In fact, due to its evocative quality, fragrance can create and stimulate wonderful memories with very little effort, time, or money. In our home the smell of rosemary reminds us of winter meals with family (as I often add it to my heartiest cold-weather stew). The scent of roses reminds Mike and me of the first perfume our older daughter received at a young age (she would often drench herself, and her bedroom, with it). And the fresh smell of mint brings to my mind that hot summer night when our entire family slept out under the stars, in the garden.

Lovely Aromas

An interesting way to recycle that unused box of Epsom salts that has been gathering dust in your cupboard is to turn them into luxurious, scented salts. Not only are salts wonderful for use in your next long soak in the tub, they make lovely air or drawer fresheners as well.

A note of caution, however: Keep these away from babies or small children, as some of the ingredients may be harmful to them.

> 2 bowls (glass or metal)
> Epsom salts
> Your favorite cologne, or essential oil
> Glycerin oil (obtain from your local drugstore, about $1.25 for a 6-ounce bottle)
> Food coloring

Mix 1 tablespoon of glycerin with a few drops of food coloring. Add your favorite aroma (perfume or oils and the like). You may use as much fragrance as you think is necessary, but note that a little oil goes a long way.

In your second bowl, measure out about 3 cups of Epsom salts. Add the aromatic oil to the Epsom salts. Be sure to mix thoroughly.

Store salts in pretty glass jars (apothecary jars are usually available—and inexpensive—at thrift shops and tag sales).

Air and Drawer Freshener

You may easily duplicate those small, wonderfully scented drawer fresheners packaged in paper envelopes and sold at gift shops for up to three dollars each. If you should open these packets you will discover that their lovely aroma arises from sweet-smelling Epsom salts (the same type described above).

Purchase small two-by-four-inch manila or white envelopes from stationery or office supply stores, or make your own envelopes from any sturdy, attractive recycled paper, such as stationery, heavy wrapping paper, greeting cards, or paper bags. Insert a few teaspoons of the premade, scented salts. If desired, add cotton as padding. Seal well, using a glue stick (hold the edges together with a paper clip until the glue has dried). You may easily embellish plain envelopes using an inked stamp prior to filling (flowers, fruits, angels, and hearts are a few classic motifs to try).

I like to make several of these at one time, and store them in the Gift Pantry, where they will remain fragrant for four to six months. These will be used in my own drawers, as well as included in gift baskets.

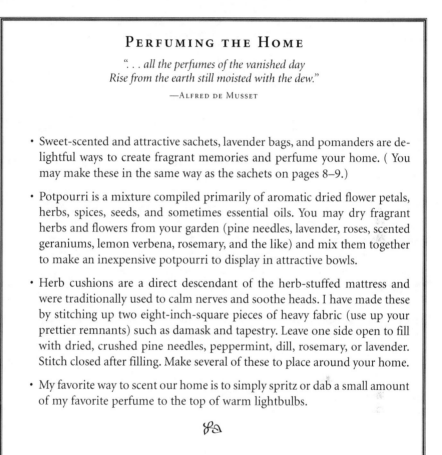

PERFUMING THE HOME

". . . all the perfumes of the vanished day
Rise from the earth still moisted with the dew."

—ALFRED DE MUSSET

- Sweet-scented and attractive sachets, lavender bags, and pomanders are delightful ways to create fragrant memories and perfume your home. (You may make these in the same way as the sachets on pages 8–9.)

- Potpourri is a mixture compiled primarily of aromatic dried flower petals, herbs, spices, seeds, and sometimes essential oils. You may dry fragrant herbs and flowers from your garden (pine needles, lavender, roses, scented geraniums, lemon verbena, rosemary, and the like) and mix them together to make an inexpensive potpourri to display in attractive bowls.

- Herb cushions are a direct descendant of the herb-stuffed mattress and were traditionally used to calm nerves and soothe heads. I have made these by stitching up two eight-inch-square pieces of heavy fabric (use up your prettier remnants) such as damask and tapestry. Leave one side open to fill with dried, crushed pine needles, peppermint, dill, rosemary, or lavender. Stitch closed after filling. Make several of these to place around your home.

- My favorite way to scent our home is to simply spritz or dab a small amount of my favorite perfume to the top of warm lightbulbs.

Illuminated Fragments
The Hearthstone

"Where glowing embers through the room
Teach light to counterfeit a gloom,
Far from all resort of mirth,
Save the cricket on the hearth."

—JOHN MILTON

The act of sitting beside an open fire is an ancient rite. All races of mankind have suc-cumbed to the luxury and pleasure found in an open blaze. The lighted hearth is a siren to the human spirit, as well as a balm to the body. Is it any wonder that the ancients be-lieved that fire came down from Heaven? Or that the ancient Romans incorporated the hearthstone blaze into the worship of their gods? Often animals yield to this lure of the flame. Our dog is never so happy as when she is outstretched in front of the fire, drowsy eyes blinking from the heat. And who was it that wrote "The fireside is the cat's Eden"? (I believe it was Robert Southey.)

It used to be, of necessity, that every home had several fireplaces. Today, with the in-vention of highly efficient wood-burning stoves and computer-controlled furnaces, our houses are heated without the aid of the open fire (and only the sternest natural-ist would venture to give up these inventions entirely). Still, it would be foolish not to use open fires as adjuncts, if for nothing more than their charm. Yet among the most curious and incomprehensible occurrences of the twentieth century was the fall from grace of the home hearth.

Happily—in this "new millennium"—I have noticed that many people are return-ing to the love of an open fire. It seems that, after a period of being thought of as old-fashioned, the qualities of repose and warmth offered by a comforting, crackling blaze are again being recognized as a luxurious joy.

EMBELLISHING THE ORDINARY

"Come, ye thankful people, come,
Raise the song of Harvest-home;
All is safely gathered in,
Ere the winter storms begin."
—HENRY ALFORD

- Scent your fire by adding dried orange and apple peels and dried herb bundles. We use lavender, rose, and lemon geranium stems—saving the flowers for more decorative projects—as well as dried cedar shavings and pine needles.

- Make scented fire-starters by soaking pinecones overnight in water scented with cinnamon oil (available for one or two dollars at the craft supply store). I have also used other scented oils for this project. Be sure to allow pinecones to dry thoroughly before adding them to your fireplace. Holiday pinecones are pinecones you have gathered, then soaked overnight in ½ pound of salt mixed with ½ gallon of water. After soaking, remove and place in recycled mesh bags. When they are thoroughly dry you may enjoy them yourself or give as gifts. When the pinecones are tossed into the fire in your fireplace they will turn pretty colors as they burn.

- If you use your fireplace for decorative use (or your allergies do not allow a blaze) group an arrangement of pillar-type candles on top of flat cookie sheets. I have seen this done in a tiered design, with shorter candles in the front, medium-sized candles in the center, and taller candles at the back. Arrange these inside a clean fireplace.

Candles

"These blessed candles of the night."
—WILLIAM SHAKESPEARE

We have been using candles as a frugal luxury in our home for years, and now it looks as if we are not alone in this indulgence. Many people are discovering that these simple, waxy lights are making home a more inviting place. Candles, with their soft, flickering light, and soothing scents such as vanilla, cinnamon, and citrus, can indulge our senses, flatter our faces, and create instant "atmosphere."

For years now I have purchased a plethora of candles at tag sales and, I am happy to say, have amassed quite a collection very inexpensively. My newest endeavor has been to make shallow candles from melted paraffin wax (heated over a double boiler), food coloring, and scented oils. As molds, I use my miniature tart pans.

I intend to make several dozen of these candles, using mateless crystal wineglasses as candleholders, filled with water. I use these "floating candles" to decorate a dinner or buffet table or, for more dramatic impact, line up several on the fireplace mantel. If time permits, I will also package sets of two or three in cellophane candy bags and use them as welcome additions to my Gift Pantry.

Candles of Good Fortune

Most of you have experienced the fun of blowing out birthday candles and opening fortune cookies. At an art fair last summer, I stumbled upon a unique way in which to combine these two fun ideas. The artist had embellished ordinary candles by applying papers with sayings and best wishes. (These gave the illusion of being inside the wax of the candle itself.) After experimenting at home, I discovered just how simple and quick these are to create. You may form your own candles of good fortune by using small votives (or tapers) on which you have written your personal good thoughts and wishes. How is this done? Quite easily with a bit of melted paraffin wax.

> White votive candles
>
> Fortunes (or whatever message you wish to send) written on small rectangles of paper, in your prettiest writing. If you have access to a computer you may wish to type these out in attractive fonts (make several on one page and cut them out with scissors)
>
> A small block of paraffin wax (available in the grocery store, and quite inexpensive)
>
> A small (no more than 1 inch wide), clean paintbrush
>
> A small sheet of waxed paper on which to set your candles

Melt the paraffin in a double boiler, according to the manufacturer's directions. (If you don't have a double boiler you may use a recycled metal can that has been set inside a pot of shallow water.) Be careful not to get water in the wax, and *never* leave hot wax unattended. Take one candle and, using your clean paintbrush, dab a small amount of hot wax onto the side of the candle, at the spot you wish to place the fortune (choose a position away from the wick, not too close to the top of the candle). Carefully press

the paper over the still-warm wax on the candle. Set candle on waxed paper. Repeat the process until you have put a paper on each candle. Then brush the outside of each fortune with a thin coat of wax, being sure to cover the entire outside of the paper with the wax.

These candles can be used; however, be certain that the paper does not catch fire as the candle burns. Do not leave these, or any, burning candles unattended.

Illuminated Fragments
Autumn Lights

"The windy lights of autumn flare . . ."
—ANDREW LANG

In honor of the season, hold a concerted lighting of candles in your home as afternoon turns to evening. Give each member of your household a small votive candle to light (perhaps make them each a special candle of good fortune), and a match with which to light it—assuming, of course, they are old enough, and responsible enough to do this. Then, at the count of three, everyone lights their candle at once. Be sure to instruct them that, when lighting, everyone must make a silent wish.

This festive celebration of the change of seasons is fun to invoke before an evening meal—especially when the dinner is composed of homemade harvest soup, salads, and bread, and, of course, illuminated by candlelight. As charming and festive as it is, this unique, and somewhat effortless, minor rite reminds us of the importance of bringing light *into* the world, even if it is for only one meal.

Chapter 13

Autumnal Offerings
◜◞

"At night the wind died and the soft rain dropped;
With lulling murmur; and the air was warm."

—CELIA THAXTER

Savoring Autumn

"Autumn is the mellow time."
—WILLIAM ALLINGHAM

The autumn season offers us the chance to look inward, and adjust to the changes that colder weather will bring to our lifestyle. As autumn winds became more forceful, and leaves fall from their trees, the days become shorter and less productive.

The early settlers complied with Mother Nature by spending their days gathering and preserving foods and supplies to sustain them during the upcoming harshness of winter. Today, with modern supermarkets and convenience foods in abundance, we can eat almost any foods, regardless of the season. While all of this is quite luxurious (and often expensive) it is my suspicion that these factors contribute to the feeling of imbalance many people express in this modern age. Perhaps, by ignoring the consumption of foods in their natural season, we are removing ourselves from the natural rhythm of life. The happy news is that each one of us may reclaim our balance by taking a dietary cue from the seasonal offerings of nature.

As the air becomes crisp with the breath of the coming winter, you may wish to make a feastlike meal of soup. The bevy of canned and dehydrated soups available to today's consumer tells me that many people are intimidated by the prospect of soup-making. Perhaps they feel it is a mysterious, elusive skill, or perhaps they think of it as an overly time-consuming task. In truth, soup is one of the simplest foods to prepare.

In my own adventures in soup-making I have discovered that while there is nothing so delicious and frugal as a home-cooked broth, using a good-quality bouillon is exceedingly helpful when time is as much of a factor as taste—and small bits of leftovers often mingle deliciously in large pots of thick soups. Hearty soup makes a supremely delicious meal that nurtures the spirit and soothes the budget—all the while allowing you the opportunity to savor the seasonal bounty offered by nature.

The Luxury of Simple Soups

"Soup of the evening, beautiful soup!"
—Lewis Carroll

Perhaps the most satisfying meals to eat during the cooler seasons are the ones that are composed of a thick, hearty soup, a crusty loaf of fresh bread or home-baked biscuits, crispy fresh salad, a luscious dessert, and a cup of good tea or coffee. This soup-and-salad meal has become a classic menu staple that can be easily adopted at home, with little expense and great success.

Many people who are not experienced at soup-making are often intimidated by the idea of preparing a homemade broth. Please don't be; broth-making is one of the easiest ways to make use of inexpensive cuts of meat; bones trimmed from cuts that were prepared for your freezer, or leftover meat and vegetable scraps; and nutritious vegetable liquids from cooking. Broth may be easily and inexpensively prepared at home, and kept in your freezer to provide a delicious base for soups, sauces, and main dishes.

Many recipes allow you to substitute canned broth for homemade stock (broth and stock are basically the same thing). And, occasionally, you may substitute small quantities of a good-quality, dried bouillon powder for the homemade variety (Knorr is one I use quite often).

Classic Chicken or Beef Stock

Omit the garlic and peppercorns if you will be freezing your stock.

For chicken stock:
   1 roast chicken carcass (for richer broth add 8 chicken necks and 4 chicken feet, cleaned and skinned)

For beef stock:
   1 or 2 large knucklebones, or other beef bones, raw or cooked; the latter will impart a rich dark color to your broth
   4 quarts water or any combination of vegetable liquids and water
   3 to 4 well-washed celery stalks, with leaves
   2 to 4 medium carrots (well washed, no need to peel)
   Scraps of raw vegetables or leftover vegetables
   1 or 2 garlic cloves
   8 to 10 whole peppercorns

Place the chicken or beef ingredients in a large kettle and cover with the water. Bring this *slowly* to a boil, over low heat, and simmer for about 1 hour (try to skim off any foam that appears on the surface of the broth as it cooks). Add the celery, carrots, vegetable scraps, garlic, and peppercorns. Loosely cover the kettle (this little detail is important because a too-tight cover can cause the stock to become cloudy, and, ideally, a clear broth is best). Continue to simmer ingredients in kettle for another 1½ to 2 hours. (Do not allow the broth to come to another boil.)

Carefully strain broth through a fine sieve, or a colander lined with a double layer of cheesecloth. Refrigerate immediately. You should have about 2 to 3 quarts of broth. Once broth has chilled thoroughly, skim off the surface fat. Use the broth to prepare the soup recipes offered in this book, or in your own favorite soup recipe. You may also freeze the broth for future use. I always make an extra-large batch of broth specifically for the freezer (packaged, labeled, and dated). When properly stored, this stock should last in the freezer for several months. Yields 2 to 3 quarts.

Note: I have made a habit of going through the cooled, strained chicken or beef bones, removing any chunks of meat that will make suitable additions to the soups I will be creating. I always use two plates when doing this, one for the cats and one for the people, and a thick layer of newspapers to hold the discards.

Clarified Stock

You may clarify cloudy soup stock easily, in this manner:

2½ to 3 quarts of well-skimmed chicken or beef stock
2 egg whites
2 eggshells

In a large kettle, bring the stock to a boil. Beat the egg whites to a froth and add them, with the eggshells, to the boiling stock. Stir continually. Reduce your heat under the kettle, and continue to stir while the stock simmers on a gentle boil for about 10 minutes. Allow the egg to settle; the egg white will capture the particles that are making the liquid appear cloudy. Cool slightly, then strain the stock through several layers of clean cheesecloth. Refrigerate or freeze. Use whenever clear soups or sauces are called for in a recipe.

Tracey's Chicken Noodle Soup

This soup holds the dubious distinction of being the very first recipe in my humble cooking repertoire. It is an old favorite in our household, especially during the cold-weather months.

2½ to 3 quarts chicken stock
2 to 4 cups diced, cooked chicken (it is important to dice meat before adding it to soups, as this prevents it from becoming overly stringy)
¼ cup finely diced or grated white onion
½ to 1 cup well-washed, finely chopped, fresh Italian flat-leaf parsley (you may substitute ½ to 1 cup fresh sorrel leaves, or fresh or frozen spinach leaves—or, in a pinch, dried parsley)
1 cup chopped celery (washed)
1 cup sliced or chopped carrots (washed and peeled)
1 to 2 large cloves fresh garlic, pressed
1 to 2 teaspoons sea salt
8 to 10 whole peppercorns
1 large bay leaf
4 to 6 cups cooked egg noodles (add these only after all other ingredients have been thoroughly cooked)

In a large soup kettle, pour in broth and add chicken pieces, onion, parsley, celery, carrots, and seasoning ingredients (reserve egg noodles). Heat to a gentle boil, then simmer for 30 to 45 minutes, until carrots are just tender. Add cooked egg noodles, and continue simmering until egg noodles have reheated. This makes about 1½ quarts. Serve soup with crusty French bread and sweet creamy butter, and a lettuce-and-tomato salad (or cucumber salad marinated in seasoned rice vinegar). For dessert serve a homemade apple pie, or simple slices of fresh apples and cheddar cheese. You have a feast! Serves 6 to 8.

Debbie's French Onion Soup

This is the best recipe for French onion soup that I have ever used. The recipe may be made in a Crock-Pot in the morning and left to cook all day. Topped with thin slices of toasted French bread and Monterey Jack cheese it becomes a frugal luxury.

  6 to 8 cups sliced yellow onions
  2 tablespoons sugar
  4 tablespoons flour
  ½ cup vermouth (Debbie's recipe calls for sweet vermouth; however, our family
    prefers the dry)
  2½ quarts chicken broth (you may use canned chicken broth, but I do not
    recommend powdered bouillon for this)
  2 cups beef broth (again, you may use canned broth, or simply make 2 cups from
    powdered beef bouillon)
  Optional: Finely diced beef or chicken pieces (leftovers work well)

Place sliced onions in a microwave-proof dish and cook on high for 6 to 7 minutes (until onions are just soft). Mix sugar, flour, and vermouth and stir into the cooked onions. Place onion mixture into a frying pan and cook over medium heat until onions are slightly golden and well coated (about 4 to 6 minutes). Do not burn! In a Crock-Pot (or large soup kettle) add broth, meat, and onion mixture. Allow to slow-cook in the Crock-Pot on low for 6 to 8 hours. (If you are cooking on the stovetop, allow to simmer over low heat for 1½ to 2 hours. Do not leave unattended.) Garnish each bowl of soup with croutons or toasted slices of French bread, topped with Monterey Jack, Gruyère, or Parmesan cheese. Makes about 1½ quarts and serves 6.

Hearty Minestrone Soup

This unusual soup is surprisingly tasty, and is a refreshing variation of ordinary vegetable soup.

1 quart beef stock (homemade, canned, or made from powdered bouillon)

1 can tomato paste (I often use about 4 to 5 ounces of pizza sauce from a large-sized can—purchased quite inexpensively at a warehouse store. These items are interchangeable because it is the tomato *taste* that is our desired ingredient.)

1 medium onion, chopped (for a more subtle flavor try using the white part of a large leek)

2 to 4 stalks celery, chopped

1 to 2 garlic cloves, minced (or simply add a teaspoon or two of pesto)

1 large bay leaf

1 to 2 teaspoons oregano (twice as much if using fresh)

1 to 2 teaspoons thyme (twice as much if using fresh)

¼ teaspoon ground cumin

¼ cup chopped, fresh parsley, or 2 to 3 tablespoons dried parsley (for best results opt for fresh if possible)

4 to 6 cups uncooked vegetables, peeled, cleaned, and diced (I put in fresh root vegetables, such as rutabaga, turnips, carrots, and potatoes, first, as they take longer to cook. After 5 or 10 minutes I then add diced, peeled tomatoes, green beans, and corn. You may use leftover cooked vegetables, but remember to add these well after the root vegetables or they will become mushy.)

Optional: 1 to 2 cups diced beef or chicken (I often use remains of previous meals for this recipe.)

Salt and pepper to taste

Put all ingredients in soup and simmer until vegetables and meat are the desired flavor and consistency (usually about 45 minutes to 1 hour). Serve with slabs of garlic bread and garnish with a sprinkling of shredded mozzarella, Parmesan, or goat cheese.

More than Bread: The Humble Biscuit

" . . . Thou shalt eat bread without scarceness . . ."
DEUTERONOMY 8:8

According to the *American Heritage Dictionary*, a biscuit is "a small cake of shortened bread." Throughout history this adjunct to the staff of life has been a blessing to the busy cook. Sadly, the secrets of simple biscuit baking have gone the way of the home-baked loaf of bread . . . a fading art. Thus, here's a convenient, modern-day alternative to the scratch biscuit that will allow you to revive the use of this old-time dinner-table staple. The plain refrigerator biscuit is an inexpensive and surprisingly tasty and versatile breadstuff. It can quite easily transform ordinary ingredients into extraordinary treats.

And while the recipes I offer here may not be the stuff of gourmet feasts, they are tasty, simple, easy-to-prepare foods that can soothe the budget, save time, and make an artful presentation at the family table. So, let us begin our exposé of the humble biscuit by borrowing from the wisdom of the eleventh-century philosopher, Amenemope, and be comforted with the knowledge that "better is bread with a happy heart than wealth with vexation."

Surprisingly Simple Homemade Doughnuts

This clever idea was a gift from a young Florida man who called in to a radio program on which I was a guest. Thank you, Frank!

> 1 or more canisters of circular refrigerator biscuits, separated (each biscuit will make one doughnut and one doughnut hole)
> A deep pan to hold oil
> Enough mild-tasting vegetable oil to fill the pan 2 or 3 inches deep
> A selection of topping ingredients such as powdered sugar, cinnamon, and butter-cream frosting

Using a small circular cookie cutter—Frank suggested using the top of a 2-liter soda bottle, as it is the perfect size for this project—cut out a circle from the center of each biscuit (put these small circles aside to cook later as doughnut holes).

In a deep frying pan, heat oil to about 375° to 400°, then *carefully* fry doughnuts—one or two at a time—for a few minutes on each side or until golden brown. (Be very careful not to let the hot oil smoke, and be cautious when working with hot oil, as even small spatters may burn you.) Fry the small biscuit circles in the same manner; these will take less time to cook, obviously, because they are smaller. The doughnuts (and holes) will puff slightly and turn a light golden brown when they have finished cooking.

With a slotted spatula, remove the doughnuts from the hot oil and place them on a paper-lined cookie sheet until you have finished cooking the entire contents of the biscuit canister. Keep doughnuts in a warm, low-temperature oven until ready to frost.

Doughnuts may be frosted with a simple glaze, made by mixing hot water and powdered (or superfine) sugar. (The hot water is important as it will dissolve the cornstarch present in most powdered sugars.)

You may also dredge cooked doughnuts in a mixture of powdered sugar and ground cinnamon (for a powdered doughnut, use sugar only). This is best done while they are still warm.

You may also ice them using butter-cream frosting (this is a good opportunity to make use of leftover frostings). Frost doughnut holes in a similar manner.

Serve doughnuts immediately, perhaps with a frosty glass of ice-cold milk, or iced tea.

Croissant Poulet

This is a deliciously frugal and fast way in which to use up leftover chicken or turkey meat. These freeze well, so you may wish to make a double batch so you will have a frugal fast food meal in the freezer for emergencies.

   2 cups diced, cooked chicken
   1 can cream of chicken soup, or make a white sauce and add chicken boullion to
      flavor
   2 to 3 tablespoons milk or water
   Dash of salt and pepper
   1 canister crescent-style refrigerator rolls
   2 to 3 tablespoons melted butter
   2 to 3 ounces cream cheese

In a mixing bowl, combine chicken, cream cheese, soup, water, salt and pepper. Separate crescent rolls into four squares. Flatten squares with your palms or a rolling pin (make certain dough becomes very flat). Spoon about ½ cup of chicken mixture into half of each square. Fold dough over the chicken mixture (fold at the perforations in the biscuit) and seal the edges of the dough so the mixture cannot leak out. Brush top and bottom of each square with melted butter.

Place each piece of flattened dough on a cookie sheet and bake at 350° for 25 to 30 minutes. Makes four servings. These are similar to the Hot Pockets available in the freezer section at the grocery store.

Breakfast Pizza

This recipe is great to prepare for the kids and their friends after a weekend sleepover.

> 2 packages refrigerator biscuits (or homemade dough, frozen bread dough available in your grocer's freezer, or ready-made packaged pizza dough generally found in the dairy case at the supermarket)
> 1 to 2 cups shredded, cooked potatoes (use leftover baked potatoes, or microwave raw potatoes until a fork slides out of them easily)
> Salt and pepper to taste
> About 1 cup shredded cheese (cheddar, mozzarella, or whatever mild cheese you have on hand)
> Optional: About 1 cup diced meats, such as ham or turkey; or crumbled, cooked bacon or breakfast sausage (this is a great way to make use of your leftover bits of meats)
> Optional: Diced fresh or canned tomatoes, green peppers, onions, and mushrooms

Use a 16-inch round pizza pan and stretch dough across the entire area, being certain to leave no area uncovered (if you are using frozen bread dough first thaw it, then cut the loaf in half with a clean pair of scissors).

Spread shredded potatoes evenly across the entire pan of dough—give the potatoes a dash of salt and pepper. Spread shredded cheese evenly over the potatoes. Sprinkle the meat and vegetable toppings evenly across the cheese.

Bake at 350° for 10 to 25 minutes. Slice as you would an ordinary pizza and serve with sparkling apple or grape juice.

Very Simple Morning Cinnamon Wreath
(a.k.a. Monkey Bread)

This is a very quick, easy, and fun recipe to make with your children. An older child can cut the biscuits, while a younger child dips them into the melted butter. The attractive, tasty results will make them think they have helped you perform a magic trick.

2 packages refrigerator biscuits
1 cup melted margarine (butter sometimes blackens in this recipe)
1 cup granulated sugar mixed with 2 tablespoons ground cinnamon
Optional: White butter-cream frosting, or powdered sugar glaze made by mixing
   powdered sugar with small amounts of very hot water or milk—consistency
   should be a bit watery
One clean pair of scissors, and a well-greased Bundt or tube pan

With scissors, cut separated refrigerator biscuits into fourths. Lightly dip each piece of cut dough into melted margarine, then quickly dip into cinnamon sugar mixture (do not overcoat). Layer pan with coated biscuit pieces (pieces must touch, but be careful not to press them together). Continue this process until all the pieces are coated and put into the pan. Bake in preheated 350° oven for 15 to 20 minutes. Cool wreath for about 5 minutes (do not allow it to cool completely) then invert onto a pretty serving plate (be careful, the sugar turns into a hot syrupy glaze). If desired, apply icing or glaze while hot.

Romancing the Remains of a Feast:
Solving an Age-Old Dilemma

"Who riseth from a feast
With that keen appetite that he sits down?"
—William Shakespeare

It is an age-old dilemma . . . what to do with the remains of a feast. Yet it isn't actually a problem of passing the food from one form to another—in itself an exciting (and economical) passage. The dilemma lies in uncovering the knowledge that magically transforms dull leftovers into a delicious feast. Once you have taken the time to familiarize yourself with the basic principles of transforming leftovers, you will find that you will actually be *planning* to have them about. The bonus lies in the amazing economy of both time and money, and the rich feeling of satisfaction that comes from having conquered the ordinary.

A proper attitude can be a great enhancer when dealing with leftovers. If you view them as old friends, you may find that they will work to your advantage. The first adjustment in your thinking is not to focus on what you *want* to make but what *can* be prepared—using only the ingredients you have on hand. For years now I have been making my menus based on this method. I make a mental game of imagining a crowd of important visitors; I must make a delicious meal for them—using only the ingredients available in my pantry, refrigerator, and freezer. This game has allowed me to create amazing meals from what at first seems to be very little.

Understand that you may serve the remains of a feast in a form other than the one in which it first appeared at your table. For example:

- If you served roast beef with baked potatoes and gravy, you need not serve the remaining beef in the same manner. Instead, dice and simmer the meat in a lightly diluted mixture of your favorite barbecue sauce for 10 to 15 minutes. Ladle the warmed meat between 2 slices of lightly toasted sourdough bread. Serve this delicious barbecue sandwich with homemade cole slaw, crudités, and home fries prepared from the baked potatoes. You may serve roast chicken, lamb, and/or pork in the same manner.

- These same meats can also be finely diced, ground in a food processor, simmered in taco seasonings with a bit of water, and used to fill homemade tacos, enchiladas, or as a meat base for tostadas or a marinara sauce.

- You may also sliver and use remaining lean meats as ingredients in stir-fry, rice, pasta, and egg dishes, and of course soups.

- If you have two or more types of leftover vegetables you can mix them to create what is called vegetable macédoines (lima beans and corn; peas and carrots; diced potatoes and carrots; asparagus and small pearl onions; cauliflower and green beans; cauliflower, peas, and carrots; zucchini and tomatoes; broccoli and cauliflower; zucchini and yellow squash; and snow peas and yellow squash slices are a few examples).

- Some restaurants serve vegetable molds that may be easily duplicated at home, using an overabundance of precooked vegetables. Simply puree vegetables (such as broccoli, squash, or cauliflower) mingled with seasonings, herbs, and a beaten egg to hold everything together, and press into molds (well-oiled small bread tins work well). Cover the filled molds with foil and place them in a larger pan containing an inch of water. Place the pan in a 325° oven to bake (about 20 to 30 minutes). Remove from water and allow to cool for a few moments. Invert molds onto individual plates and serve immediately.

Illuminated Fragments
The Spell of Home-Baked Bread

"Efficiency of a practically flawless kind
may be reached naturally in the struggle for bread.
But there is something beyond—a higher point,
a subtle and unmistakable touch of love and pride beyond mere skill;
almost an inspiration which gives to all work that finish which is almost art—which is art."

—JOSEPH CONRAD

Many people regard bread as a nourishing food, necessary for sustaining life. Yet, to those of us who have admired its mysteries, smelled its fresh-baked aromas, and sampled its vast variety of textures, it surpasses the realm of the ordinary and metamorphoses into the most luscious of all luxuries.

The aroma of home-baked bread is enchanting. I can think of only one thing more delectable than savoring the scent of home-baked bread, and that is the taste of it. A fresh-baked loaf of bread, be it white, wheat, or rye, is a simple way to liven up an ordinary meal. The next time you are faced with a boring afternoon, you might want to try your hand at the art of bread-making. By so doing you may indulge yourself, your family, and your friends with this age-old pleasure.

If you are not so inclined, or haven't the time to indulge in the actual process of start-to-finish bread baking, an acceptable alternative is the frozen loaves of bread dough found in the freezer section of your grocery store. These are very reasonably priced (about sixty cents per loaf) and are extremely easy to prepare.

ANGEL'S BREAD

This is the tastiest bread I have ever eaten. It came from a former neighbor who was kind enough to share her recipe with us. I have used it many times, and continue to enjoy the luxurious smell and taste of what I have aptly named "Angel's Bread."

1 tablespoon salt
¾ cup sugar or honey
2 tablespoons vegetable oil
3 cups hot water
2 packages dried yeast
4 cups white flour (approximate)
4 cups whole wheat flour (approximate)

Combine salt, sugar, vegetable oil, and water in a large bowl. Let cool to lukewarm and add dry yeast. Mix well and let it bubble. Add and mix flour. Knead well for 10 minutes. Dough may be sticky; continue to add extra wheat flour until it doesn't stick to your hands too much (you may need to add up to 1½ cups of extra wheat flour until the stickiness is gone). Oil the top of your mixture with 1 tablespoon of oil, cover with a clean hand towel, and allow the dough to rise to the top of the bowl in a warm (but not hot) place in your kitchen. Divide dough into halves and place into two greased loaf pans. Allow the dough to rise to the top of the pan, but not over the sides. This usually takes 2 or more hours.

Bake in a preheated 400° oven for 10 minutes, then turn down the temperature to 350° and bake for 20 to 30 minutes more. When tops are golden brown, loaves are done. Every oven cooks differently so watch closely the first time you bake. Butter the tops while the bread is in the loaf pans and then turn out to cool (racks work best). Relish your luxury!

ৡৡ

Chapter 14

The Autumn Gift Pantry

~

"The wondrous gift is given."

—Phillips Brooks

Packaging Gifts of Noble Origin

"Every gift of noble origin
Is breathed upon by Hope's perpetual breath."

—William Wordsworth

During this season of abundance and harvest, I am thinking of the many wonderful gifts I can compose from nature's noble bounty. As special as these gifts may be, they become superlative when the packaging in which they are presented is artful, attractive, and frugal.

Magical Jars The most attractive jars for jams, jellies, and preserves are simple mason jars, which lend an old-fashioned charm. You can also use mason jars for a bevy of gifts other than preserves. I keep them on hand in a variety of sizes in order to send soup home with a friend, or to package flavored popcorns, nuts, well-dried fruits, homemade pancake mix, granola, and the like. These traditional jars look even more lovely when their metal caps are embellished in an attractive manner. Boxes of mason jars are available in a variety of sizes at grocery or hardware stores, and are often quite reasonably priced. Or look for them at thrift shops, flea markets, and yard sales. Keep in mind that if you will be using them for actual canning purposes they should have no chips or cracks, no matter how small, especially at the top of the rim.

Apothecary Jars These may be collected throughout the year and added to your Gift Pantry and used to present gifts of food, or store-bought candies. I have presented this type of jar filled with individually wrapped chocolates and hard candies, as well as firm homemade cookies, sturdy fudge squares (you may wish to wrap these in cellophane or waxed paper beforehand), and nuts (flavored or plain). With an attractive ribbon around the rim, and a pretty tag hanging from the lid, you have a lovely token of your friendship to give to a neighbor, friend, or hostess, or to include as part of a gift basket.

Lace Doilies Create a polished, finished gift package by tying lace doilies onto the tops of mason jars, using raffia, silken cord, or satin ribbon. You can easily make lace doilies by cutting rounds of lace from scraps you have on hand. (You can hem the raw edges, use a fray-reducing product, or sew satin binding or fringe along the edges.)

Jar Covers Make your own jar covers by cutting circles from papers humble or grand—parchment, handmade art papers, brown craft paper, or plain white freezer paper. Take this concept a step further, and photocopy old black-and-white botanical prints and use these to cover your jar lids, for an unusual effect. Commercial paper doilies and scraps of attractive fabrics look lovely as well.

Wrapping If you wish to wrap the entire jar, as opposed to merely the lid, take a square of paper three times as wide as the jar is tall. For example, if the jar is four inches tall, you will need a twelve-inch square of paper. Place the jar on its side, about an inch away from the paper's edge, and roll. Fold the ends of the paper that are under the jar first (neatly) and fasten with tape. Next, gather the top of the paper and tie it tightly with raffia or ribbon. This will create a paper collar that will stand up and form a ruffle at the top of the jar.

Cellophane Candy Bags These inexpensive candy bags (twelve bags for about a dollar) are available at cake, candy, and craft supply stores, and come in a variety of sizes. I use these to package an assortment of goodies from the kitchen. These bags can hold dried herbs; repackaged pancake, cake, or muffin mixes; dried soup, rice, and pasta mixes; dehydrated vegetables and fruits; cookies; home-cooked or purchased candies; fresh-baked sweet breads, miniature bundt cakes, muffins, and shortbread wedges; and fresh produce such as garlic or shallot bulbs, kumquats, limes, lemons, and lady's apples. Just about any item from the kitchen or garden will look attractive in such a package. These bags are an invaluable re-source to me. I use them for many purposes outside of the kitchen as well, such as to package dried flower petals or potpourris; to present fresh herbs and flowers from the garden; and to hold seeds, soaps, and the like.

Cans of Bread I have been known to implement the time-honored habit of bak-ing breads in a variety of recycled tin cans. This is an adaptation of the traditional Boston Baked Bread, where bread dough is baked inside a clean, well-oiled can instead of a bread pan. You may bake several of these ahead of time and freeze them (well wrapped in freezer paper or plastic freezer bags) in the can, two or three weeks before the holiday. When the holiday season arrives, simply thaw your bread (still in the can) then decorate it with an attractive tulle bow, or a thick tassel of raffia, and paste purchased or homemade labels onto the can fronts (this is another opportunity to use labels you have designed, as described on the next page).

Unusual Tokens Throughout the year, I collect pretty ceramic crocks (I use small crocks to present homemade herb and honeyed butter—larger ones are lovely to bestow dried soups and mixes in); sugar bowls (inside which I place packets or cellophane bags filled with homemade flavored sugars); teapots (filled with tea bags or packages of loose-leaf tea); attractive teacups and coffee mugs (for individual tea bags, flavored coffees, mulled cider mix, instant cocoa powder, and the like); and dinner plates and saucers to present homemade cakes, cookies, and shortbread. Look for new or vintage flatware and serving pieces: attractive knives can accompany gifts of herb and honey butters; old-fashioned sugar and jam spoons accompany homemade or store-bought jams, jellies, and flavored sugars; wooden spoons and ladles are paired with gifts of soup and powdered punch mixes; whisks are companions to muffin or pancake mixes.

Gift Tags

"Remove not the landmark . . ."
—AMENEMOPE

A tag need not merely mark who a gift is for. With a bit of thought and ingenuity you can transform ordinary papers, office supplies, and throwaways into a thoughtful element of packaging.

Labels Create simple handwritten labels to apply to the front of your jars. These may be cut from scraps of paper you have around the house and applied with a glue stick. If you would like to get a bit more creative, perhaps design a special label for all of your homemade kitchen gifts. These may be duplicated by photocopying or printing techniques. Use a piece of copyright-free art as your logo, or ask an art student to create a design for you. Unless you plan to have your labels color-photocopied or printed (in which case they will be much more expensive) make certain your design looks attractive in black and white. And, of course, if you have access to a home computer there are many simple programs on the market that can enable you to create your own attractive designs easily and inexpensively.

Office Tags Office supply stores are brimming with inexpensive paper goods that are attractive and unique for your purposes. A single walk down the retail tag and inventory product aisle will garner a cornucopia of novel markers to use on special gifts. Metal-rimmed hanging tags, rectangular cardboard mailing and luggage tags, and the tiniest manila or white change envelopes are charming when used as markers for presents (loop fine strands of satin ribbon or raffia through a corner of the tag to hang it from gifts). If you are feeling creative, you may wish to embellish these with patterned ink stamps; dried herb petals; tiny seashells; antique buttons; dried rosebuds; a fresh ivy leaf; attractive stickers; or a hand-lettered greeting or a favorite motto, using a fountain pen or fine-point marker and your best penmanship. Slip tiny candies, coins, or secret messages inside of the change envelopes for an added delight.

Custom-Made   Design your own tags and have them photocopied on heavy paper, such as card stock (about ten cents per sheet at the office supply or stationery store). If you give thought to your design you may be able to fit four cards (unfolded) onto each sheet of paper.

Illuminated Fragments
A Magical, Ancient Liquid

" . . . Bedewed with liquid odors . . ."
—HORACE

Vinegar represents a true metamorphosis—the transformation of simple juices into a tart, acidic flavoring. This magical ancient liquid has been associated with health, prosperity, and gastronomy for millennia. Hippocrates, the father of medicine, prescribed it; Caesar's legionnaires drank it with water as a thirst-quencher during battles and long journeys; and Cleopatra was said to have dissolved a perfect pearl in vinegar and drunk the concoction as a beauty treatment. The French gave vinegar its modern name: *vin aigre,* meaning "sour wine."

In today's modern diet vinegar appears in numerous foods. Most salad toppings contain at least small amounts. Mustard, ketchup, barbecue sauce, and pickles contain vinegar. Main dishes are often accompanied by vinegar: German sauerbraten, English fish-and-chips (with malt vinegar), and Japanese sushi (with rice vinegar). Vinegar is a delicious, frugal contribution to our culinary pursuits.

TYPES OF VINEGAR

- Cider vinegar, made from the fermented juices of pressed apples
- Wine vinegar, distilled from the juices of fruits such as grapes and berries
- Italian balsamic vinegar—a darker, slightly sweet aged vinegar from the juice of white Trebbiano grapes (this type is very popular in gourmet cookery)
- French wine vinegar, a.k.a. red wine vinegar—also a favorite of gourmet and humble palates alike

Homemade Herbal Vinegar

Fresh herbs such as mint, basil, tarragon, hot chili peppers (about 2 handfuls of
leaves per quart of vinegar works well, or 4 to 6 peppers)
White wine vinegar or white rice vinegar
Pretty bottles to store herbal vinegar (I recycle pretty imported wine or beer
bottles for this purpose), plus clean cork stoppers
Nonreactive pan and funnel

Combine herbs (reserve about ¼ of the fresh leaves) and vinegar in pot. Heat until very
hot but not boiling; keep at high heat (not boiling) for about 5 minutes. Let vinegar
cool until you can safely handle the mixture. Strain through a colander to remove
herbs. Pour cooled, strained mixture into sterilized bottles, using a funnel. Drop small
amounts of fresh herbs into each bottle. Let vinegar stand for about 3 weeks in a warm
place. Try to shake bottles at least once a day. Embellish your family's meals with this
treat, or store in your Gift Pantry.

Lavender-Flavored Vinegar

This year I have put most of my collection of attractive glass bottles to use holding
lavender-infused vinegar, made by steeping fresh lavender blossoms and stems in very
hot—not boiling—white wine vinegar. After plugging the filled bottles with clean
corks, I seal them by applying a coat of paraffin over the corks and lip of the bottles.
Also, I often tie a gift tag to the neck of the bottles (using my ever-present raffia) to explain what is inside and suggesting uses for this treat. These bottles are added to our
Gift Pantry, or used as the secret touch in some of my recipes.

THE GIFT PANTRY INVENTORY LIST FOR AUTUMN		
GIFT RECIPIENT & DATE OF ENTRY INTO GIFT PANTRY	GIFT ITEM(S) PURCHASED OR CREATED	WHEN TO PRESENT THE GIFT & PACKAGING IDEAS

Part IV
The Magic and
Majesty of Winter

~

"O Winter, ruler of the inverted year!"
—William Cowper

Chapter 15

Festivals of Winter

❧

"A feast of fat things . . ."

—Isaiah 25:6

Winter's Contrary Reign

"Faith declares what the senses do not see, but not the contrary . . ."

—Blaise Pascal

Winter is a season of contraries—solemn and festive, active as well as dormant, natural yet supernatural. Thus, it is little wonder that I find myself, as the season again approaches, cloaked with equal amounts of retrospect and anticipation regarding the many and bright festivals of the season.

Feast-fires are lit, and continue to glow, from the first short day until well into the new year. Yet, because we live in a culture in which the holiday of Christmas reigns over the other seasonal festivals, I do not describe the winter holidays in chronological order. Instead, I devote an entire separate chapter to Christmas and its accompanying rites of celebrating, decorating, and gift-giving. And New Year's Day is not included in the season of winter. Because endings are really nothing more than disguised beginnings, I felt it appropriate to conclude *Frugal Luxuries by the Seasons* with the start of a new year.

Saint Nicholas Day

*"On December sixth, Saint Nicholas' birthday, we put up the
Advent calendar and the Christmas pyramid."*

—Tasha Tudor

December 6 is the birthday of Saint Nicholas. This traditional European feast day is a
minor celebration in our home. The ritual begins on the evening of the fifth as we
bring out, and officially hang, our holiday stockings for the Christmas season.

As Saint Nicholas Day dawns, we find the children digging inside the toes of their
respective stockings, seeking out the small gifts that mark this day. A few silver dollars,
and perhaps the first candy cane of the year, is all they will find. Yet the value of these
inexpensive tokens is more than tangible; they express the *spirit* of the season, and hint
at the magical fun that is still to come. Often, the advent wreath is put out on this day
as well—along with our collection of tiny crèche figures. And if time permits, we will
bake a special dessert.

I have discovered that small gestures such as these inspire the gift of wonder in the
children, and in myself. As well, the simple celebration of Saint Nicholas Day allows us
to launch the new holiday season, and to savor its pleasures to the fullest extent.

Simple Saint Nicholas Day
One-Bowl Cake

This cake, especially when it has been baked in a Bundt pan, looks quite wreathlike.
You may wish to double your batch and make a second Saint Nicholas Day cake for a
good neighbor or friend.

Bring all ingredients to room temperature before blending. Preheat oven to 375°.
Grease and flour 2 9-inch layer cake pans or one standard Bundt cake pan.

1 cup sugar
½ cup butter or margarine
2 eggs
1 teaspoon vanilla, or ½ teaspoon each vanilla and almond extract
1½ cups sifted flour (cake flour is my preference, but all-purpose flour works well
    too)
½ teaspoon salt
2½ teaspoons baking powder
½ cup milk or water

In one large mixing bowl, cream the sugar and butter until light and fluffy. Add the eggs, one at a time, beating well after each addition. Add vanilla and almond extracts and beat again. Sift flour, salt, and baking powder and add to butter mixture, alternating with the milk. Mix only until blended. Pour into prepared pans and bake for 20 to 25 minutes (if you are using a Bundt pan, cook 30 to 35 minutes at 350°). Remove cakes from pans and cool on a wire rack before icing. Ice this cake with an easy buttercream frosting, or sift a thick layer of powdered sugar across the top and serve with ice cream or peach sauce.

The Festival of Hanukkah
(The Feast of the Dedication)

"It was a miracle of rare device . . ."
—Samuel Taylor Coleridge

The Feast of Hanukkah, which lasts for eight days, starts on the twenty-fifth day of the month of Kislev (usually in the month of December), at about the same time as the winter solstice.

The eight-branched menorah is the central symbol of Hanukkah. In fact, the Hebrew word for menorah is *hanukiyah,* from which the holiday derives its name. During the holiday it is traditional to light this ritual lamp as a reminder to the observant of the ancient tale of faith triumphing over adversity, and of light, renewal, and freedom.

When the Syrian Antiochus IV became ruler of Judea (modern-day Israel) during the second and first century B.C., he began religious persecution of the Jews, and ransacked the holy Temple of Jerusalem, overturning the menorah that had always been kept lit. A small band of Jews, the Maccabees, fought this persecution and, despite the lopsided odds, miraculously succeeded in regaining power. Thus, the first miracle of the festival of Hanukkah recalls the victory of Judas Maccabeus and the rededication of the Temple of Jerusalem.

The second miracle of Hanukkah was revealed when it came time to reconsecrate the temple. Oil was necessary to fuel the temple's sacred lights, but only one small jar could be found that had not been desecrated by the Syrian soldiers. As the Jews preferred one day of illumination to a continued darkness, the menorah was lit using only the small amount of oil that was available. When the next morning came, they discovered that the menorah remained lit—and it continued to burn unwaveringly for eight straight days.

Hanukkah is a rich holiday, filled with songs, good foods, and gift-giving. On the first night, only one candle is kindled; on the second night two, and so on. Always kindled from the left to the right, the candles should be lit as soon as possible after nightfall. Traditional blessings are recited, and the song "*Mo'oz Tzur*" ("Rock of Ages") is sung. In households that contain young children, you may find the family going from room to room in a Maccabean march.

At Hanukkah time gifts are frequently exchanged (often one or two each evening), and special foods are served, such as latkes (potato pancakes) and blintzes (filled crepes). In essence, Hanukkah is an occasion of great exuberance. Religious schools often present cultural programs such as pageants, plays, and oratories retelling this ancient tale of wonders. In Israel, bonfires are often lit on the hilltops, and torches (*lapidim*) are carried from town to town, and city to city, by special runners, in commemoration of the Festival of Lights. All of this jubilation is welcome at a time of year when the days are shortest and the darkness longest.

Savory Cheese Blintzes

To make cheese filling you will need:
  1 pound strained cottage cheese (allow cottage cheese to drain in colander in the refrigerator for at least 4 hours or, for best results, overnight—remember to put a dish beneath it to catch the whey)
  1 egg
  1 tablespoon melted butter
  1 teaspoon salt
  ½ teaspoon sugar

Combine all ingredients and mix well. Refrigerate until it is time to fill the blintzes.

To make blintzes you will need:
  2 eggs
  1 cup water
  ½ teaspoon salt
  ⅔ cup flour

Stir together all of the ingredients for the blintzes, blending as for a pancake batter. Prepare a small lightly oiled or nonstick frying pan; be sure it is hot, but not smoking. Drop a small amount of batter into the frying pan, enough to create a small (about 6–inch) thin pancake. Cook as you would pancakes. (Separate the cooked blintzes with small squares of waxed paper as you take them from the pan, until ready to fill.) Fill the center of each circle with about one teaspoon of the cheese mixture, and fold the sides of the blintz—first turn the top down over the filling, then the bottom, and, finally, both sides. Repeat the process until all the blintzes are filled. Lay filled blintzes side by side in a shallow, oiled baking dish. Reheat them in a 350° oven until they are light brown (about 15 to 20 minutes). Serve with a dollop of sour cream. Makes about 12 blintzes.

Twelfth Day (Epiphany)

"The world will never starve for wonders; but only for want of wonder."
—GILBERT KEITH CHESTERTON

In olden times, Twelfth Day was sometimes referred to as the Feast of the Three Magi, or Little Christmas. Epiphany is still a feast of the first rank for many Christians. Falling on January 6, this festival commemorates the manifestations of Christ to the gentiles, in the persons of the Magi, and His baptism in the river Jordan (which is thought to have revealed His divinity). As well, it is a celebration of the revelation of His power, as shown at the wedding feast of Cana, during which Christ worked His first miracle: transforming water into wine. Until the fourth century A.D., the birth of Christ was also celebrated on this day in the East, and is observed so still by the Eastern Orthodox church.

The Minor Miracle of Fudge

Because this feast day is one on which to ponder miracles, I think it only appropriate to prepare a simple treat that illustrates a minor but useful form of wonder-working—that of invoking the alchemy that will transform simple ingredients such as sugar, butter, milk, and cocoa into deliciously creamy fudge.

It is especially fun to have your children help you to prepare this recipe. Once it is ready to eat, perhaps you would like to share this tasty, minor miracle with a neighbor or friend.

16 ounces powdered sugar, sifted
½ cup powdered cocoa (unsweetened)
¼ teaspoon salt
½ cup butter or margarine
¼ cup milk
1 teaspoon vanilla extract
Optional: ½ cup finely chopped nuts (such as walnuts or pecans)

In a 2-quart, microwave-safe glass bowl, combine sugar, cocoa, and salt. Add the butter; no need to blend. Microwave contents of bowl on the highest power for about 2 or 3 minutes. Add milk and stir with your whisk until it is well blended. Microwave again (on high) for 1 minute. Stir in vanilla and nuts. Pour into a greased 8-inch square pan. Refrigerate until the fudge becomes firm. Cut into small squares, and savor the miracle of transforming ordinary ingredients into a delicious candy. Yields 1½ pounds.

Saint Valentine's Day

"Get some fresh hay, then, to lay under foot,
Some holly and ivy to make fine the posts;
Is't not Valentine's Day?"

—BEN JONSON

It is said that Saint Valentine was a devout and serious bishop, who was executed in Rome on the fourteenth day of February (about 270 A.D.). He lost his life because he defied Emperor Claudius II's decree that all adult male citizens of Rome should become soldiers, and never marry. Valentine continued to unite couples in marriage despite the emperor's ruling. When he was canonized as a saint, the day of his death was dedicated to him.

The customs celebrated on our modern Saint Valentine's Day are of very ancient origins. A few customs, however, have become extinct over the centuries. In the England of olden times, this day was kept as a great gala, and houses were ornamented in evergreens to honor it. The highlight of the day's ceremonies was always the choosing of a valentine, or sweetheart, for the upcoming year, the choice being left to chance. (One custom held that the first unattached member of the opposite sex seen by an individual on Saint Valentine's Day became his or her valentine.) The cavalier was expected to escort his lady at all social gatherings, as well as execute all of her commands.

"All mankind loves a lover," noted Emerson. And today, Saint Valentine's Day is widely recognized as devoted to romance. But it is also a day of *friendship*. Innocent valentine cards and candy are often exchanged by schoolchildren. And who does not remember decorating an empty shoe box with pink paper and lacy doilies? This treasure box would hold the expected surprises of the day and, every so often, a happy unexpected memento or sentiment.

Heart-of-Buttons Brooch

"Fine art is that in which the hand, the head, and the heart of man go together."
—John Ruskin

A graceful way to recycle buttons (new and antique), small charms, and odd earrings is to turn them into pins, or brooches.

- First, form a base for the pin by cutting heart shapes from materials on hand. Often I use recycled Styrofoam from cups or well-washed meat trays. Heavy cardboard also works. Or, you can purchase thin, precut wooden shapes from craft and hobby stores.

- After you have prepared the base, decoupage a scrap of wrapping paper or fabric over it.

- Using the plainest and flattest as a bottom layer, cover the base with an assortment of buttons. Use a variety of sizes. Don't worry about the base showing between them; the second and third layers of buttons will cover any gaps. Fasten buttons to the base and each other by using a glue gun or rubber cement.

- Apply the more attractive charms and buttons carefully over the gaps left by the first layer. Repeat until you have created a level, moundlike, shape.

- Secure a pin-back, available at your local craft or hobby store, to the plain side of your project to transform it into a brooch. Or attach a slender silken cord (firmly) to the back of your project to create a necklace.

This venerable project is a lovely way to make use of those beloved vintage and antique buttons that have been passed on to you. You might also create a lasting memory, and preserve family history, by using sentimental buttons culled from your children's outgrown clothing, old uniforms, special dresses, and so on. It is also a fun project to do with children, using inexpensive plastic buttons recycled from discarded garments.

If time and materials permit, we make several button brooches at one sitting to stock the Gift Pantry.

❦

Valentine Cookie-Pops

1 cup softened butter
¾ cup granulated sugar
1 large egg
1 teaspoon almond or vanilla extract
10 to 12 drops red food coloring
2¾ cups all-purpose flour
1 teaspoon baking soda
1 teaspoon cream of tartar
Several clean Popsicle sticks
One 3-inch, heart-shaped cookie cutter (or just cut a heart shape from paper, trace it over the dough with a butter knife, and cut it out)

Cream together butter and sugar in a large mixing bowl. Once this becomes fluffy add egg and beat heartily. Mix in the vanilla and food coloring. Add the dry ingredients. Blend until ingredients are well combined, and have formed a dough. Gather the dough into a ball, flatten with the heel of your palm, and cover it well with plastic wrap. Chill the dough in the refrigerator for about 3 hours. (To save time, you may wish to prepare the dough the night before.)

On a lightly floured wooden cutting board, roll out the dough until it is about ⅛ inch thick. Cut out heart shapes using your cookie cutter or paper template. Place one end of a Popsicle stick in the center of the heart, so that it protrudes from the bottom of the cookie dough. Add another heart over the stick, to sandwich it in place. Pinch the sides of the cookie dough so that the two pieces will stay together.

Bake the cookies on an ungreased cookie sheet, in a preheated 350° oven, for about 10 to 12 minutes (remove them from the oven before the edges start to brown). Keep the cookies on the cookie sheet until they have completely cooled. Decorate them using pink-tinted icing (or allow your children to ice them for you). Embellish your cookie-pops with candy hearts, sprinkles, or messages written with frosting. Yields about 1 dozen cookie-pops (depending on the size of your cookie cutter).

The Birthday of President Washington

"George Washington, Commander of the American armies, who, like Joshua of old,
commanded the sun and the moon to stand still, and they obeyed him."

—Benjamin Franklin

An ancient proverb of unknown origin states that "the first step toward greatness is to be honest." However, I would venture to say that honesty is not merely the first step toward greatness, it *is* greatness itself. Perhaps this is why a simple example of honest behavior—the legendary tale of George Washington and the felled cherry tree—has carried on for more than two hundred years. Washington's honesty in the face of punishment reassures us, from generation to generation, that he who is honest in small ways will be rewarded greatly. More importantly, it also subtly tells us that the habit of being honest can provoke other noble characteristics in an individual, such as courage and leadership.

Honesty inspires an alchemy that transforms other things to its own high quality. Another example occurs in Washington's address to his humble troops prior to the Battle of Long Island (August 27, 1776). He openly told his men that the time was "near at hand which must probably determine whether Americans are to be freemen or slaves . . . The fate of unborn millions will now depend, under God, on the courage and conduct of this army. Our cruel and unrelenting enemy leaves us only the choice of brave resistance, or the most abject submission. We have, therefore, to resolve to conquer or die." Washington and his troops, despite the glaring odds against a victory, went on to win the battle.

When first reading these noble words, I was struck that *I* am one of those "unborn millions" whose fate was positively affected by the courageous actions taken by those men, more than two hundred years ago. Not only did this illumination renew my longstanding respect for the great heroes of the American Revolution, but it was a strong reminder of the tremendous power our own actions (or nonaction) will hold over the future. Perhaps the manner in which you live today will not affect the fate of an entire nation, but it will impact the lives of the future generations of your own family—whether the resulting influences will be positive or negative is entirely up to you.

I am privileged to honor this day on which a good and honest man was born . . . a man who was pivotal in securing the freedoms that most Americans currently enjoy.

Cherry Brownie Torte

This delectable dessert—the cherries are symbolic of the day—is very easy to prepare, tastes delicious, and makes a lovely presentation.

While you enjoy it with your family and friends, invoke the name of our nation's first president, give honor to his memory, and appreciate the still-fresh fruits of his labor.

1 package brownie mix (19- or 20-ounce box of any variety), plus any ingredients called for by the manufacturer
1 21-ounce can cherry fruit filling
2½ cups frozen nondairy whipped topping, thawed (You can substitute whipped cream for the nondairy topping if you plan to serve this dish *immediately*.)
¼ cup toasted, slivered almonds (If you have only raw almonds, toast them in the oven at 325° for about 5 to 7 minutes.)

Preheat oven to 350°. Grease and flour 2 9-inch round cake pans. Prepare the brownies according to package directions—use the cakelike version. Divide brownie batter evenly between the two cake pans and bake for 18 to 20 minutes (do not overbake). Allow brownies to cool in pans for 10 minutes, then remove from pans and allow to cool completely (use a wire rack for best results).

To build your torte, place one brownie layer on a pretty serving plate. Top this with 1½ cups of the whipped topping, spreading it to about ½ inch from the edge. Carefully spread half of the cherry filling evenly over the whipped topping. Top this with the second brownie layer. Spread remaining cherries over the top (again to within ½ inch of the edge). Sprinkle the toasted almonds over the top. Dollop the remaining whipped topping around the edge of the torte (if you have a pastry bag with a piping tip, use it to pipe the whipped cream around the edges of the top layer). Cut into wedges with a serrated knife, and serve with a cup of good hot tea. Makes 12 servings.

Illuminated Fragments

Joy

"She says, 'But in contentment I still feel the need of some imperishable bliss.'"
—Wallace Stevens

The idea has been transmitted throughout the ages that joy is akin to an immense, precious jewel—a single gem of such rarity that to seek it is a futile waste of life, time, and effort. If the truth be known, joy is not a single stone, but a mosaic, composed of a multitude of small, sparkling fragments. These radiant fragments lie within your path every day. Each, taken separately, may seem to hold very little value. Yet when gathered and set they transform into that often elusive—much desired—intangible we refer to as *joy*.

Perfecting the art of wise, joyful living has been an object of humankind since the beginning of thought. And while most people, ancient and modern, have sought out its secrets, they all might agree upon one point: Happiness does not come automatically, but is arrived at only by dedication. Yet, paradoxically, you must not focus on it in an exclusive fashion.

True joy is not achieved by the absence of troubles. By my own definition, "imperishable bliss" is simply the cultivation and mastery of the skills needed to overcome adversity with grace, dignity, and a sense of self-worth. Doing so requires that you extract the necessary lessons from each life experience, and keep a record of them so that you—and possibly other members of the human race—may take away something of value.

Chapter 16

Winter Home Graces

❦

"A sweet attractive kind of grace."

—Matthew Roydon

Cultivating Winter Home Graces

"Now stir the fire, and close the shutters fast,
Let fall the curtains, wheel the sofa round . . .
So let us welcome a peaceful evening in."

—William Cowper

This time of year, more than any other (especially after the major holidays have passed), is the ideal time for you to delight and astonish those you love with graciously prepared, thoughtfully presented foods. These will provide sustenance for the body, and warmth for the spirit.

The creative sleight of hand that transforms an ordinary day into a holiday or celebration is the details: the cluster of berries and evergreen (snipped from the juniper trees in the garden) that have been artfully arranged in a crystal vase; the birds that flutter in and out of a feeder perched just outside the kitchen window; the fragrant chocolate torte baking in the oven; the leftover holiday turkey and ham that have been transformed into a rich and delicious soup—all these ignite the warmth of home, hearth, and family in the dull winter days that lead us out of the holidays.

As well, winter home graces can be found in the impromptu picnic served in front of a gentle fire on a cold winter evening—along with a bit of music and good company. They are seen in the long-stemmed glass goblets (no two of which are alike) that grace each place at the family table for a Twelfth Night dinner. And you will see them at the dolls' tea party held on Saint Valentine's Day. All of these activities take very little time to implement, but make lasting impressions on children, as well as adults, who understand that something delicious has happened to turn a boring day into a festive gala.

Money is *not* the key to creating home graces. Neither is spending hours slaving in the kitchen to make absolutely everything from scratch (unless, of course, this is your joy and passion). Still, those of us with busy lives need to know that we have *permission* to buy prepared foods. We are *allowed* to use mixes in the kitchen (budget permitting)—especially when doing so contributes to traditions of family, food, and fun. Recognizing the fact that it would not be humanly possible to implement every home grace that sounds attractive allows us to delight in those things that we choose to do—and not lament over what has been left undone.

The Alchemy of Flatware

"They pursued it with forks and hope . . ."
—LEWIS CARROLL

Although today we take flatware for granted, there was a time when most foods were eaten with the fingers. While the knife has been around for more than one and a half million years and is thought to have been used by *Homo erectus,* the spoon is a mere twenty thousand years old (dating back to the Paleolithic age—also found in Egyptian tombs). The shape of early spoons can be traced back to the origin of their name. In fact, the word itself is a derivative of the Anglo-Saxon word *spon,* meaning "chip," a thin, slightly concave piece of wood used to dip into soups or porridge.

By comparison, the common fork is an infant. Although our word *fork* is extracted from the Latin *furca,* meaning "farmer's pitchfork" (one of the most ancient of tools, dating back to about the fourth millennium B.C.), small forks for eating did not appear until about the eleventh century A.D., at which time they were considered ridiculous, and frowned upon. For almost five hundred more years the fork remained a disgraceful instrument. It wasn't until the eighteenth century that the fork became an acceptable, if not fashionable, eating utensil, probably to emphasize class distinction. Thanks in part to the French nobility of the eighteenth century the fork became a symbol of refinement, status, and luxury.

Today, I find myself drawn to vintage pieces of flatware (usually silver or silver plate). My collection is neither valuable, complete, nor in good condition. In fact, I am often at a loss as to how to make use of my many beautiful, but sometimes dilapidated, pieces. Still, I continue to acquire them, often for a mere pittance, at yard sales, thrift shops, and flea markets. Once, I purchased an entire bin of vintage silver flatware for a mere five dollars. Obviously, this acquisition prompted my imagination to find artful uses for these lovely items.

- For less valuable plated pieces (on which the silver plating has started to wear thin) I sometimes drill a hole at the top of the handle of a fork, knife, or spoon, so I may use it as an ornament for our holiday tree. I often spray-paint these using a gold or silver color (chrome paint works well if you like a very bright, shiny appearance). Once the paint has dried, I thread a pretty scarlet ribbon through the hole and hang the utensil on our holiday tree (always keeping sharp edges and points away from the little ones) or use them to decorate wreaths for the kitchen (adding real pomegranates, lady apples, and citrus for an all-encompassing food theme).

- Use your better-quality knives, forks, and spoons (they needn't match) on your table as attractive serving ware. If you have a large enough collection of un-matched pieces to create several place settings, polish them to a high gleam (store them in resealable plastic bags to keep them shiny for a longer period) and use them at your next dinner party. Or surprise your family by serving an ordinary meal using your favorite silver pieces. For many years we used our own collection of mismatched flatware on a daily basis.

- I often add my prettiest knives and spoons to my Gift Pantry. Silver or silver-plated knives are polished to a high gleam, tied with a French ribbon, netting, or strands of raffia, and given away with home-baked breads, homemade jams and jellies, and/or herb butters freshly made and offered in ceramic crocks. Spoons, treated in the same manner, are often tied to jars of homemade jam or jelly, or as an accom-paniment to teacups and coffee mugs.

- If you wish to create an elegant picnic basket for yourself or to give as a gift, at-tractive flatware is a charming addition: Collect and polish place settings for two or four (depending upon the size of the basket) along with a set of attractive vin-tage plates, and coordinating cloth napkins and tablecloth (vintage look lovely, and are in keeping with the antique theme).

- Make architectural statements using your most beautiful pieces of antique flat-ware. Cross two spoons and wire these together—cover the wire with raffia or rib-bon—and secure them above or on your kitchen door, or over a window, as you would a piece of architectural salvage. You may wish to paint a thin layer of clear lacquer over well-polished silverware in order to prevent tarnish. (Do this only with less valuable pieces, as lacquer must be removed by soaking with acetone, and acetone may damage silver. Never eat from lacquered flatware.)

Winter Tokens and Traditions

"An outward and visible sign of an inward and spiritual grace."
—THE BOOK OF COMMON PRAYER

In ancient times, denizens of Scandinavian and North German countries saw the first snowfall of the winter as heralding the season of feasting and drinking. Today, during the holiday season, we find that our modern grocery markets are laden with traditional holiday foods—dressed with evergreens and ribbon rosettes, they serve to remind us of past times and traditions. With such well-laden tables it would seem there could be room for no more. Still, it may be worth making the space for an attractive centerpiece you have created. You may do this by stacking tiered cake plates in graduated sizes, and lining them generously with small sprigs of evergreen. Doing this enhances even the humblest of foods, and imparts an elegant look to your table. On the topmost plate, place a pretty drinking glass containing a small bouquet of flowers from your florist, or winter greens and berries from your garden.

- Extend a gift to your community by decorating your home on the outside. Celebrating the holiday season in this manner says "Happy Holidays" to everyone who passes by. Looping garlands of birdseed along an evergreen is a thoughtful winter treat for your winged friends. And remember to present a decoration to someone who would not normally trouble themselves, but would appreciate the gift given, and the time spent.

- If you are entertaining, set out an attractive tray or basket filled with small wrapped gifts for your guests. May I suggest the following: small picture frames; holiday ornaments; special gifts of food; packages of fresh greenery (such as miniature rosemary or ivy wreaths, or small swags); dried herbs or potpourri; or a homemade mix of three-bean soup. You may also wish to present them with the recipes for the meal you have served. These may be handwritten or made up on the computer. Roll each recipe page into a scroll, tie with a festive holiday ribbon, and store in an attractive basket until it is time to distribute them. At the end of the evening offer your guests a parting gift from the tray and/or basket.

- Spend an afternoon writing Christmas cards for an elderly friend who may be unable to write out his or her own correspondence. Afterward take the friend for a drive around the neighborhood to look at holiday decorations and lights. With your heart in the proper place, the possibilities are endless.

- Remember to take advantage of the mood-altering effects of music. I listen to Christmas music throughout the year—whenever I need an uplifting moment, holiday music provides the necessary spark that transforms my mood from glum to glad.

- Spend January dreaming of gentler months ahead, and nurturing the new year by way of plans and dreams. Set aside a quiet time to concentrate on marking your calendar with all of the enticing ideas and resolutions you have set for each upcoming season. Record all of your quintessential pleasures and unique ideas, then savor and implement them all year through.

- Create tradition. The winter festivals seem to be the time of year in which our hearts seem most hungry for the reassurance of tradition. It is a comfort to know that *some* things will never change. In a sometimes frenzied modern world, traditions are the things that can keep us sane—adding that much-needed continuity that threads one year to the next. Special ways in which to celebrate a holiday, the warmth of home, aromas from the kitchen, certain kinds of foods, music, and even a specific style of wrapping and presenting gifts, can conjure a variety of very good thoughts, provoking childhood fantasies as well as memories.

The Joy of the Winter Table

". . . to the general joy of the whole table."
—WILLIAM SHAKESPEARE

There is something about winter feasting that alludes to mystery as well as celebration. And while this is generally a joyful time of year when family comes home and relatives gather, the season can also become a bit overwhelming for those in charge of households and, more specifically, kitchens.

A festive dinner and a great meal can come merely from the presence of well-cooked food, presented attractively, composed of a few items that are unique for the season (ice cream and sorbet are frugal luxuries in summer, as fresh fruits are in winter), and/or favorite ingredients of the particular diners.

The kitchen is often referred to as the soul of the home. Yet in winter, more than at other times of the year, the kitchen embodies much of the soul of the *season*. A gifted host or hostess knows that hospitality consists of more than making an attractive table and preparing meals. It is the ability to make family feel like guests, and guests feel like family, that will bring ease, welcome, and comfort to all who sit at his or her table. The following suggestions are designed to help you do just that.

- Serve food of love. Despite myriad recipes in modern magazines and cookbooks, most people do not want something *too* different from the traditional fare of the culture or country to which they belong. For example, America has the traditional turkey, but the original Christmas bird, British lore tells us, was the goose, and sometimes even the swan. Throughout much of Europe, the traditional Christmas feast features a pork entrée.

- The old Anglo-Saxon word for wassail was *wes-hâl,* or "be whole." Enjoy a modern-day version of the Christmas wassail bowl using mulled or spiced cider, warmed with sugar and spices. The old wassail bowls were usually made of silver or pewter, and were immense. If you don't possess your own wassail bowl, substitute a large, clear glass salad or punch bowl, and use an attractive silver dipper to serve forth your brew.

- It was an old European tradition that every person in the household should stir the Christmas pudding and make a wish, and that some "answers" to the ever-present question of what the future held would be garnered from the pudding as well. How? Placed into the pudding before it was cooked were tiny trinkets of silver: a coin foretold riches; a thimble warned that someone would remain an old maid; a button indicated a bachelor; a wedding ring promised marriage. Each of these portents pertained to whoever received that specific trinket in their portion of the cooked pudding. (The old saying "the proof is in the pudding" most likely was derived from this practice.) Today, it is customary to put a coin or trinket into the batter of a Christmas cake (make certain it is of a size that is too large to choke on or bite into). The person who is served the trinket is considered to have good luck for the coming year. Fanciful activities such as these, especially in more humble abodes, enliven the holiday with very little effort, money, or time.

- Every country boasts of a traditional Christmas cake. The French bake large flat "cakes of the three kings" for Epiphany and, for Christmas, miniature cakes called *naulets,* shaped like the Holy Child, are often given as gifts. In old-time Germany many believed that loaves of bread baked at Christmas held magical powers if the dough was moistened with the dew of Christmas night. Serve your own holiday breads in an elevated fashion. Placed upon attractive pedestaled cake plates the holiday bread at your house will take a place of honor.

Pedestaled in Triumph

"Why comes temptation, but for man to meet
... And so be pedestaled in triumph?"
—ROBERT BROWNING

Footed serving plates are one of my frugal luxuries. I can think of no finer way in which to showcase simple foods to perfection. I collect and use these pedestaled wonders to highlight both the humble and the grand.

- One tried-and-true trick I sometimes use to fill out a less-than-abundant buffet table is an abundance of sandwiches, carefully cut into small triangles and stacked pyramid-style, atop a doily-lined cake plate.

- I also use these artful devices to arrange and serve chunks of hard cheeses, salami, and crackers (rest these on gentle tufts of romaine lettuce or fresh herbs).

- Our daily breads may benefit from similar treatment. I cannot tell you how many times I have served simple muffins; sliced soda breads; humble buttermilk biscuits; triangles of just-baked bread spread with sweet, herbed butter; or old-fashioned cinnamon toast on my favorite footed cake plate.

- So diverse are these footed wonders, I can put them to work elevating simple serving bowls filled with soups and sauces (doing this adds dimension to your table setting).

- In my mania for serving foods in an elevated fashion, I have been known to turn sturdy, wide-based wineglasses or crystal candleholders upside down and use the bottoms as a serving surface. Be certain that your glasses or candleholders are properly proportioned so that your new invention will not be top-heavy and tip over. I use these to present a single cupcake, one beautifully decorated cookie, or to showcase a very tiny bouquet of flowers and herbs.

Illuminated Fragments
Become Indebted to the Common Life

*"A grateful mind
By owing owes not, but still pays, at once
Indebted and discharged."*
—JOHN MILTON

I once read that the human race can be divided, roughly, into two groups: those who think they are giving more than they get, and those who think they are getting more than they give. The first kind are always speaking about the sacrifices and gifts they make, and how burdensome life and people can be. The second group feel indebted to the common life, and set their lives and minds to seeing goodness in even the smallest blessing. These people recall how long they have been on the receiving end of life's bounty. Their minds will rummage among their memories and uncover the many forgotten reasons for gratitude. The secret to untangling life's knotted threads is to know which group you belong to, and—should you belong to the first group—decide if you want to remain a member.

If you continually believe the world is your enemy, it will become so. If you are constantly thinking that others are cheating you, the belief itself cheats you out of many possible friendships and, more importantly, peace of mind. Conversely, you become free from this fretfulness if you concern yourself with cultivating a deep spirit of appreciation for what your life currently offers you. As a result, you may discover that you have been granted a type of immunity to uneasiness.

Chapter 17

Christmas: A Time of Grace

~

"Some say that ever 'gainst that season comes
Wherein our Savior's birth is celebrated,
The bird of dawning singeth all night long;
And then, they say, no spirit can walk abroad;
The nights are wholesome; then no planets strike,
No fairy takes, nor witch hath power to charm,
So hallow'd and so gracious is the time."

—WILLIAM SHAKESPEARE

The Wondrous Circle of Christmas

"The circle of our Christmas associations and the lessons that they bring, expands!
Let us welcome every one of them and
Summon them to take their place by the Christmas hearth."

—CHARLES DICKENS

Christianity holds the belief that both the material and the spiritual were created by God. It is no surprise then—in a religion that views humankind as a fusion of the tangible and the intangible—to discover that one of its most honored holidays celebrates the concept that a spirit (God) took a material form (the Christ). The noble purpose of this incarnation? The redemption of mankind.

Throughout most of the two thousand years since the birth of Christ, Christmas has been celebrated (for the most part) with both serious spirituality and festive jubilance. Abstract notions such as the Incarnation and the Nativity have kindled such joy in the hearts of Christian believers that, throughout history, they have sought natural things to convey the supernatural. Used in moderation, these physical *things* symbolize entirely abstract ideas, and make them come to life.

Degrees of Celebration

" . . . That is best which is capable of producing the greatest degree of happiness . . ."
—GEORGE MASON

Just as each of you has chosen your own unique style of frugal wisdom and practices, you may also choose to what degree you wish to implement the art of celebrating Christmas. Joy is found in the fact that each year need not mirror the last. Your choices may reflect your current attitude, your financial situation, or both. Regardless of the circumstances that guide your decision, the realization that *you hold the power to choose* how you will celebrate the holiday will free you from the frenzied pace that tends to hover over us at this time of year.

I have experienced lavish holidays during which I enjoyed decorating each nook and cranny of our home—setting out visible evidence of my passion for festivity. The fresh evergreen wreaths (in which I tucked ruby red roses, set in small water-filled vials) that graced each window of the house were only the beginning of my endeavors. Each gift I presented had been thought out, purchased or carefully created, perfectly packaged, and ceremoniously delivered. I happily expended tremendous amounts of energy to celebrate every facet of the holiday season in such a detailed fashion.

Still, as Shakespeare reminds us, "What are we if not human?" Some years present larger than usual limitations on what you can accomplish, such as restraints on time, energy, enthusiasm, or finances. But even during less lavish celebrations I continue to moderately decorate the house and give gifts. However, the decorations are few and well chosen; the gifts practical (often in the form of money, gift certificates, or items ordered from a catalog) and humbly packaged. (I often succumb to my youngest daughter Rosie's pleas to let her help wrap them. Her small hands jubilantly perform this task and the results are often charming imperfections.) Should *you* wish to celebrate more simply, it is perfectly permissible for you to say, "This Christmas we will be doing things a bit differently from last season." Once this announcement has been made (and the children, and other family members, are assured that you haven't identified too strongly with Ebenezer Scrooge) you may feel that a tremendous pressure has been lifted from you. Consequently, you might discover that you find a renewed joy in the seasonal tasks that you *are* performing. Why? Possibly because you do not feel quite so obligated to perform them.

The material things of this world, when used properly, are good, and are indeed gifts from God. This is one of the most important reasons that we celebrate at Christmas. Yet, there is a time for temperance and a time for luxury (and a time to blend the two). You must remember that you have the power, and the responsibility, to choose the degree of celebration that is right for you and your family at this particular season of your life. Keep in mind, however, that lifestyles, attitudes, and circumstances can change over time. You may peacefully, without remorse, alternate your celebrating style from one year to the next.

How to Kindle Christmas

"Truths kindle light for truths."
—LUCRETIUS

"Happiness is a sort of atmosphere you can live in," notes the writer Adela Rogers St. Johns, and I can think of no festival that encourages us to devote ourselves to creating an attractive, happy atmosphere as much as Christmas.

The decorating of houses, as part of winter festivals, harkens back to antiquity. In the years before the rise of Christianity, the second half of December was the time of several pagan celebrations. In ancient Rome, Saturnalia, which began on December 17 and lasted until December 23, was dedicated to the god Saturn. In northern Europe the winter solstice, which included the Festival of Yule, began on December 21. And December 25 was considered by the ancient Romans to be the birth date of the Unconquered Sun (*Sol Invictus*). Such occasions were very deeply ingrained in the lives of the people and were retained by the common folk—even long after Christianity became a major influence. In response, the early church chose to absorb and transform this season of the year by Christianizing it.

The second-century church teacher Clement of Alexandria recorded what earlier teachers believed—that Jesus was born on either December 25 or January 6. Therefore, the original purpose for celebrating on the date of December 25 (*Sol Invictus*) was changed, so that it imparted Christian beliefs. Thus the familiar order of life was not altered; only the meaning and emphasis of the various festivals were changed. In this way, Christians sought to capture the worthy aspects of the old cultures. Thus, certain things that we now associate with Christmas are actually older than Christianity. These ancient traditions have become akin to vessels whose contents have been transformed.

A Kindlier Hand

"Ring in the nobler modes of life
With sweeter manner, purer laws . . .
The larger heart, the kindlier hand . . ."

—ALFRED, LORD TENNYSON

The use of evergreens as Christmas decorations is a prime example of the use of pagan symbols in our contemporary traditions. Long before the advent of Christianity, evergreen boughs and wreaths were used as winter adornments. It was a pagan custom of Norse origin to beautify dwellings with pine branches, ivy, and holly in the winter. They imagined that these plants possessed some form of magic power because of their ability to retain their green leaves, even in the harshest northern snow and cold. And a species that brought forth its fruit at this time of year, such as holly, amazed them even more.

Saint Gregory the Great of Rome encouraged his clergy in mission lands to adopt (whenever possible) local customs, and to reinterpret them with Christian influence. For example, holly was lovely when made into garlands that embellished public buildings and private homes during the winter season. Thus, the holly leaves, with their sharp points, came to symbolize the crown of thorns, while the red of the holly berry evolved into the symbol of the blood of Christ.

In the days of America's founding fathers, colonists decorated their fireplace mantels (and other areas in and around their homes) with bountiful displays of evergreens gathered from the local woods. Although country folk often did not have the money or time to spend on ornate or exotic details, they used nature's gifts bountifully. Gathering aromatic greens, they mixed them with colorful fruits (such as apples and squash borrowed from their fruit cellars or attics). They also added colored, air-dried flowers that had been preserved during warmer seasons (yellow yarrow and cockscomb being favorites). These simple supplies were fashioned into all manner of adornment, and were used to transform cold rooms into festive havens during winter's stormy months.

Nature offers us bountiful greens to enjoy and display throughout each season. As a wise and frugal decorator you should gather whatever greenery is inexpensively, and easily, available to you. Use nature's gracious gifts to garnish your home and hearth throughout the year—particularly during the winter season. In so doing, you will discover (especially when snow drifts heighten during the coldest winter days) that a crackling, hearty fire and the scent of evergreens have the ability to comfort the soul.

Garmenting Trees for Celebration

"Put on her garments of gladness."
—Judith 10:3

No outward decorative symbol is so essential to modern Christmas as the evergreen tree. Yet, the origin of the modern Christmas tree is rooted in fourteenth-century German customs. At that time, the German people celebrated the feast of Adam and Eve on December 24, by staging what was called a "Miracle Play." The decorations for this event included a fir ("Paradise") tree, hung with apples to symbolize the forbidden fruit in the Garden of Eden. It was primarily due to this custom that the evergreen tree eventually acquired the name *Christbaum*, literally "Christ-tree," and later transmuted into the English *Christmas tree.*

Jeweled Branches

"Choose wisely then, each ornament and frosted tinsel skein
For branches that have worn jewels of gleaming mountain rain."
—Elizabeth-Ellan Long

Today, the Christmas tree, sparkling with tiny lights and artful ornamentation, is the prettiest sign of Christmas. The manner in which you decorate your tree can set the mood for your entire holiday. The tone may range from charmingly romantic to whimsically amusing, or prettily formal. If your family is at all like ours, however, you have probably been acquiring a variety of Christmas tree ornaments for many years. Although it is exciting to each year bring them from their boxes, there may come a Christmas when you wish to try something entirely new. When this occurs you may enjoy developing a theme for your holiday tree.

Planning a theme tree can be creative and fun for your entire family, and can make a simple tree seem more special. First and foremost you must decide what theme you wish to follow. Do this by deciding what activities you and your family enjoy, or look around your home to see what sort of objects and materials are easily and inexpensively available to you. Keep in mind the general style of your home. If the room you plan to put your tree in has a particular look you may either follow that look as your theme or provide a contrast to it. To give your imagination a starting point, here are a few ideas for garmenting celebratory trees:

Floral Motif Use a selection of dried flowers tucked into the tree, or tied into little bouquets and hung among the branches. The generous use of fresh, or preserved, tufts of white baby's breath throughout the tree adds a touch of delicacy, and lends an air of romance. You may include other accoutrements, such as garlands, bows, or ornaments, that carry through your floral theme. I have glued dried rosebuds from my summer garden onto the center of large raffia bows and used these to embellish our holiday tree (these look pretty on packages as well).

Melody Tree William Shakespeare tells us that "if music be the food of love, play on." Celebrate a love of music by covering your tree with scrolls and full pages of sheet music. (Photocopy vintage sheet music, roll it into a scroll, and tie it closed with red or gold satin ribbons. Or leave the paper flat and attach the sheets to the tree with a ribbon threaded through a corner.) Add miniature instruments, and wrap small gift boxes in the same style of photocopied sheet music. Place these inside the branches of the tree. You might also roll the sheets into cones with red ribbon handles, and fill the cones with bouquets of dried flowers, small gifts, or candies. Use additional red or gold ribbon to garland the tree, as well as to tie onto branches in simple bows.

Natural Wonders Embellish the prettiest fresh tree you can find with pinecones, fresh or dried fruits, herb bundles, seed pods, and thick garlands of inexpensive raffia threaded among the branches, or tied into several large bows. As a finishing touch—and as a useful filler for hiding bare spots—add clusters of dried hydrangea blossoms tucked throughout the tree's boughs. (Use white and gold spray paint if blossoms are discolored once they have dried.) Add tiny all-white lights.

Memory Tree Capture family memories by transforming small, sentimental items into ornaments. We have used our children's smaller, outgrown toys to easily achieve this effect. Clancy's wooden toy soldiers, Katie's miniature woolen teddy bears, and Rosie's baby rattles, plus a hodgepodge of silver-plated baby banks and drinking cups, very tiny baby booties and bonnets (hand-knit by their great-great-aunt Evelyn), and several wallet-size (about two inches square) silver-plated picture frames (purchased from a discount store) with family pictures inside are all perfect ornaments. A few picture frames can also hold fabric relics from cherished childhood blankets, dresses, and cloth toys, giving each child special sentimental reminders of their youngest years. We surrounded this memory tree with the classic American Flyer diesel toy train Mike and I purchased for Clancy on his second birthday.

Wee Trees Unlike most theme trees, this tree is for the children to decorate on their own. My husband and I put tiny, twinkling, multicolored lights onto a small, fresh evergreen tree. The children then add the paper chains and foil-paper snowflakes they have created during the weeks beforehand, as well as tiny baskets, favorite teddy bears, and other small toys. Cookies and candies are also hung from the tree with raffia bows. And finally, strands of computer-paper lace serve as snow white garlands. As an adjunct to the family tree, wee trees (live or artificial) can be placed in your children's bedrooms.

The Giving Tree   You may wish to decorate your tree with the old-fashioned method of placing gifts *inside* the branches as well as beneath it, as Victorian-era Americans were fond of doing. Or, take this tradition one step further: Wrap and hang or tie an assortment of tiny gift-filled boxes onto your tree. You may also wish to create little gift sacks (similar to the type of pouches jewelers use) from wide strands of ribbon such as grosgrain, satin, or chiffon. (These are easily made by cutting ribbon into 12-, 10-, or 8-inch lengths; folding the ribbon at the midsection; and stitching up the sides.) Tie the tops of the gift sacks with pretty ribbon, cord, or lace. Give the top edges a finished look by cutting with pinking sheers, hemming, or using a commercial no-fray product.

The Language of Nature

*"To him who in the love of Nature holds
Communion with her visible forms, she speaks
A various language."*
—William Cullen Bryant

The symbolism and beauty of traditional greens are a welcome gift in any season, yet they are especially treasured during the winter months as you endeavor to "deck the halls." Henry David Thoreau once observed that "heaven is under our feet as well as above our heads." If you take a walk in your own garden and woods you may be surprised at the beautiful, frugal bounty available to you. In your own backyard you may find traditional, and unusual, greenery that will allow you to easily and inexpensively dress your home for the holidays (and other festive occasions).

Rosemary   Rosemary is a symbol of remembrance, and is said to have once had only white flowers. There is an ancient tale relating that, during the flight to Egypt, the Holy Family stopped for a rest. Mary took off her blue cloak to rinse it in a running brook. She spread it over the branches of a flowering rosemary shrub in order to dry. When she removed her cloak it had acquired the delicate aroma of the herb, and the tiny white flowers had transformed to blue. I cannot help but think of this magical tale whenever I harvest rosemary branches from my father's garden. I use these fragrant boughs to construct aromatic wreaths in a variety of sizes, to use as wall hangings, centerpieces, garlands, and gifts.

The Bay Laurel   The bay laurel (a.k.a. bay leaf) dates back to ancient Rome as a symbol of glory. I have often purchased dried bay leaves (in bulk) and used them as tags for gifts (I write on them with a special gold pen bought at a stationery or craft supply store). I have often transformed plain, craft-paper packages by gluing laurel leaves onto the top of the package, in a heart or wreath shape (if time permits, I will first spray-paint the leaves gold, silver, or copper) topping with a generous bow of raffia at the center.

Ivy   Ivy, one of my favorite plants, is an ancient symbol of dependence and fidelity. I use it lavishly when decorating. I have twined ivy into wreaths to hang on doors and walls, and used miniature ivy wreaths on the Christmas tree, or as napkin holders. Ivy is also a wonderful addition to a buffet table. Arrange clean vines artfully around important dishes such as the punch bowl and the meat platter, or add them to simple bouquets of flowers, ferns, and herbs, for an especially elegant effect.

The Cherry Blossom   The cherry blossom has long symbolized knowledge and wisdom. In some parts of eastern Europe a holiday custom advocates gathering small cherry branches indoors at the beginning of advent. Placed in water, they will often bloom with lovely blossoms by Christmas Day. An ancient superstition from the same region allows that if a single woman tends a cherry sprig, and it blossoms on Christmas Eve, she will be wed in the next year.

THAT ANCIENT AROMA OF CHRISTMAS

"At Christmas I no more desire a rose
Than wish a snow in May's newfangled mirth;
But like of each thing that in season grows."

—WILLIAM SHAKESPEARE

The aromas of cinnamon, cloves, and other spices have been associated with this gracious time for centuries. What better way to impart the spirit of the holidays to yourself, your family, and friends who visit your home than by cultivating the scents of the season. Here is a recipe I devised to simmer on my stove during the holidays, when I am too busy to bake.

> 3 teaspoons ground allspice
> 4 full-size cinnamon sticks (or 8 to 10 tablespoons ground cinnamon, available, and quite reasonably priced, at warehouse stores or health food stores that sell it in bulk)
> 10 to 20 whole cloves
> 1 fresh ginger root (about 3 inches long, grated) or 2 heaping tablespoons of ground ginger

Mingle these spices well, then pour them into a rarely used teakettle, an attractive pot, or a Crock-Pot. Add a quart of water and bring to a very gentle boil. Turn the heat to a low simmer and your home will be infused with the inspiring scents of Christmas. Add water as needed, and be careful to never allow the pot to simmer until it is dry.

While you are composing your medley of delightful scents you may wish to make a few extra batches to include in your gift baskets, or as hostess gifts (use only dried ginger in these). Package this mixture in small apothecary jars or cellophane candy bags (secure the bags with a rubber band around the top and conceal this with an attractive ribbon and card).

Note: This mixture is not for consumption, and should not be left unattended when simmering.

෯

Terrestrial Little Things

"We find great things are made of little things.
And little things go lessening till at last
Comes God behind them."

—Robert Browning

While you are trimming trees and wreathing evergreens, also take the time to reflect upon your life, your goals, and your blessings. Appreciate what you possess and make a silent vow to improve tangible and intangible areas of your life, and your character. These small acts can richly enhance your joy of living.

Decking the halls for the winter is in itself an act of generosity and love. It is by consistent, small, considerate actions that you can elevate the season's pleasures beyond the realm of obligation. The following suggestions are designed to inspire you. They offer unique and creative ways in which you may inexpensively dress your home for Christmas, thus extending to family and friends visible evidence of your caring.

Enhancing a Little   Make a small tree seem much larger by setting it atop a trunk or a table, to give it height. Drape a floor-length tablecloth over the table before situating the tree, then use the remaining area of the tabletop to set gifts upon. Surround the floor around the tree-laden table with various sizes and shapes of attractive baskets, prop open an antique trunk, or display a doll's stroller (one year we placed our antique wicker bassinet near the tree as part of our holiday decorating). Use these vessels to display a stuffed bear or doll collection; to collect an overflow of presents; and/or to hold a bounty of dried flowers or pinecones. A child's chair, or attractive doll furniture, placed nearby, with a doll or stuffed bear nestled in it (and dressed for the holidays) is another whimsical touch that allows a little to seem like more.

Collecting Cutters   I've been collecting cookie cutters for over a dozen years; I find these to be fun, frugal, and useful items. Throughout the year I purchase them new, often at sale prices, or vintage at yard sales, thrift shops, and flea markets. Needless to say, I have an overabundance of them. So, during the holidays, I often choose my favorite cookie cutters and, using ribbon, hang them from the tree as ornaments. I have also been known to dangle a small collection of my prettiest cutters from tiny cup hooks placed on the inside of my wood window trim.

Mason Lights   A collection of old mason canning jars, especially tinted ones, filled with sand (about a quarter to a third full depending upon the size of your candle and jar) in which you have placed a votive candle can embellish the holiday mood. Place this collection on your windowsill, on the fireplace mantel, or in the center of your table. Leave the lid off (perhaps propped against the side of the jar) and enjoy the glow of candlelight. Or you can combine tinted and/or clear mason jars (perhaps in graduating sizes) and loosely fill them up with a curled strand of tiny white Christmas lights (electric or battery operated). Embellish the rims of select jars with raffia, or tulle bows, and enjoy the lovely results.

Tip of the Pinecone   Before using pinecones to decorate you may wish to place them on a cookie sheet, in a warm oven (about 250°) for about an hour. The heat will cause the cones to "blossom" and thus open more fully. (And the scent is enhanced as well—at least while they are warm.)

Extraordinary Ornaments   Ornaments are not only for your tree. Use them to spice up gift packages, to hang on doorknobs, as window-shade pulls, as place cards at a party, or pile an old collection in a clear glass vase, or on a cake plate, to display as a centerpiece.

Adorning Books   Adorn your holiday home with attractive vintage books. Think of books as art objects and display them as you would your favorite collectibles. Wrap a group of three with attractive ribbon, as you would a gift. If they are of no further use as books (perhaps damaged or outdated), spray the covers with gold, silver, or white spray paint and wrap with ribbon. Use these as a pedestal-type base on which to display flowers, baskets, ceramic figurines of angels, and the like.

Nature's Bounty   If you live in a warm climate as we do, you may find that the leaves from most citrus and eucalyptus trees are lovely and fragrant at this time of year. These types of leaves hold up quite well—looking lovely even after several weeks. Trace a mantel, outline a doorway, and thread or curve these gifts of nature into circles of celebration.

Festive Teacups   I enhance my lovingly collected treasures with the blessings of nature from my garden, the produce department at the grocery store, or clippings

garnered from neighboring trees and shrubs (always with permission). Occasionally I secure my most festive teacups onto garlands that surround windows and doorways, by threading a sturdy, attractive ribbon through the cup handles, and tying them firmly onto a well-supported portion of the garland. I have yet to lose one to breakage, but several have been commandeered by friends who fell in love with a particular design. If you are reluctant to risk your good cups in this manner, consider acquiring attractive teacups of lesser quality or value (such as those with hairline cracks or small chips) exclusively for this purpose. You may also embellish holiday trees in a like manner, and holiday wreaths look enchanting with child-size china teacups attached to them.

Fruits of the Season Bowls of fresh fruits and nuts—lemons, limes, oranges, pomegranates, apples, pecans, walnuts—are lovely holiday statements. Place fruits in your most attractive bowls in strategic areas of your home—perhaps inserting a sprig of rosemary or pine as an embellishment. If your house doesn't get overly warm in winter, the fruit should last for at least two weeks (be sure to choose only the freshest, unblemished fruits for this job—and check periodically and remove any moisture in the bottom of the bowls). After the holidays have passed you may wish to use the fruit and nuts in baking and cooking. Commercially freeze-dried or dehydrated fruits are available as well. These are much lighter in weight than fresh fruit (and are *not* edible), and may be reused for several years; however, they are much more expensive. You may also slice and dry apples, oranges, and other citrus fruits. These dried fruits are lovely as tree ornaments or to enhance a homemade potpourri.

Rustic Skirts For a rustic, old-time effect, drape an old quilt—not a valuable one—around the base of your tree instead of using a tree skirt. Or use tablecloths, bedcovers, and curtains that have irreparable damage or stains on them. Just pleat the cloth to hide the damaged areas as you wind it around the base of your tree. To make a more whimsical statement, I have used a very ruffled, layered, vintage petticoat as a (literal) tree skirt. Ours had an elastic waistband, and was easily slipped under the bottom of the tree before we decorated it.

Prisms of Light Ever since I saw the movie *Pollyanna* years and years ago, in which the title character opens the heart of a bitter old woman by showing her the magic of rainbows inside chandelier glass, I have been a collector of crystal chandelier prisms. I often take them from dilapidated light fixtures found at yard sales and flea markets. Cleaned and sparkling, these make lovely additions to your holiday tree, imparting the look of sparkling icicles. When the light catches the crystals they cast tiny rainbows throughout the room.

Paper Ornaments Last year I found some very attractive heart-shaped notepads. Each paper was embellished with roses and ivy. So infatuated was I with their motif that I decided to find a way to hang them on my holiday tree as ornaments. I easily reinforced them by sandwiching two pieces of notepaper over a thin layer of cardboard. While I was watching a favorite movie classic, I cut two dozen heart shapes out of card stock (I recycled the backs of old greeting cards for this purpose, using a piece of the notepaper as my template). Next, I glued one notepaper onto each side of the heart with a glue stick. Using a small paper-punch, I made a hole at the top of each heart in which to loop a piece of ribbon for hanging. The results were, for under four dollars and an hour and a half of my time, a unique set of pretty ornaments for the tree.

Enhancing Early Light:
Creating a Pierced Tin Lantern

"There was a time when meadow, grove, and stream,
The earth, and every common sight,
To me did seem
Appareled in celestial light . . ."
—William Wordsworth

Before the advent of electricity or the modern flashlight, many American settlers used lanterns created by piercing designs into pieces of tin, and setting sturdy candles inside. The patterns on the tin lantern would cast out uniquely shaped shafts of light. Neighbors often identified one another by the unique designs punched into the family lantern. This lantern was a necessity indoors as well as out, and many a chore was accomplished by the light from lamps such as these.

You may create your own decorative lantern, much like those the early American tinsmiths made, by recycling a clean tin can of any size.

> Clean tin can (any size will do)
> Hammer and pliers
> Tap water and freezer
> Sturdy nail (in the size you wish your perforations to be)
> Old towels
> Heat-proof plate
> Sturdy candle

Smooth down any sharp edges at the top of the can by turning them under with the pliers. Fill the can with water, and freeze until water has turned into solid ice.

Fold an old towel to make a nice, thick cushion and lay it on the floor (you may want to do this job in the garage, or out of doors, in order to protect your flooring). Place the can (with ice still inside) on its side, on top of the towel.

Use your hammer and nail to punch holes in the can, making a design as you go. (If your design is more complex than, say, an asterisk, you might wish to first draw the design onto the can itself, using a marking pen.) Repeat your pattern on all sides of the can, leaving about a half inch of unperforated area around the bottom so that wax will not drip from the holes.

Place your pierced lantern in the sink and allow the ice to melt. When the ice has melted, dry the can thoroughly.

Set a short, thick candle into the lantern after dripping a bit of melted wax onto the bottom to keep your candle in place.

Set your lantern on a heat-proof plate, and enjoy the flickering design.

If you are feeling exceedingly creative or ambitious, you may design and make several of these lanterns and use them to line your walkway in much the same manner as luminaries are used. A successful alternative is to use metal cheese graters. Center a votive candle on a heat-proof plate (wide enough for a food grater to sit on at an even level). Place a metal cheese grater over the candle. You may embellish the handle of the grater with a heat-proof ribbon or bow. These makeshift lanterns cast wonderful patterns of glowing light.

ॐ

Candlelit Graces

"Then be ye glad, good people, this night of all the year,
And light ye up your candles, for His star it shineth clear."

—OLD CHRISTMAS CAROL

Throughout history, light has been identified as a symbol of good—of knowledge and understanding. The Jewish Sabbath observance begins with the ritual lighting of candles by the woman of the house. This is a reminder that light was one of the first acts of creation. The Sabbath ends with the man of the house spreading his hands toward a lighted candle, as if longing for it, and saying a prayer. Early Christians had a custom of saying a blessing when the household lamps were lit: "Praise God who sends us the light of heaven." Yule candles used long ago in England and France were so large that holes were chiseled into the stone floors in order to serve as holders. Christmas dinner lasted until the candles had burned completely.

In some Christian churches there is a Candlemas service. Our family attended one such service last Christmas Eve. As the worshipers entered, each was given an unlighted candle. At the close of the service, the priest lit one candle from the altar. The servers then lighted their candles from his, and carried them to the congregation. In turn, this person lighted the next person's until, wick by wick, candle by candle, the entire church was filled with the luminescent glow of candlelight. It felt to me that this gentle light radiated not only to the walls of this church but far beyond. The glow, however, was not the tangible one wrought by candles. It was, instead, akin to a mysterious, *intangible* light—waxing strong and piercing the darkness of the world's night. When reflecting on this rare experience I cannot help but think of a quote from the wonderful writer Rumer Godden, who wryly noted that "candles, like angels, have the oddest disguises."

Illuminated Fragments
· *Patience*

*"Patience is the guardian of faith, the preserver of peace,
the cherisher of love, the teacher of humility."*
—L. W. YAGGY

If I had to possess only one virtue I would find it hard to choose between patience and faith. Still, isn't patience an irrevocable necessity for faith? And (please tell me I am not alone in this) doesn't it seem that we find ourselves requiring the quality of patience more often than the other virtues? Patience is a shield with which you can defend yourself; it's a guardian of faith, a strengthener of character, and the conservator of happiness and home peace.

Examples of patience are found throughout nature. The fruits of a garden take months in their growth and perfection. Waters patiently erode flatlands into majestic canyons and, as Granville Sharpe observed, "slowly deposit their rich alluvial soil at river's end." A human being takes many years to grow from infancy to adulthood. And the richest, most enduring relationships are those built on the foundation of time.

I find it intriguing that patience has sometimes been defined as "genius." The success of many great people has often been attributed to their having possessed the power of patience. They were satisfied to work diligently (with a goal in mind), waiting for the results with patience and faith. "Courage and industry," noted Granville Sharpe, "[might] have sunk in despair, and the world [might] have remained unimproved and unornamented if men had merely compared the effect of a single stroke of the chisel with the pyramid to be raised, or of a single impression of the spade with mountains to be leveled."

Those people who have not chosen to cultivate this characteristic, even to a small degree, are impoverished. For without patience the petty annoyances of life will drop you into despair and irritation. In turn, these will lead the impatient person into a life of prolonged restlessness and uneasy thoughts. For patience comforts us in poverty and moderates us in prosperity. She teaches us to be cheerful in the face of adversity as well as to forgive those who have caused us injury. Patience adds an otherworldly beauty to the person who cultivates and possesses it. And the home in which patience is nurtured and practiced will possess the most valuable adornment of all . . . serenity.

Chapter 18

The Winter Gift Pantry

~

"I am in the habit of looking not so much to the nature of a gift as to the spirit in which it is offered."

—Robert Louis Stevenson

Blessed "No"

"Blessed is he who has found his work; let him ask no other blessedness."
—Thomas Carlyle

Each of us tries to do more than we should during the holiday season. To stay stress-free, and allow time for those projects you truly enjoy, you must learn to say no. Choose activities that you really wish to indulge in and do only these. If you love creating gifts and decorating the house, as I do, do so to your heart's content. However, it is okay to buy a cake mix, or use refrigerator cookie dough, or buy pumpkin pies (if your budget permits) in order to save precious time—using it to savor the season in a relaxing fashion.

The holiday season is more than just a time for shopping madly; it is a time when, through the act of sharing, we gain much more than we give. Any gift that is well considered, regardless of expense, is a grace not only to the recipient, but to the giver as well. "The excellence of the gift," noted Charles Dudley Warner, "lies in its appropriateness rather than its value."

Faithful Budgeting

"He that is faithful in that which is least is faithful also in much . . ."
—LUKE 16:10

The calends of January, a pre-Christian winter festival, was celebrated by the ancient Romans during the first three days of the year (immediately after the Saturnalia). This holiday, full of omens and portents for the future was (much like our modern Christmas) celebrated with evergreens and lights. It was also the precursor to the modern-day custom of gift-giving during the holidays. Ancient writings tell us that tables everywhere were well laden; luxurious abundance was found in the houses of the rich, and in the houses of the poor better food than usual was put upon the table. The impulse to spend seized everyone . . . a stream of presents poured itself out on all sides. Banishing all that was connected with toil, the Calends festival allowed the people of old to give themselves up to uninterrupted pleasures.

Today, gift-giving during the winter holidays is practically mandatory—so much so that I am reminded of the story regarding the Roman emperor Caligula. It is said that, one New Year's Day, he announced he would stand on his veranda to receive gifts of money—if the amount did not satisfy him, the giver was publicly shamed. Why is it that this attitude has been somewhat preserved over the centuries? To those of you who dread opening the mail after the holidays, due to the abundance of bills you have accumulated, beware of the calends. To help keep your holiday bills in check consider implementing the following strategies.

Creating a budget Decide *before* you shop the total amount you can afford to spend for holiday shopping. Next, divide that amount among the people on your list.

Tracking Your Spending One of my favorite ways to organize my holiday finances is to establish an envelope system. This is done by designating an envelope for each person on my holiday gift-giving list. On the outside of the envelope I write the person's name, the amount I have budgeted to spend on him or her, and any gift ideas that I might have in mind for that particular individual. Inside the envelope I put the designated amount of cash I will spend on that person. When I do my holiday gift shopping, I take the cash-filled envelopes (and *no credit cards*) and spend only what I have budgeted.

Drawing Lots   To reduce your holiday spending further, you may decide to draw lots for names of family members. As a result, you need buy a gift only for the person whose name you have drawn. Your family may wish to draw names annually, or create a list where givers and recipients are rotated each year. (This strategy is particularly helpful in reducing holiday spending in very large families, and among large groups of friends or coworkers who exchange gifts.) You might also designate a limited amount to spend on each gift, in order to ensure that no feelings are hurt or no one feels slighted.

Giving from the Heart   Eliminate the concept that the expense or size or novelty of your gift is vitally important in expressing your love. Instead, realize that a true friend and loved one will value a gift for the simple reason that it has been given by someone whom they care for—and who cares for them.

Bazaar Bargains   Many people love handcrafted items, and enjoy giving them as gifts. However, not everyone can find the time or enthusiasm to create them. Even so, you may still give beautifully handcrafted items. Appropriate gifts can often be found at craft sales and bazaars for nearly the cost of the materials—and often this money goes to worthy causes. For this purpose, seek out sales that are sponsored by charitable organizations in which the items are donated by the crafts people. These sales usually offer lower prices than sales where the artisans sell their own work.

Planning Your Shopping   Organize your shopping by writing down the specific stores you wish to visit. And to eliminate backtracking, map an orderly shopping route. This is an especially useful strategy when visiting shopping malls. If you are unfamiliar with the mall, call ahead and ask them to mail or fax you a map of their establishment. Use this map to make your plans. Implement this same strategy, to a lesser degree, when shopping at the larger department stores.

An Envelope for All Receipts   I put receipts and sales tags from the gifts I purchase into the gift budget envelope (mentioned earlier) of the particular recipient. If you don't care to implement the gift budget envelope system, perhaps carry a single sturdy envelope with you into which all receipts and tags can go. Make an effort to read all warranties before you buy large-ticket or electronic items. This will save you headaches after the holiday. And make an effort to shop only at reputable retail establishments so that if there is a problem with the gift you may easily return it. Always inquire about a store's return policy before you buy anything.

The Art of Gift-Giving

"The only gift is a portion of thyself."
—RALPH WALDO EMERSON

Although there is no other aspect of the holiday season that creates more anxiety than selecting thoughtful gifts for family and friends, the art of gift-giving need not break your bank account or drain your time and energy. Here are a few ideas to help make your holidays artfully simple.

Gift Certificates   Gift certificates are always a welcome present. Who would not enjoy receiving the promise of a meal to savor at a favorite restaurant? Your presentation will be even more creative when you wrap the gift certificate with a menu from the same restaurant!

Simply ask for a menu when purchasing the gift certificate. Take this idea further by wrapping gift certificates from video stores in discarded movie posters from the same store (many of these establishments give these away for free, or sell them for fifty cents or a dollar each). Borrow this same strategy for gift certificates to movie theaters.

The Gift of Memory   A loving gift for older or grown children and grandchildren is to assemble a special book, or recipe box, with a collection of all of your favorite family recipes. Don't forget to gather recipes from grandparents, aunts, uncles, cousins, and so on. Each year you may add new recipes as well as appropriate sayings and footnotes as to what is most remembered about that particular recipe. This thoughtful gesture will provide a lovely gift that will grow with your children, or offer your grown children a true box of memories from their youth.

Adopt a Needy Family   If you exchange gifts at your office you might want to start a new tradition. Instead of giving gifts to one another, jointly adopt a needy family. Gifts of donated money, food, clothing, or toys can be presented to the family in need.

Pinecone Bird Feeders A lovely children's hour activity during the cold weather season is to convert simple pinecones into gifts for the birds. Lay out newspaper on the table and tie about two feet of strong string to the top of the cone. Using rubber gloves, take a butter knife and press peanut butter thoroughly around the cone. Fill a large empty coffee can halfway with sunflower seeds, add a peanut-butter-covered pinecone, then put the lid on tightly. Have the children take turns shaking the pinecone inside the can. After removing the pinecone, have the children press the sunflower seeds firmly into the peanut butter. Wrap the cone in waxed paper and tie with a ribbon. The children may wish to give these to friends and neighbors to hang on their outdoor trees—make some for your own trees as well. Be sure to have the children help you tidy the mess! One word of warning: This project works well only in cold climates, if the temperature is above 45° to 50° the peanut butter may melt off.

Practical Giving One Christmas, a friend of mine gave her elderly parents and in-laws an emergency kit to keep in the car. It contained a first-aid kit, bottled water, enough canned food to last one person for two to four days, a flare, and a thin, insulated blanket bought at a camping store. Packaged in a sturdy plastic box, these are the kind of practical gifts that people seldom think to buy for themselves.

Floral Treasures This past Christmas, my friend Debbie gave me the wonderful gift of a month's worth of flowers! Each week (or whenever the flowers in my original bouquet became wilted) I was presented with a fresh bouquet she purchased and delivered herself.

Recycled Treasures Monogram a set of vintage stemware for a newlywed couple's first Christmas, have a child's name engraved on an antique silver baby's cup or spoon, or delight a friend who enjoys antique books with one she has long appreciated from your own collection. Gifts need not be new, or purchased, to have value. My mother knew a woman who took an antique clock from the wall and gave it as a Christmas gift to a friend who had always admired it.

Simple Gifts from Your Kitchen

"We set around the kitchen fire an' has the mostest fun . . ."
—JAMES WHITCOMB RILEY

In this era of frantic, overextended days a gift that takes time is especially cherished. A homemade Christmas gift from your kitchen is a twofold treasure. Not only does it often taste much better than store-bought products, it offers with it the ultimate gift of time. Giving gifts garnered from your own time and effort is a lifetime experience and one we are never too old, or too young, to savor—as the giver and the recipient.

Herb or Honey Butters

Flavored butters are a lovely way to enhance the ordinary. A simple ingredient such as honey or chives blended with creamy butter is a lovely addition to home-baked or store-bought bread, or muffins, and is very easy to make.

Package herb butter in crocks you have collected throughout the year, or purchase inexpensive white ramekins from a discount store or restaurant supply store for a dollar or two each. Include a vintage silver butter knife you have polished to a high gleam. Embellish it with a lovely golden ribbon or tuft of white tulle tied into a puffy bow.

> 1 cup butter at room temperature
> ¼ to ½ cup quality vegetable oil, such as safflower or corn
> 3 teaspoons honey or 3 teaspoons dried ground sage (6 of fresh). You may also substitute garlic for herbs, or blend other herbs such as oregano, thyme, and parsley
> Electric beater, food processor, or blender

Beat butter until creamy. Add oil, then herbs or honey. Continue beating until all the lumps have disappeared and the butter is the constancy of a half-melted milk shake. Pour into clean crocks or ramekins. Refrigerate until ready to present with a fresh loaf of homemade bread, muffins, or rolls.

Chocolate Stirrer Spoons

These chocolate stirrer spoons, used to stir coffee or hot cocoa, are a lovely frugal luxury. Package a dozen of these chocolate-coated spoons inside an attractive coffee mug, with gourmet coffee or instant cocoa.

12 heavy-duty plastic spoons
10 ounces semisweet chocolate, broken into small pieces

In a shallow pan bring one inch of water to a boil. Reduce heat to a simmer. Place the semisweet chocolate in a deep 2-cup metal mixing bowl (or melt in the microwave, on high, stirring every 30 seconds until melted). Set bowl inside water in pan. Stir constantly until melted (about 5 minutes or so). Dip plastic spoons into melted chocolate until well coated (avoid coating the handle of the spoon). Set spoons on waxed paper to cool. When chocolate has hardened completely slide each spoon inside a cellophane candy bag, and tie a ribbon around the handle to close.

Note: You may make this fun activity even simpler by using candy melts. Candy melts look like large chocolate wafers and are created especially for dipping purposes, and they melt quite easily in the microwave (follow the manufacturer's instructions). You can usually find them at craft and candy supply stores (they are more expensive than chocolate chips but a bit easier to work with).

A Gift of Knowledge

"So far as it goes, a small thing may give analogy of great things, and show knowledge."
—TITUS LUCRETIUS CARUS

Yard sales are known for unearthing heirlooms and treasures. Imagine my satisfaction when I came home from such a sale with this recipe for "Very Flaky Pie Crust." It was a gift from a very lovely lady who was conducting the sale in preparation for her and her husband's move to a retirement facility. The recipe is over seventy years old and, I was informed, "never fails so long as you chill it in the freezer for five minutes or so before filling." I use it often with great success and would now like to share it with you.

This recipe makes two one-crust pies, or one double-crust pie.

Very Flaky Pie Crust

4 tablespoons cold unsalted butter, margarine, or shortening
2½ cups flour
1 tablespoon sour cream
3 to 4 tablespoons ice water

In a large mixing bowl, cut the butter into long strands and mix with flour and sour cream, just until it looks like large gobs of wet sand. A tablespoon at a time, add ice water until all the dry flour has been worked into the mixture (be careful; too much water will cause a brittle crust, too little will cause a dry crust). Work very quickly (don't concern yourself too much with what your dough looks like at this point). Form dough into two round balls and chill in the refrigerator for about 1 hour. When dough has chilled properly, roll it out *quickly* onto a lightly floured surface. Be careful not to overwork your pastry, as this will toughen it; the object when rolling dough is to not press the flour too firmly into the fat.

Note: The secret to a very flaky pie crust is the chemistry that occurs during cooking. Flakiness in pie crust is caused by the cold fat particles, each separated and surrounded by flour, reacting to the oven heat. I have noticed that cooking the pie at 350° from the beginning of baking creates a soggy bottom crust. To prevent this, I always put a pie into a 400° oven for the first five minutes, and then turn the oven down to whatever temperature the recipe calls for. I have never had a soggy crust when implementing this little technique.

I often prepare enough dough to shape several crusts at one time. I store these in pie pans, in our freezer, where they are ready and waiting to be filled with luscious apples, juicy peaches, or creamy, spiced pumpkin. I place dough-filled pie pans inside a large self-sealing plastic freezer bag, stacking three or four pans and separating each with a large square of waxed paper or plastic wrap. You may also freeze dough in plastic freezer bags, as flattened circles. To make an especially attractive and luxurious double-crust pie I slather the top of the uncooked pie crust with egg yolks and sprinkle a liberal amount of granulated sugar on top of the egg (enough that any wet areas are absorbed by the sugar).

While you are bargain-hunting at tag sales, be sure to stock up on pie pans. There seems to be an abundance of aluminum pie tins in our area; I am able to purchase them for about ten cents each. I have enough to keep the freezer stocked, as well as to give them (filled with pies) as gifts.

Charitable Luxury

"The luxury of charity."
—Oliver Goldsmith

"Should a vine expect acknowledgment for bearing a bunch of grapes . . . do bees create honey in order to be thanked?" inquired Marcus Aurelius in the second century A.D. The question is rhetorical in nature, and provokes thought. Indeed, why should a person who has performed a deed or kindness *look* for gratitude? To do so seems to contradict the act.

In the twelfth century A.D., the subject of charity was also broached, this time by the wise philosopher Moses Maimonides. Maimonides delineated what he titled "The Eight Degrees, or Steps, in the Duty of Charity." He created a structure upon which the first step was giving "with reluctance and regret." Happily, by the time an individual evolved to step number eight (the "most meritorious of all") he or she was, ideally, able to *prevent* poverty and need through the charitable acts of allowing others to "earn an honest living and not be forced to the dreadful alternative" of begging.

Regardless of the century, true giving is always born from a generosity of spirit, and not from a desire to receive an abundance of glorious accolades, or to have monuments built in your honor. Throughout the ages, the wise implemented this philosophy of anonymous charity, and understood it as being beneficial, not only for the recipients, but for the givers.

ℰ

Techniques for Elegant and Easy
Gift Packaging

". . . A moment's fondness to be bestowed."
—Wilkie Collins

- Create a plan *before* you wrap your gifts. I find joy in creating a unified color scheme for all the packages under our tree. Thus, make a plan before buying or creating papers, ribbons, and other embellishments for gift packages. I have found it quite useful to use a very large, deep butler's tray to hold all of my gift-wrapping accoutrements during the holidays. I find this tray an invaluable time saver, as it keeps all the necessary tools for elegant wrapping in one convenient place—my wrapping paper, small baskets in which I have tucked my scissors, tapes, glue stick, and spools of ribbons, special gift tags, a vintage teacup filled with colored pens, and tie-on ornaments and accessories I will use to embellish gift packages. When presents need to be wrapped, I set up my tray to serve me nearby. When not in use, it is tucked on top of an armoire, under a bed, or on the shelf or floor of the closet.

- To create crisp corners on packages, trim away excess paper before you close the ends on your package.

- To keep your scissors from disappearing in the midst of a wrapping frenzy, tie a long loop of colorful ribbon or string to their handles. This trick will help you find them when they are hiding under wrapping accoutrements.

- If you are wrapping a sturdy gift box with a fitted lid, try wrapping the top of the box separately from the bottom.

The Luxury of Ribbons

"I'll tell you how the Sun rose—A ribbon at a time—"
—EMILY DICKINSON

Now is the season in which to make use of the wondrous ribbon collection you have been gathering throughout the year. Pull from your Gift Pantry the fine organdy and wired French-style ribbons you bought on sale after last Christmas, and mingle them with the more humble ribbons you have made from vintage clothes garnered at tag sales and flea markets. I have been using ribbons made from recycled fabrics since my college years, when I used pinking sheers to make strands of red-and-white gingham ribbon from one of my father's cast-off shirts. I have also had no qualms recycling pieces of ribbons that I have received on gifts, and thus my generous lidded basket is filled with layer upon layer of ribbon treasures. (To bring new life to crushed, out-of-shape bows, use a warm or hot—depending on the bow's material—curling iron. Always test the effects of the hot curling iron on a discrete corner first.)

Bestowing

"The manner of giving is worth more than the gift."
—PIERRE CORNEILLE

The manner in which a gift is bestowed can be as important (or more so) than the gift itself, or its wrappings. Without graciousness, the loveliest gift will lose meaning and value. Giving is an act of emotion, for regardless of its size or cost, it is a symbol of love, friendship, or honor.

As well, the manner in which a gift is presented to another can serve to enhance and enrich a holiday that may be somewhat barren, due to lack of finances, time, or other circumstances of life.

Riddle Tags   It is an old Swedish tradition to attach a little rhyme to packages, offering hints as to their contents. For those years in which you have more imagination than budget, the riddle tag might be a welcome amusement to help enhance Christmas morning festivities. Our family members read the poems, one at a time, then try to solve the riddle. We also enjoy writing a "praise" on the tags of special gifts, to describe its recipient. For example: **To:** *the hardest working, brightest student in the sixth grade.* **From:** *the Proudest Parents in Garden Grove.* Each tag is read aloud when the gifts are handed out and everyone tries to be the first to call out the correct name. Small details such as these create rich memories, and enable us to savor our special moments a bit longer.

A Basket of Fun   In order to enhance the holiday for yourself and your children, purchase twelve *inexpensive* gifts (candy, puzzle, book, pencil, water colors and paper, pens, markers, coloring book, crayons, rubber stamp, stickers, silver dollar, etc.) for each child. Wrap each gift individually, and set in a basket next to the tree (if you have more than one child, I would advise you to place each set of gifts in a separate basket). Make a tradition of opening one little gift in front of the lit Christmas tree every evening (after dishes are done). This ritual may begin on December 12 (which will have you opening the last gift in the basket on December 24). Or you may begin on December 26 and proceed until Twelfth Night (January 6). Choosing to do this activity *before* Christmas helps younger children to handle the waiting, as well as enables them to count down the days; if done *after* Christmas, it helps to relieve the post-holiday blues that sometimes take hold of the best of us. If you are feeling especially ambitious and indulgent, double the amount of gifts in each basket and do both. Or, follow this same strategy beginning on December 1, and end on the 24th, as a type of Christmas countdown activity.

Juilklapp   In Sweden or Denmark this word means "Christmas-box" or "gift." Today the word has evolved to mean a gift package in a sphere shape, composed of layers of rolled crepe paper. Small trinkets such as costume jewelry, small toy cars, trading cards, doll shoes, candy, and money are wrapped between the layers of the crepe paper as it is rolled into a ball shape. To make a juilklapp, take a roll of crepe paper and wind it into a small, sturdy ball shape (in much the same way you would ball yarn). Once you have formed a circular core, lay a small gift, such as a quarter, on top of the ball. Continue wrapping the paper around the coin and paper core until its shape is hidden. Continue wrapping several small gifts until your juilklapp is about the size of a softball. (If you like, you may substitute torn or cut lengths of fabric for the crepe paper.) It is very enjoyable to watch the children unroll this long stream of paper, and see their delight as the presents drop out!

Treasure Hunt   To extend the joy of bestowing a very special gift (perhaps the number-one item on a child's wish list) you may enjoy wrapping a box with only a clue inside. This clue will lead to the whereabouts of that special gift (clues should be more fun than difficult). For example, "With your pretty eyes of blue, look in Daddy's tennis shoe." In the shoe you may put another clue, which could either lead to the gift, or prolong the treasure hunt! I recommend opening the clue-gift last. If you are doing this for more than one child, you might find it more enjoyable having each of them follow their clues one at a time, so the entire family can take part in each adventure.

Illuminated Fragments
The Gift of Appreciation

"You can't appreciate home till you've left it, money till it's spent . . ."
—O. Henry

Appreciating the everyday blessings of our lives is sometimes more difficult a task than one might imagine. Many times it takes the absence of these blessings to appreciate them in full. A few years ago Mike, the children, and I finally convinced my father to take a much-needed vacation. Reluctantly, he packed his bags and headed toward the Midwest to visit family in his hometown. Meanwhile, we stayed at my parents' home to care for my mother.

For years I have taken for granted the use of my legs, arms, hands, and the gift of speech. I was reminded, however, in this concentrated two-week lesson, how important these blessings are. I was left with a renewed appreciation for my father's commitment to my mother, and for my own health. I vowed to never again take these things for granted.

Many of us unconsciously ignore the simplest treasures of life. It is quite easy to do. We get caught up in the necessary tasks of living, often overlooking these basic blessings. Perhaps you should ask yourself, who and what in your own life are you currently overlooking? Are you grateful for the use of your legs? For the ability to communicate your thoughts and ideas through speech? Do you appreciate your family and the friends you have chosen, warts and all?

Appreciation is a very real force. I once read that people can literally *think* themselves into happiness. That is, by appreciating the hot water for a bath and the comfort of a warm clean bed, these simple things became more valuable. The act of appreciation blesses and enhances every aspect of our lives, as well as the lives of those we touch. Some ancient religions actually built their entire philosophies around the concept of enriching experiences through appreciation and imagination.

In *Anne of Green Gables,* the title character is an orphan who in her early years (which are somewhat abusive) keeps her sense of dignity and self-worth alive by the generous use of imagination and appreciation. It is this concept that gives the person who makes use of it the power to transform ordinary things or occasions into extraordinary ones.

It is also important to remember the basic fact that everyone responds to appreciation. Don't you want to be with and give more to the person who expresses true appreciation for your character and thoughts?

The holiday season offers us many blessings, and one of them is the chance to take inventory of our lives, and appreciate the many gentle kindnesses and tender blessings that are bestowed upon us. Remember that what you *focus* on grows. With this thought in mind, begin appreciating what you already possess, rather than lamenting over those things you lack, and witness the magical richness that can result.

HOLIDAY PREPARATIONS: GIFTS–DECORATING–CRAFTS– BAKING–WRAPPING		
PROJECT	MATERIALS NEEDED	TIME FRAME / CHECK WHEN DONE

The Gift Pantry Inventory List for Winter

GIFT RECIPIENT & DATE OF ENTRY INTO GIFT PANTRY	GIFT ITEM(S) PURCHASED OR CREATED	WHEN TO PRESENT THE GIFT & PACKAGING IDEAS

Epilogue

New Year's Day:
Old Threads, Long Tangled,
Become Straight

~

"Here is home.
An old thread, long tangled, comes straight again."

—Marjorie Kinnan Rawlings

New Year's Day

"This festival has been made the season for gathering together of family connections, and
drawing closer again those bonds of kindred hearts, which the cares and pleasures . . . of the
world are continually operating to cast loose: of calling back the children of a family, who have
launched forth in life, and wandered widely asunder, once more to assemble about the paternal
hearth . . . there to grow young and loving again among the endearing mementoes of
childhood."

—Washington Irving

The old-fashioned New Year's Day custom of visitors dropping by throughout the day,
shaking hands, extending wishes for good fortune and happiness for the new year, in-
dulging in laughter, and paying courtly compliments has declined to near extinction.
Still, many people enjoy celebrating the day, and my own heart "keeps open house"
as well.

Open House

*"My heart keeps open house,
My doors are widely flung."*
—THEODORE ROETHKE

After the hectic bustle of Christmas is past we often celebrate the new year by inviting friends and family into our home. I spread out a buffet meal, using my prettiest dishes, put on our most inspiring music, and prepare the dining table for any impromptu games that might transpire.

The back room is transformed into a cozy nest for the children to view videos and play board games, should they become bored of adult activities. The house is filled with fresh evergreens cut from the garden, along with a dozen or so red winter roses, scattered amongst the greenery to remind us all that the new year brings with it fresh and fragrant beginnings.

Organizing a Feast

This amount serves about twenty guests very generously for well under a hundred dollars. If you wish, you may easily lower costs by transforming the feast into a semi-potluck buffet.

Family members may contribute by bringing their favorite liquor and/or dessert.

- Silver platter lined with cold cuts (roast beef, ham, and smoked turkey, and slices of cheddar and Monterey Jack cheeses: about 8 pounds finely sliced)
- Fresh French rolls, croissants, and rye breads, in damask-lined baskets (breads purchased from local discount bakery)
- Small cut-glass containers or ramekins filled with herb butters and mustards
- Bowls of thinly sliced tomatoes, pickles, and lettuce
- Crudités: carrot sticks, sweet pepper strips, zucchini rounds, and broccoli florets—served with sour cream dill dip
- Large cut-glass bowls of fresh fruit and fruit cocktail (large cans of fruit cocktail are available for only a few dollars at warehouse stores, or make your own using diced fresh apples and oranges; frozen strawberries and blueberries; and diced, canned pineapple)

- Small clear glass casserole dish of black-eyed peas, traditional, for good luck (we use the canned or frozen variety)
- Fresh pretzel twists, potato and corn chips, and freshly-popped popcorn in linen-lined baskets
- Desserts of fresh-baked apple crumble, served in attractive ceramic pie plates; homemade dessert breads sliced and arranged on doily-lined footed glass cake plates; and a batch of holiday cookies from premade frozen dough
- Hot spiced apple cider on the stove in a blue enamel spatterware pot with matching dipper
- An adult drink center featuring sparkling cider or champagne punch, with an herbed ice circle (make the ice ring a few days in advance, using a tube-shaped cake pan, and lemon geraniums or mint from the garden)
- Another drink center featuring attractive glass pitchers filled with fresh brewed iced teas, lemonade, and fruit punch, all garnished with fruit slices
- Ice bucket and glasses arranged on doily-lined silver trays
- Baskets filled with attractive, quality paper napkins, or our collection of cloth napkins, laundered and freshly folded and pressed
- Pretty silver flatware, polished, and arranged in a buffet holder for guests' convenience
- Stacks of blue-and-white china plates arranged in the proper manner near the meats and vegetables; smaller plates near the dessert tray

A Scottish Custom

"Custom, then, is the great guide of human life."
—DAVID HUME

Serving shortbread is a tradition throughout the year in Scotland. However, on New Year's Day it is mandatory to have on hand, so that it may be served to "first-footers."

What are "first-footers," you ask? Quite simply, they are the first few people who enter your home during the new year. It is considered very good luck to serve "first-footers" this traditional cookie of Scotland.

Shortbread, usually shaped in a special mold, is extremely easy to make. However, you can make this recipe without a mold by shaping the dough into a circle and baking it on an ungreased cookie sheet.

Oatmeal Shortbread

1 cup all-purpose flour
3 tablespoons powdered or granulated sugar
½ cup cold butter (I recommend using only butter, and not margarine, in this
    recipe)
⅓ cup quick-cooking (but not instant) rolled oats
Optional: granulated or powdered sugar for garnish

Combine flour and sugar in a mixing bowl or food processor. Cut in butter until the mixture begins to cling together. Stir in oats. Do not overmix. (If you are using a food processor, be certain your butter is well chilled before adding it to the flour and sugar, then pulse for about 5 to 10 seconds—do not overprocess.)

Roll or pat dough into a flat, 8-inch circle. Place dough onto an ungreased cookie sheet. Use your fingers to press and shape a scalloped edge. With a small knife, cut the circle of dough into 16 pie-shaped wedges. Leave the wedges together. This will keep the shape intact (the wedges will expand when baking, and reconnect the circle). Or, press dough into a lightly floured shortbread mold then turn it out onto an ungreased cookie sheet before baking.

Regardless of whether you mix by hand or use a food processor, the secret to a very flaky shortbread is to chill the dough in the freezer for 5 minutes before you place it into the hot oven. If desired, sprinkle (prior to baking) the top of your shortbread with granulated sugar. If you wish to garnish it with powdered sugar, do so after baking.

Bake shortbread in a preheated 325° oven for 25 to 30 minutes, or until the bottom begins to brown and the center has set.

While still warm, cut the shortbread circle into wedges, along the same perforations you made before baking. Allow it to cool on the cookie sheet for about 5 to 10 minutes, then transfer to a wire rack until it has cooled entirely.

Serve homemade shortbread on your favorite holiday plate or tray. If you are giving these rounds as gifts, you may wish to recycle interesting vintage dinner plates—wrap entire plate, topped with shortbread, with cellophane and add a pretty bow. Occasionally I find attractive, well-priced wooden cutting boards and use them to serve or present my homemade shortbread.

Humble Graces

"God resists the proud and giveth grace to the humble."
JAMES 4:6

Benjamin Franklin has been widely quoted as having once endeavored to attain moral perfection. He drew up a list of the twelve virtues that he thought would embody the traits of a good life. In a special little book, he allotted one page to each virtue. He then drew seven lines on each page, one for each day of the week. His plan was to try to focus his mind on one virtue for an entire week at a time, using the notebook to keep track of each daily violation. He thought that he could attain the good and avoid the bad with the help of his good conscience.

One day he showed his list to an old Quaker friend, who gently informed Mr. Franklin that he had omitted one very necessary virtue: humility. I find it quite interesting that his list was revised as follows: Temperance, silence, order, resolution, frugality, industry, sincerity, justice, moderation, cleanliness, tranquility, chastity, and humility (listed last). It seems that even Mr. Franklin, in all his wisdom, had a lifelong battle with pride.

Now, please don't misunderstand me. There are different sorts of pride. For example, it is perfectly fine to take pride in the quality of honest work, such as a thorough job of cleaning house, or exerting your best efforts for your employer. This sort of pride is very constructive, and often motivates you to action by igniting your enthusiasm.

Unfortunately, there is another sort of pride that can cause you to stagnate and stop growing. It blinds us to the idea that we are imperfect beings. This type of blinding pride has been described as being much like the light inside a car. When you turn it on at night, it transforms the car windows into mirrors. You can see your own reflection, but you cannot see *outside* the car, thus making driving difficult and unsafe. Therefore, in order to have a clear view of the road ahead of you (or the road behind) you must focus your interior light away from yourself.

The opposite of pride is humility. And, contrary to what many people think, humility is not just an ornamental grace. It is the foundation of all other virtues, because it encourages spiritual growth. And such growth (in my humble opinion) is one of the primary reasons for existence.

Illuminated Fragments
The Spirit of Resolve

". . . The dauntless spirit of resolution."
—WILLIAM SHAKESPEARE

William Shakespeare once noted, "Our bodies are gardens, to which our wills are gardeners: so that if we will plant . . . why, the power and . . . authority of this lies in our wills." It is true, resolve is a wondrous force, and earnest resolution almost seems to carry with it a tinge of omnipotence.

In my humble opinion, the most amazing fact regarding the power of resolve is that we all possess it. It is not restricted to the very rich; we need not be genetically predisposed toward it, and we are not born into it. The power of resolve is available to you, as sure as you are reading this book. In the next moment you may make use of this life-changing force—and every moment after that—*if you so decide.*

The resolution to create and self-publish our newsletter, *Frugal Luxuries* (formerly *Frugal Times: Making Do With Dignity*) in 1993, changed my life. That single decision led to writing my first book, *Frugal Luxuries,* as well as the humble volume you are now reading. It has allowed me the privilege of forming new friendships, and touching the lives of others—kindred spirits who are living a similar lifestyle, and have a strong desire to share and to learn the simplest and best ways to balance both the material and spiritual sides of our existence.

How did I access the power of resolve? By making the simple decision that I no longer was satisfied by writing only in my journal. I wanted to express myself to a wider audience and share what I felt were valuable life lessons, as well as learn from the experiences of others.

Resolutions are set into motion by the simple act of writing them down. There is something magical about the process of giving thought to, and writing out, your dreams, goals, and resolutions. By the simple act of setting them onto paper, you send an unconscious message to your central nervous system (similar to entering data into the hard drive of a computer). Consequently, you find yourself working (often subconsciously) to fulfill the commands you have set in motion. And when you combine resolve with a bit of perseverance and effort, you have a formula for success.

An ancient adage tells us that if we plant a grain of wheat, we can eventually feed the world. This metaphor came to mind when first I realized the power of a single resolution. I view it as being akin to the manner in which a seed is planted and, if it is cared for, eventually becomes a mature, fruit-bearing plant.

Will today be the day *you* make use of this miraculous force? Will today be the day you resolve, with certainty, to untangle the knotted threads of life by focusing on what is of value in *your* life? Will you make the decision to live your future hours cultivating positive qualities such as perseverance, confidence, and appreciation—and experience them daily? Will this be the day you resolve to coordinate your everyday life with your true spirit?

Now is the moment for you to make or change your own resolutions. Vow not to allow your circumstances to control you. Instead, control your circumstances by your reactions. True resolution is the force that transforms your ideals into reality.

ॐ

ACCESSING THE POWER OF RESOLVE
Please take a brief moment to set your power of resolve into motion by writing out your dreams, goals, and resolutions for the future.

_____

_____

_____

_____

_____

_____

_____

_____

_____

_____

ॐ

Appendix A

~

Kindred Spirits

". . . Like kindred drops, been mingled into one."
—WILLIAM COWPER

The Luxury of You

"Type of the wise who soar but never roam,
True to the kindred points of heaven and home!"
—WILLIAM WORDSWORTH

We feel tremendously blessed and grateful for all of the gracious letters and notes that have been sent to us by a multitude of kindred spirits. It seems that each of you has a special quality, a simple grace that reveals an elegant and eloquent spirit . . . as well as a sincere appreciation of the frugal luxuries within your own lives.

Some correspondents have been with us since the inception of our newsletter in 1993. Others have more recently discovered our merry band of kindred spirits by way of our book *Frugal Luxuries*. It matters not when they joined us; what is so awe inspiring is that this is a very unique and special group of people, with an intelligent, caring, and generous spirit. It is rare that I get a letter that does not reflect this simple graciousness.

You cannot imagine how delightful it is to mingle minds with so many kindred souls, to know that there are others in this world who understand that the beginnings of happiness and riches of any kind are created by making the best of what you have.

Our lives have been incredibly touched and enriched via long lovely letters; heartwarming cards; and encouraging, kind notes from so many of you readers—so much so, that I felt that this abundance of intangible riches was far too valuable to keep to myself.

As you will soon discover, this chapter is comprised primarily of letters and ideas that were so generously contributed by other like-minded individuals. It was conceived with the hope that you will enjoy learning, as we did (and do), of the many clever, artful, and inexpensive ways in which others cultivate and savor frugal luxuries within their own lives.

It is my strongest wish that, after reading this book, your life will be further enhanced by the practical ideas offered here—and your soul comforted by the knowledge that you are not alone in your quest to appreciate, enhance, and enjoy your life . . . regardless of the size of your budget.

May I suggest that you set this chapter aside until you can capture a quiet moment to relax (perhaps with a favorite beverage) and mingle minds with other kindred spirits?

Warmly,

Tracey McBride and Family

Dear Tracey,

I recently received a copy of your newsletter. I very much enjoyed reading it, as well as your book, Frugal Luxuries. *It is wonderful that folks are finally addressing such subjects. I have long practiced making my house a happy and peaceful home, and doing so on a very tight budget.*

It seems that in today's culture there is a collective attitude that dismisses doing things that are frugal or practical—even comforting—as a waste of time and energy. The folks who cultivate that negative attitude just "don't get it" and, in my opinion, will lose out in the long run. However, I choose to stand my ground and will continue cultivating a lifestyle that I enjoy, and that my family loves. (I simply cannot imagine a life without all of the frugal luxuries that life and God have to offer.)

I have been married for twenty-three years, and my husband and I have two teenage sons (ages seventeen and nineteen). We also have a "good ol' " southern extended family, and we love to get together on Sunday afternoons and other family occasions. Traditions mean a lot to us. Still, getting teenagers, especially boys, to notice efforts made by Mom may seem like an impossible task . . . but mine do.

My sons are big guys, with even bigger hearts and souls, so I frequently hear little praises and comments from them. "I love pulling up in the driveway and smelling that fire in the fireplace," or, "The guys say that our house always smells so good!" Or, simply, "It's good to come home, Mom." I cannot tell you how much I love hearing remarks such as these. And do you know what? The things that the boys are noticing cost little more than pennies of money and moments of time to implement, yet they create memories that will last a lifetime. It seems that we have learned to enjoy each day as it comes. It is a gift.

Living in a middle-class community just outside of Atlanta, Georgia, brings many challenges to us all. The "never enough" society in which we live is often hard to ignore. Adults as well as children are constantly bombarded with advertisements (and peer pressure) to own flashy cars, expensive stereo systems, designer clothes, and the like. It appears that the philosophy of "buy more—spend all of your money" is being adopted by so many people without thought to the long-term consequences of such decisions. It saddens me that people are trying to secure happiness and contentment by collecting things. Unfortunately, this philosophy often leaves little time to recognize and enjoy all the true treasures that life has to offer.

Family, home, traditions, shared experiences, similar values and goals (combined with simple joys, like laughing together at a family joke, or reminiscing about shared life lessons) is the glue that holds us all together. Obviously, in order to experience these riches, a family will need at least one person who possesses the love and desire to cultivate and remember such things.

For those who haven't much of a family to hold together, you will always be given the opportunity to weave friends into your life (you may wish to make a conscious effort to do this, if you haven't already done so). In our home, many of our friends are just like family to us.

I don't live in a big or fancy house. Still, by the grace of God, I don't have to be away at an office job all day. Long ago I made the decision (along with my family) that it was not worth the trouble or financial benefit to do so. I found that, financially, I was barely breaking even when working outside of the home. With the car expenses, money spent on clothing, makeup, lunches out, and buying convenience foods—due to lack of time and energy—the money I was earning melted like butter on a hot knife.

Today, my family appreciates more the many things that I can personally do for them, by providing a safe, nurturing, and loving home. My husband and I are now able to be in the stands at the boys' sporting events—or in the audience when it is important to be there. And, because of this personal involvement, we have met other, like-minded parents, thus establishing many lasting friendships.

I do realize, however, for some people this lifestyle is quite difficult, if not impossible, to achieve—due to financial circumstances. Others may simply enjoy being away from home. Circumstances and attitudes will vary with the individual. However, I strongly felt that my primary job was to be a cultivator. I longed to be at home, and in my yard and gardens.

So, now, when my jeans are looking a little too faded, and my walking shoes are showing excess wear, I simply count my blessings. I remind myself that I am one of those lucky human beings who is able to experience the frugal luxuries of life.

Today, I opt for a walk at the park rather than a trip to the mall. Our family chooses hamburgers cooked on the backyard grill rather than a dash through the fast-food drive-through. And now, when I spend money on things, I know they won't end up being stored away in a closet or box. Instead, I am investing in what matters . . . things that are intangible yet have so much more substance. These treasures will be stored away in my heart, and in the hearts of my family.

In closing, I just want to remind you and your readers to make every day special. Put some flowers on the table, use those cloth napkins that have been cluttering your linen closet, and light those candles that have been sitting in those pretty candleholders for two years. Most importantly . . . turn off the television set. Use your "good stuff." Let your family know that they are the special guests that all those pretty things were packed up for.

It is the moments of life that weave the fabric of our days. God has given each of us gifts, and we must use these to build a full and giving life.

Thank you, Tracey, for sharing your Frugal Luxuries, your thoughts, and your knowledge, with us all. Even all the way over here in Georgia!

Through you, all of us kindred spirits can find and communicate with each other . . . offering support and sharing ideas.

God Bless You.

Sincerely,

Carole Turner
Georgia

ℰᴑ

Dear Tracey,

I have just finished reading your book Frugal Luxuries, *and wanted to tell you how much I savored each and every chapter. Like you, I wear many hats—wife, mother of three (ages four to thirteen), nurse, author, laundress, housekeeping engineer, and so forth.*

I have always tried to make a warm and "homey" home, but with the business of life it is often difficult.

My friend and I have made a commitment to live more frugally . . . and finding your book was like a confirmation of that resolve.

My husband and I have also implemented a plan to become debt-free (including mortgage) that spans the next five to six years. We plan to achieve our goal by living frugally.

I have discovered that by planning better, watching for specials, utilizing coupons and so on, I have already trimmed two hundred dollars per month from our family grocery bill. My husband is amazed and delighted. Plus . . . our family is eating much better!

I laughed when I reached the end of your book and found the section on "Kindred Spirits" in the Appendix. I was thinking you were a kindred spirit all the way through the book.

You also brought to mind a lot of the little things that my grandmothers and aunts used to do to make a cheerful home—thank you for rekindling those memories.

Warmly,

Peggy Stoks
Minnesota

Dear Tracey,

Thank you . . . you have made me feel better about being "frugal." For two generations this is the manner in which we have lived. What you teach in your book is interesting and informative.

Because money is sometimes tight, we use our imaginations and ingenuity to get things done within our budget.

I would like to share with you the frugal way my husband went about building an entrance, a sun room, and two decks, onto our home . . . all for only fifty-nine dollars.

When building, he would often gather free or inexpensive construction materials simply by asking others (who had recently completed a building project) if they had extra, unneeded, building materials. If the answer was "yes," he would then offer to purchase it. Very often, however, the people would offer it at no cost, on the condition that my husband would haul the materials away. He would then use the materials in our own building projects.

How glad it makes me feel to know that there are people like you who show others that being frugal can be an honorable trait . . . a skill to be proud of (not embarrassed about).

I hope you write more books . . . I was so glad to know that there are, what you call, "kindred spirits" out there. My own spirit is a little lighter just knowing that others are doing similar things as I am, and enjoying them.

Thank you.

Robin Dougherty
New York

Dear Tracey,

All of my life I have been learning from my mother ways to save money . . . but you have brought a true beauty to the subject through your book, Frugal Luxuries.

It seems that the attitude of the modern world in which we live tells us that in order to be fulfilled and entertained we must always spend a lot of money. In my opinion this attitude is not only expensive, it is boring!

As a twenty-year-old woman, I have always felt myself to be a bit of an outcast among my peers. I have concluded that a person can only become involved in a finite number of commercially inspired activities before being caught up in a shallow mind-set (such as going to the movies, the mall, and eating at expensive restaurants—every weekend).

Since I was a young girl I have enjoyed cooking, creating, gardening, and art. Instead of reading magazines such as Glamour *or* Vogue . . . *I have read* Woman's Day, Family Circle, Reader's Digest, *and the like.*

My husband and I were married and owned our own home by the ages of nineteen. Now, I am about to become a mother. We live in our frugally decorated home, with a nice yard, along with our beagle, Abigail. Our days are filled with God . . . reading, trying new meals, gardening, and simply being creative. We are both active in our church and derive much contentment, joy, and peace from this.

Many times I have been made to feel that I am strange because I believe it is important that my surroundings be attractive (right down to the Hamburger Helper being served attractively . . . even on busy nights). But you have reassured me that I am normal when aspiring to live beautifully, but simply, in every aspect of my life.

Thank you dearly for being a kindred spirit. You have given me self-confidence in who I am . . . an individual who is searching for deeper meaning in life (and this you cannot find at any store).

God bless you in all your work.

Yours,

Tabitha Higgins
Ohio

A Child's Birthday Tea

"Come, O come, ye tea-thirsty restless ones—
the kettle boils, bubbles and sings, musically."
—Sir Rabindranath Tagore

Dear Tracey,

I love your newsletter, as I knew I would! I will be waiting for the next issue to arrive (hopefully, with patience). I'm so excited to know that you are working on a second book. I'd love to send you some of my fun ideas. For example, let me tell you about my daughter's sixth birthday party.

She wanted a tea party, which thrilled me since I love tea, and tea things. We used my good dishes, which are white with pastel flowers. The tablecloth was a pink sheet on which I laid a lace curtain panel. We served peanut-butter-and-jelly sandwiches, ham-and-cheese sandwiches, pink heart-shaped cookies, chips, peach iced tea poured from two cute teapots I found at a local discount store, and the crowning touch, two cakes made in the shape of teapots.

I made the cakes from two boxed, white cake mixes (bought on sale—of course) and baked two cakes using my seven-inch (approximately) Pyrex bowl, as well as twelve extra cupcakes (all from the same two cake mixes). I inverted each bowl-shaped cake onto a doily-covered plate, and frosted them with pink frosting. For the teapot lids, I cut a cupcake in half length-wise and used half of it turned upside down. I frosted the top with the same pink frosting and added a Hershey's kiss for the final touch. I decorated each cake with flowers and squiggles of white frosting (please keep in mind that I'm not an expert cake decorator). For the handle and spout I used a candy cane cut in half. The curved end served as my handle, and the straight portion made a perfect spout. The cakes turned out very cute, and my children loved them.

We played "Pin the Lid on the Teapot," which I made from a piece of poster board and some gift wrap remnants. For the party favors, I purchased a pretty set of pale blue teacups that were shaped a bit like a flower for fifty-nine cents each at the same discount store where I found the teapots. I filled each cup with candy, wrapped them individually with pink tulle (purchased on sale) and tied them with a pink ribbon bow (thirty-three cents per roll).

It was a wonderful party, and ended up being much more lovely than I had hoped! It was such fun coming up with inexpensive ideas while keeping the event elegant and attractive. I thought you might enjoy hearing about it. (I loved your chapter on Katie's Garden Tea Party in Frugal Luxuries.)

I look forward to my future newsletters. Bless you in your work.

Sincerely,

Beth Whitlow
Texas

ɠə

The Beauty of a Hand-Wrought Gift

"That irregular and intimate quality of things made entirely by the human hand."
—WILLA CATHER

Dear Tracey,

How delighted I am to read in your newsletter that you will be writing a second book! You have a talent for putting the desires of my soul into words. Your efforts to cultivate the gifts of heart and home are so appreciated. I, too, am unwilling to give up style, beauty, and happiness while trying to live within our means.

I have many frugal ideas that I would like to share with you. However, the first is the enclosed card I made for you. I love to send notes of encouragement and good thoughts to friends and family. I believe that sending them in a handmade card speaks volumes more than my words. Making cards is also an outlet for my creativity.

Several friends and I get together every few months and let the children play while we madly make cards and share ideas. The cards are not only attractive and thoughtful, but incredibly inexpensive!

How to Make Marian's Greeting Cards:

- *Buy 8 x 11-inch pieces of card stock (about six cents apiece) at a photocopy store.*
- *Cut each sheet of card stock paper in half—then fold that in half. You will end up with two 4 x 4-inch cards.*
- *From fabric, cut out designs (i.e., hearts, flowers or other shapes—I often make a quilt-type pattern) and iron them on the front of each card. Use inexpensive iron-on webbing to adhere fabric to paper (follow the manufacturer's directions).*
- *Outline, or "quilt," around the fabric design to make a border, or write a message. A Micron 01 pen works best, but a ballpoint pen will work in a pinch.*
- *Embellish each card with raffia (I often tie it into tiny bows), ribbons, buttons and so forth.*

Again, best wishes on your new book. I am anxiously awaiting its publication. Remember, take time out for you and your family amidst the work.

With Love,

Marian Underdahl
Idaho

The Very Thing I Seek

Dear Mrs. McBride,

I just finished your first book. You have hit upon the very thing I seek. I long to live a more simple lifestyle, one that embraces quality more than quantity. I've gathered so many things (junk, really) in my twenty-eight years, and yet I feel like I have nothing of value . . . and because I can't enjoy it all I enjoy none of it. Your book opened my eyes to the fact that by having too many things I can't appreciate all that I have. By streamlining my possessions I'll be able to fully enjoy those things I choose to keep, because they are not competing with other things for my attention. I feel I've always known this truth, but until now I didn't know how to embrace it and make it my own.

At the moment, my husband and I have no children (we've only been married about a year and a half). We just bought a house in April, and hope to start a family within a year. I long to be able to stay at home to raise our family. So far we've been able to pay off our credit cards monthly (avoiding interest!) and only have our house and one car financed. We save money by using what we call the "Ten-Ten-Eighty Plan." From each paycheck, we give ten percent to our church, put ten percent in our savings account, and live off the other eighty percent. This has worked quite well for us so far, though we're still not sure about my being able to stay at home when the kids come. But your book has given me some useful tips and ideas on how we can simplify our lives so that we can be frugal and still live abundantly, making room for what we consider important: a warm, inviting home, plenty of family time, my staying home with the children, and the list goes on.

I wanted to thank you for writing your book, and I hope that you will write another. I know I've got a rough road ahead of me—old habits are hard to break—but I've got a glimpse of a frugal, yet luxurious, lifestyle, and I'm looking forward to achieving it. Thanks again!

Sincerely,

Jennifer Neuman
Illinois

A Better Place

"When I was at home, I was in a better place."
—WILLIAM SHAKESPEARE

Dearest Tracey,

Originating from Massachusetts, my family was taught about being frugal early on in our lives. We learned about squeezing the "Yankee dime," from our grandparents, aunts, uncles, and parents—just as a normal way of thinking and acting.

My mother was (and remains) a super cook and, to this day, she still scrapes the butter wrapper to get that last smidgen of butter, and still uses her finger (clean!) to get the last drop out of the eggshell (perhaps this is why her cakes are always so moist and yummy!). Of course, paper towels (an early luxury) were often found drying over the kitchen faucet—after all, they were only used to dry already clean hands, and could be reused! Diluted shampoo, kept in a recycled, clean catsup bottle over the washing machine, was used to remove "ring around the collar," as well as on grimy cuffs and other stained areas on clothing.

My favorite way of having frugal fun is to save quarters. (We collect these in a pretty, salt-glazed pottery pitcher.) Every three months, my husband and I treat ourselves to our "quarterly night out." It is amazing to me that we usually have about fifty to seventy dollars to spend from this quarter collection!

Before our date, I take the quarters with me to our local video rental store, dry cleaner, minimarket, bookstore, and so on, and exchange them for bills as I am transacting my necessary business. These small establishments truly enjoy and appreciate receiving the quarters, as they use them for making change. (And this saves my husband and me the trouble of lugging a bunch of jangling quarters to our favorite restaurant.)

These "quarterly nights out" are such a treat for my husband and me—especially because we feel so frivolous and decadent! We have found them to be such a nice way to splurge on ourselves, and support our time out together (and the strategy is relatively painless, financially, and very enjoyable to boot)!

I thought you and your readers might enjoy hearing about all of the above, and per-haps be inspired to create your own frugality and fun in a kindred manner!

Warm regards from a faithful reader . . .

Susan Vrh
California

ℰℬ

Spiritual Luxury

Dear Tracey,

This week I went to our mall to look at a copy of Spiritual Literacy *at one of the bookstores. Instead of buying that book I bought yours! I cannot tell you how I am en-joying* Frugal Luxuries. *You have been able to articulate the way I think but am not al-ways able to express . . . I work at living the life you describe in your book. Daily I go about my activities in a peaceful and gentle way.*

After two decades of not working [outside the home], I took a job in a shop down-town—a job that I thoroughly enjoyed. However, after two and a half years, I gave my resignation. For me, the reason was "to have time to lean on the end of my broom after sweeping." Your book suggests this same simple attitude about daily life. To most, I would think, it all sounds too simple or maybe like a fairy tale—but I am living proof that it all works.

Keep sowing the seeds of simplicity. I love it—a truly lost art.

Carolyn McDonald
Texas

ℰℬ

A Stitcher's Frugal Luxury

Tracey,

This weekend I was fixing up a new set of sheets. As I made the pillowcases, I thought of you and your newsletter, and decided to share some of my own frugal luxuries with you.

I like to buy one-hundred-percent cotton bedsheets because they are more comfortable for sleeping, but they are more expensive than the cotton/polyester blends. To save money when I buy a set of queen-size sheets, I compare the costs of a twin flat sheet and a pair of queen-size pillowcases. Usually the ready-made pillowcases are far more costly than the twin sheet, with a price difference of twenty to thirty dollars.

I buy the twin flat sheet and make my own pillowcases, using a pillowcase from my linen closet as a pattern. Sometimes the upper hem edge of the sheet has special trim, such as a ruffle. Then, only one open end of each pillowcase gets the special trim.

There's more sheet fabric left after I cut out two pillowcases, so I can use the extra fabric to make one additional pillowcase, some throw pillows, or to trim towels. A double flat sheet would provide enough extra fabric for a second set of pillowcases plus extras.

Just a few straight seams and very basic sewing skills are all that's required to make a pair of pillowcases—you might want to give this simple project a try.

Best Regards,

Mary Mualari
Minnesota

Dear Mrs. McBride,

I recently purchased your book, Frugal Luxuries, *at a bookstore on a whim. I was pleasantly surprised to discover in your work suggestions for entertaining and living graciously on a budget. I have read Martha Stewart's magazines and books, and enjoyed the idea of gracious living, but my budget did not allow me to put many of her ideas into practice. Your book helped me to educate myself about methods of "budget" gracious living.*

I am currently engaged, and my fiancé and I are making plans for the purchase of our first family home. Although neither of us has a large income (I am a kindergarten teacher; he works in a machine shop factory) we will be able to make a substantial down payment. However, after we do purchase a house, we will be anxious to save money with the goal that I can some day quit teaching in order to have children.

Thank you for all of your hard work on your book and newsletter. I appreciate it!

Sincerely,

Melissa Whittle
Tennessee

WELCOME ... ALL KINDRED SPIRITS!

Almost daily I receive gracious letters and short notes that are brimming with lovely ideas (tangible and intangible), and good wishes. Among my most comforting and prized intangible treasures is the knowledge that I am *not alone* in my desire to make my home, family, and lifestyle as lovely, peaceful, and gracious as possible.

I would so enjoy including more of your lovely letters and useful ideas in forthcoming books, and in our newsletter, *Frugal Luxuries.* Please consider taking a few moments of your valuable time to share with other kindred spirits your thoughts, ideas, success stories, and positive philosophies on the subject of frugal luxuries.

Reading your letters is such a pleasure, and it is our hope that you will continue to feel free to contribute any ideas and topic suggestions you might have for the newsletter—clippings from magazines and newspapers that you think would interest us are always a welcome pleasure to read—and please tell us about books you think we should know about, as well as brochures from inns and/or bed-and-breakfasts that you have enjoyed (and even menus that you find interesting). Your suggestions are welcome contributions that will enhance the lives of those who read them.

I thank you in advance for being so very generous with your knowledge of how to manage a frugally luxurious, appreciative, and gracious lifestyle—regardless of income. Although we may not be able to respond to each letter that we receive, please know we appreciate each contribution. I am so looking forward to reading your insightful and helpful letters.

Please feel free to write to us at:

Frugal Luxuries-KS
Post Office Box 5877
Garden Grove, CA 92845

Please note: All correspondence becomes the property of Tracey McBride and may be edited and published.

Appendix B

❧

Bibliography

*"The true University of these days
is a Collection of Books."*

—Thomas Carlyle

Alcott, Louisa May. *Little Women.* Kingsport, TN: Grosset & Dunlap, 1947.
Allen, James. *As a Man Thinketh.* Mount Vernon, NY: Peter Pauper Press, 1898.
American Heritage Dictionary and Electronic Thesaurus. Boston: Houghton Mifflin Company, 1987.
Anderson, Joan Wester. *Where Miracles Happen.* New York: Ballantine Books, 1995.
Barnes, Emilie. *More Hours in My Day.* Oregon: Harvest House Publishers, 1982.
Bartlett, John. ed. *The Shorter Barlett's Familiar Quotations.* Boston: Little, Brown, 1980.
Beeton, Isabella. *Beeton's Book of Household Management.* London: S.O. Beeton. 1859–1861.
Betty Crocker's Cooking Calendar. New York: The Golden Press, 1962.
Book of Christmas, The. Pleasantville, NY: The Reader's Digest Association, Inc., 1973.
Concise Columbia Encyclopedia. New York: Columbia University Press, 1990.
Durant, Will. *The Story of Philosophy.* Garden City, NY: Pocket Books, 1953.
Emerson, Ralph Waldo. *Essay on Self-Reliance.* New Canaan, CT: Keats Publishing, 1973.
Fisher, M.F.K. *The Art of Eating.* New York: Collier Books, 1990.
Frankl, Viktor E. *Man's Search for Meaning.* New York: Pocket Books, 1984.
Hamilton, Edith. *The Greek Way.* New York: W. W. Norton & Company, Inc., 1930.
Henry, Lewis C. *Best Quotations.* New York: Fawcett World Library, 1965.
Holy Bible. New Jersey: Omega Publishing House.
Jewett, Sarah Orne. *The Country of the Pointed Firs.* New York: Anchor/Doubleday, 1989.
Jhung, Paula. *How to Avoid Housework.* New York: Fireside, 1995.
Lewis, C. S. *Mere Christianity.* New York: Macmillan, 1960.
Lewis, C. S. *The Four Loves.* New York: Harcourt Brace Jovanovich, Inc., 1960.
Living Bible, The. Wheaton, IL: Tyndale House Publishers, 1971.
MacDonald, George. *The Christmas Stories of George MacDonald.* Elgin, IL: David C. Cook Publishing Company, 1982.

McBride, Tracey. *Frugal Luxuries.* New York: Bantam Books, 1997.

McGuffey's Eclectic Reader, Volumes 5 and 6. New York: Van Nostrand Reinhold, 1920.

Microsoft Corporation. *Microsoft Bookshelf.* 1987–1992.

Newman, Lewis. *The Jewish People, Faith and Life.* New York: Lewis Newman, 1953.

Panaati, Charles. *Extraordinary Origins of Everyday Things.* New York: Harper & Row, 1987.

Plato. *Five Great Dialogues.* New York: Walter J. Black, 1942.

Porter, Sylvia. *Sylvia Porter's Money Book.* New York: Avon, 1974.

Proust, Marcel. *Swann's Way.* New York: Vintage, 1970.

Quinn, Jane Bryant. *Making the Most of Your Money.* New York: Simon & Schuster, 1991.

Robbins, Anthony. *Awaken the Giant Within.* New York: Fireside, 1991.

Savage, Terry. *Terry Savage Talks Money.* New York: Harper Perennial, 1990.

Schaeffer, Edith. *L'Abri.* Wheaton, IL: Tyndale House Publishers, 1969.

Schofield, Deniece. *Confessions of a Happily Organized Family.* Cincinnati, OH: Writer's Digest, 1984.

Shakespeare, William. *A Shakespeare Treasury.* Selected by Levi Fox. Norwood, England: no publisher or date given.

Stoddard, Alexandra. *Daring to Be Yourself.* New York: Avon, 1990.

Treasure Chest, The. Edited by Charles L. Wallis. New York: Harper & Row, 1965.

Tudor, Tasha. *A Time to Keep.* Chicago, IL: Rand McNally & Company, 1977.

Wilder, Laura Ingalls. *Little House in the Big Woods.* New York: Harper & Row, 1971.

Appendix C

∽

Resources

"Most people live . . . in a very restricted circle of their potential being.
They make use of a very small portion of their . . . soul's resources."
—WILLIAM JAMES

The NFCC is the nation's oldest and largest nonprofit organization, providing education and counseling services on budgeting and credit. NFCC members are located in 1,300 offices across the United States, Puerto Rico, and Canada. Many members operate under the name Consumer Credit Counseling Services. To locate the closest NFCC member office, call 800-388-2227, or visit the NFCC Home Page at http://www.nfcc. org.

Spring

Heard's Country Gardens
14391 Edwards Street
Westminster, CA 92683
A charmingly unique nursery that offers an abundance of free and very useful advice, sometimes about gardening, and other times about life in general. A visit to this store is a soul-soothing experience.

Keepers Antique Store
11931 Valley View
Garden Grove, CA 92645
(714) 898–6101

Springdale Country Store
15802 Springdale
Huntington Beach, CA 92649
(714) 893–6514
(714) 373–4547

Summer

Room Service Interiors (formerly Vintage Rose)
14461 Edwards
Westminster, CA 92683
(714) 373–4547
This lovely store specializes in accoutrements found in cottage-style interiors, offering a cozy mix of old and new. Owner Cathy Jarrell also consults with those who want a cottage look at home or in an office.

Petticoat Lane (women's consignment clothing)
15051 Edwards Street
Huntington Beach, CA 92649
(714) 891–4090
Voted Best Consignment Store in Orange County by the *Orange County Register,* with very good reason, as this store almost always has fabulous merchandise at very reasonable prices.

Wearagains (children's consignment clothing)
15051 Edwards Street
Huntington Beach, CA 92649
(714) 898–3400
This wonderful store is conveniently located next door to Petticoat Lane, thus offering one-stop bargain shopping for mother and child! I am a loyal customer of both establishments.

National Association of Resale and Thrift Shops
157 Halsted Street
Chicago, IL 60411

Mary Mulari (Mary's Productions)
P.O. Box 87FS
Aurora, MN 55705

Autumn

Connie Sheerin
Crafts A La Cart
85 West Baltimore Avenue
Lansdowne, PA 19050

Mrs. Cubbison's Food Inc.
132 S. Peerless Way
Montebello, CA 90640

Harriet Beecher Stowe House Visitor Center
71 Forest Street
Hartford, CT 06105
(203) 525–9317

The American Woman's Home, by Harriet Beecher Stowe
($12.95 each, add $2.50 for postage and handling. CT orders add sales tax.)
Available from
  The Stowe-Day Foundation
  77 Forest St.
  Hartford, CT 06105
  (203) 522–9258

Winter

Service 1st Carpet Restoration
Dying and Water Extraction
(714) 253-5548
Gary Stewart, the owner of Service 1st, gave Mike and me a mini-education in carpet dying
  and care. We discovered that, contrary to common belief, carpets cannot be successfully
  dyed a different color than their original hue. However, if you have a good quality carpet
  that you love, and the color has badly faded, or been bleached out in areas, you may be the
  perfect candidate for carpet dying—and the cost is but a fraction of what you might pay
  to replace it.

State College Distributors: Carpet, Hardwood, Ceramic Tile
1620 S. State College Blvd.
Anaheim, CA 92806
(714) 935-0533
The Silverbergs, owners of State College Distributors, found the perfect quality flooring for
  our new home at less than half the cost of what it sold for in retail stores. Because they are
  positioned to sell at a discount, their prices are almost always lower than national chains.
  And the customer service was excellent. In fact, they even shared a secret with us: If you
  want to get the lowest price on flooring, try buying it in late winter (after the holidays) as
  this is the slowest time of the year for flooring retailers.

With Love and Appreciation

"Who so loves believes the impossible."
—ELIZABETH BARRETT BROWNING

I would like to acknowledge the multitude of God's graces that have touched me deeply throughout my life. I continue to be blessed with a rippling circle of support, love, friendship, good thoughts, inspiration, and faith. For this I am deeply grateful.

Grace, like love, possesses the unique quality to magnify—once it is appreciated. I first learned this lesson when I was eight years old, as I asked my mother how she could love each of us children equally. (Because I was the fourth and last child in the family I was concerned that her supply of love had diminished by the time I arrived.) Standing at the white enamel stove, preparing dinner, she quietly listened to my question, sensing my childish need for reassurance. "That's the funny thing about love," she answered. "You never run out of it. The more you love the more love you *have* to give." Quite satisfied with this answer, I went about the business of childhood. Mother's simple wisdom has been a guiding force in my life ever since.

Warm appreciation and love is also extended to my father, from whom I have received myriad intentional—and unintentional—gifts, all of which I count among my most precious blessings.

Foremost in the many graces I have been privileged to receive is my love for—and the love and friendship of—my husband, Mike. His unfailing (and often blind) faith in my limited abilities has enabled me to stretch and grow into a person who more fully appreciates the wisdom, wonders, and miracles that surround us daily.

Our children, Katie, Clancy, and Rosie, have been the greatest gifts of my life. The deep love I have for each of them continues to be the driving force behind my every good effort and thought.

I extend heavy doses of gratitude to my former editor, Emily Heckman, who continues to be the quintessential kindred spirit. To Christine Brooks I offer my warmest thoughts and thanks for her very clear thinking, and generous, patient spirit. I also must send my appreciation to my copy editor, Connie Munro, for her kind and sensible contributions (and for creating the illusion that I have some command of the English language). To my editor, Robin Michaelson, I can only extend my deepest appreciation and thanks for adopting and caring so tenderly for this little book. You are a wonder.

A special portion of thanks must be extended to my agent, Sandra Dijkstra, who has offered me the opportunity to learn and to grow while under her banner (even though she may struggle with the *frugal* portion of my philosophy, she is quite in tune with its *luxury* aspect).

A private note of appreciation must be extended to Claudine Murphy, who was instrumental in the publication of my first volume of *Frugal Luxuries*. Thank you, Claudine. Ours was a brief but blessed friendship. Please accept my apologies for being so tardy in acknowledging it, and you.

To Debbie Supnick and Kelly Ehrlichk, I extend warmest gratitude, best thoughts, and friendship. Their generosity and kindnesses have contributed many blessings to *Frugal Luxuries,* and to me.

In the *terre-a-terre* of existence I would like to thank my friends Debbie and Jack—and their children, Chrissie and Jessica—for their unwavering friendship and abundant help. To my kindred spirits Belinda Davis, Hillary Wassman, Terry Wing, and Lisa Simington, I send my best thoughts and thanks for your kindnesses and gracious support (as well as all those complimentary lattes and lunches). I offer my warm appreciation to Michelle Martz (as well as the entire staff of C.C.H.B.) for her continued support, understanding, and friendship. And to Alexis Larson, whose talent brought us the lovely line drawings within this book, I am truly grateful. May your lives be filled with wisdom and joy.

To the multitude of kindred spirits we have been privileged to meet via our newsletter and books, I extend my deepest appreciation. You are a very special group of people who have proffered a multitude of support, kind words, good thoughts, creative ideas, and friendships. You have (as Wentworth Dillon advised) chosen "an author as you would choose a friend," and continue to be a constant source of inspiration and joy. It is my great pleasure and honor to know you.

To those of you who have only recently discovered our philosophy, I extend my warmest welcome. The invisible hand that guided you to pick up this book, take it home, and incorporate the philosophies into your life urges you to uncover the miraculous graces that await you in every season.

Recipe Index

Index

Adams, John Quincy, 99
air and drawer fresheners,
   180–81
Amenemope, 203
American Woman's Home,
   The (Beecher sisters), 174
Anne of Green Gables
   (Montgomery), 258
appetizers: simple ham
   spread, 23; tray of crudités,
   97
attitude, 37–38
autumn: bargains, 138;
   equinox, 156; festivals of,
   151–72; flowers in season,
   116; gift pantry, 200–205;
   home graces, 174–85;
   savoring, 187; warm up to,
   177

bargains, season by season,
   137–40
bay laurel, 236
basket(s): alternatives to
   traditional gift, 145–46;
   Easter, 21; of fun, 256; key,

61; mail and bills, 61; May,
   28–29; mending, non-
   clothing, 65
beans, ham hock and, 24–25
Beecher, Henry Ward, 87
Beecher sisters, 42, 174
beef: garlic-and-rosemary
   roast, 152; leftovers, 197;
   stew, 157; stock, 189. *See*
   also corned beef
Beethoven, Ludwig van, 129
biscuits, 193
bleach, chlorine, uses for, 53
bluing, liquid, 54
Book of Common Prayer, The,
   224
books, adorning, 239
breads, 193–99; Angel's
   (home-baked), 100;
   biscuits, 193; cans, 202;
   challah, 162–63; cinnamon
   wreath, 196; croissant
   poulet, 194–95; doughnuts,
   193–94
breakfast: fruit crisp, 33–34;
   pizza, 195
Bridges, Robert, 8

bronze or brass cleaning, 55
brownie torte, 219
budgeting: Christmas,
   246–48; clothing/school
   supplies, 130–31
bunny tracks, 21
buttercream frosting, 19
buttons, heart-of-, brooch,
   216

cake plates and pedestals, 227
cakes: buttercream frosting,
   19; Christmas, global, 226;
   crushed strawberries with
   white, 104; easy Easter
   bonnet, 18–19; fairy, 97;
   Saint Nicholas Day
   one-bowl, 210–11
Caligula, 246
candles, 184; decorating
   fireplace interior, 183;
   good fortune, 185–86;
   graces, Christmas, 243;
   making, 184; Mason lights,
   239; pierced tin lantern,
   242–43

About the Author

When Americans look for frugal luxuries they turn to Tracey McBride. By way of her books, newsletters, and repeat appearances on television shows such as *The Carol Duvall Show, Smart Solutions,* and NBC news (Los Angeles affiliate), Tracey McBride shares her wisdom on how to savor the intangible gifts we receive when we create

nurturing homes, share luscious yet low-cost meals with family and friends, master our budgets, learn to combine style and thriftiness, and cultivate our dreams and imaginations without spending a cent.

Surrounded by books at an early age, Tracey took refuge in their counsel as she sought simple ways to transform the mundane into the magical. As the youngest of four children, and the only girl, Tracey assumed many of the household chores as her mother struggled with the debilitating disease multiple sclerosis. Tracey developed her passion for home-keeping as she taught herself how to craft something from nothing and make "every day a feast," all the while remembering what is truly of value in life—time, loved ones, and an inner sense of prosperity.

After attending college, Tracey taught kindergarten classes at a small elementary school in southern California. She was married in the 1980s, and swimming against the tidal wave of women entering the workforce, Tracey McBride chose to simplify her life by quitting her job after the birth of her three children. The following decade allowed her the apprenticeship needed in order to cultivate and master the skills she believes have been lost to much of her generation: budgeting, cooking, sewing, and making a comfortable and peaceful home.

In 1993, Tracey McBride began sharing her observations with others in her *Making Do with Dignity* quarterly newsletter (now renamed *Frugal Luxuries*). Her unique philosophy of marrying luxury with economy has caused a tremendous stir in the voluntary simplicity movement, and is the focus of her books *Frugal Luxuries* and *Frugal Luxuries by the Seasons.*

Tracey McBride teaches and lectures on behalf of numerous organizations, supporting children's charities such as Mary's Shelter. She lives in southern California with her family, four cats, and an errant labrador, in a cottage she purchased at a rummage sale. Visit her website at www.frugalluxuries.com.

We Cordially Invite You to Join Us

"We are lovers of beauty without extravagance . . ."
—Thucydides

Our newsletter, *Frugal Luxuries* (formerly *Frugal Times: Making Do With Dignity*) was established in 1993. Our goal was, and remains, to blend beauty, grace, and spirit with the practical details of living. Regular features such as Gracious Moments, Home Peace, The Alchemy of Artfulness, Creative Recycling of the Ordinary, Seeds of Time, Home Graces, and our longtime favorite, Frugal Luxuries, have been a breeding ground for the alchemy that transforms the ordinary into the extraordinary.

You are warmly invited to mingle minds, exchange ideas, and comfort your soul through this medium. If you would like to join us in our endeavor to make do with dignity, you may do so by sending a check or money order for $18:

> Frugal Luxuries Newsletter
> Post Office Box 5877–00
> Garden Grove, CA 92845

Thank you, and welcome!

Printed in the United States
by Baker & Taylor Publisher Services